LET EVERY NATION KNOW

John F. Kennedy in His Own Words

ROBERT DALLEK *and* TERRY GOLWAY

SOURCEBOOKS MEDIAFUSION™
AN IMPRINT OF SOURCEBOOKS, INC.®
NAPERVILLE, ILLINOIS

Published by Sourcebooks MediaFusion, an imprint of Sourcebooks, Inc.
P.O. Box 4410, Naperville, Illinois 60567-4410
(630) 961-3900
Fax: (630) 961-2168
www.sourcebooks.com

Library of Congress Cataloging-in-Publication Data

Dallek, Robert.
  Let every nation know : John F. Kennedy in his own words / Robert Dallek and Terry Golway.
       p. cm.
  Includes bibliographical references and index.
  1. Kennedy, John F. (John Fitzgerald), 1917-1963. 2. Presidents—United States—Biography. 3. United States—Politics and government—1961-1963. 4. Presidents—United States—Messages. 5. Speeches, addresses, etc., American. I. Golway, Terry, 1955- II. Title.
  E842.D27 2006
  973.922092—dc22

                          2005037973

        Printed and bound in the United States of America.
            LB 10 9 8 7 6 5 4 3 2 1

To Hannah Claire Bender
and Kate and Conor Golway:
the next generation

Contents

On the CD

The audio on the accompanying compact disc has been selected by the authors to enrich the experience of this book, to allow you to experience the words of John F. Kennedy in his own voice. These selections represent some of the most remarkable moments of his presidency and offer a window to the mind of the man. At the start of each chapter in the book, you will find an icon and track number denoting the corresponding speech on the CD. We encourage you to use and we hope you enjoy this mixed-media experience of the life of John Kennedy.

1: Address to the National Press Club • *January 14, 1960*

2: Acceptance Speech, Democratic National Convention • *July 15, 1960*

3: Address to the Greater Houston Ministerial Association • *September 12, 1960*

4: The First Debate, Chicago • *September 26, 1960*

5: The Second Debate, Washington, D.C. • *October 7, 1960*

6: The Third Debate, New York and Hollywood • *October 13, 1960*

7: The Fourth Debate, New York • *October 21, 1960*

8: Address to the General Court of the Commonwealth of Massachusetts • *January 9, 1961*

9: The Inaugural Address • *January 20, 1961*

10: Announcement of the Creation of the Peace Corps • *March 1, 1961*

11: Proposal of the Alliance for Progress • *March 13, 1961*

12: Speech to the American Society of Newspaper Editors • *April 20, 1961*

13: White House News Conference • *April 21, 1961*

14: Address to the American Newspaper Publishers Association • *April 27, 1961*

Preface

JOIIN F. KENNEDY IIAD ONE OF THE BRIEFEST PRESIDENCIES IN American history. And yet, it is one of the most chronicled and, for millions of Americans, one of the most remembered of their lifetime. His thousand days in office were filled with crises at home and abroad. Some of those crises resonate today, in an age when we are reminded of how vulnerable we are to unimaginable catastrophe. John Kennedy was president at a time when the world teetered on the brink of a nuclear apocalypse. Berlin and Cuba were the hair triggers that so nearly brought the United States and the Soviet Union to all-out war.

All the while, the Kennedy White House was confronted with an uprising in the South as African Americans took to the streets to demand that Washington live up to its rhetoric about the importance of freedom and liberty.

Some of the issues John Kennedy faced will sound familiar to readers in the twenty-first century. The most famous fiasco of the Kennedy administration—

the failed invasion of Cuba—was born of faulty intelligence. The president, though once a journalist himself, saw fit to ask newspaper publishers to censor themselves in the interests of national security. And power in Congress was wielded by southern white males (Democrats then; Republicans now).

John Kennedy's words, delivered more than four decades ago, read and sound as fresh as the nightly news, with one major difference: John Kennedy did not speak in sound bites. The phrase had not yet been invented. He spoke in literate paragraphs, and his speeches were filled with references to history and literature that have all but disappeared from American political discourse.

So to the question: Why a book about Kennedy speeches? Because the words he used to inspire a nation are as relevant today as they were at the time.

That certainly seems curious. After all, Kennedy's term was brief and his legislative accomplishments were minimal at best. All his principal initiatives—an $11 billion tax cut, federal aid to elementary, secondary, and higher education, health insurance for the elderly and the indigent, a civil rights bill banning segregation in places of public accommodation, and departments of housing and urban development and transportation—were pending in Congress when he died on November 22, 1963.

In foreign affairs as well, there were major shortcomings: the Bay of Pigs invasion of Cuba in April 1961; secret assassination plots against Fidel Castro; imperfect performance at the Vienna Summit conference in June with Nikita Khrushchev; and the expanded U.S. involvement in the Vietnam War that lead to 58,000 American deaths.

Despite these limitations, John Kennedy is seen by most Americans as one of the four or five great presidents in U.S. history. Opinion surveys over the last forty years consistently include JFK in the front rank of presidents with Washington, Lincoln, FDR, and, most recently, Ronald Reagan. True,

Kennedy rescued the world from a nuclear war by using diplomacy to resolve the Cuban Missile Crisis peacefully. He also negotiated a limited nuclear test ban treaty that inhibited the proliferation of weapons of mass destruction. Nevertheless, his overall record hardly compares with those of even near-great chief executives like Theodore Roosevelt, Woodrow Wilson, and Harry Truman, to mention just three twentieth-century presidents.

What then accounts for Kennedy's exceptional standing among the forty-two men who have held the highest office? His assassination is certainly one element of the public's regard for him. But it is hardly a full explanation. In 1941, forty years after William McKinley was assassinated at the start of his second term, not many people considered him a great or outstanding president. At best, he had joined the group of nameless, faceless characters who had occupied the office in the last third of the nineteenth century.

Kennedy's youth and charisma go far to explain his enduring hold on Americans and, indeed, people around the world. His youthful good looks, charm, wit, and intelligence, which were so evident at his innovative live tele-vised news conferences, are frozen in our memories. He remains an exciting forty-six-year-old president who inspired hope for a better America and a more peaceful world. The premature deaths of his brother Robert and of his son, John Kennedy Jr., have undoubtedly added to the sense of enduring tragedy about him and a conviction that had he lived, we would be a less troubled nation.

JFK also commands approval as a heroic president who, despite lifelong physical maladies, including constant back pain, served courageously in World War II and performed effectively in the White House. Revelations about his response to medical problems have marked him as a man of strong character, which has been so much in question because of widely publicized accounts of compulsive womanizing.

The principal reason for Kennedy's popularity, however, is his inspirational rhetoric. Substantive presidential accomplishments seem to have less of a sustaining hold on Americans than does memorable presidential language in public addresses. Americans know more about Washington's Farewell Address than about any specific episodes in his presidency. Dwight Eisenhower, for all his considerable achievements both before and during his presidency, is largely remembered for a single speech at the end of his eight-year term warning the country about the military-industrial complex.

Kennedy, for example, asked Americans to put the national interest ahead of their personal interests and to do away with war before war did away with mankind. These were calls to sacrifice and high-minded ideals that Americans loved. (For instance, although Woodrow Wilson's promises to end war and make the world safe for democracy fell short of realization, his appeal to the country's better angels has assured him of a continuing place in the front rank of presidents.)

It is interesting that the only other post-World War II president to maintain high standing with a majority of Americans is Ronald Reagan. Like Kennedy, his rhetoric continues to inspire hope for a better, more prosperous, more peaceful America. Almost everyone seems to recall Reagan's description of his time in office as "morning in America" and a moment when "the pride is back."

No one should underestimate the effects of the power of language on presidential reputation. The highly popular Kennedy is remembered for several speeches and the effectiveness of his televised press conferences. The access to JFK's audio and written speeches provided by this book will once again inspire those who heard and read them over forty years ago, but it will also win new converts to the Kennedy mystique among the millions of Americans who were born after 1963.

Kennedy speaks during a 1952 campaign stop,
using crutches because of his chronic back pain.

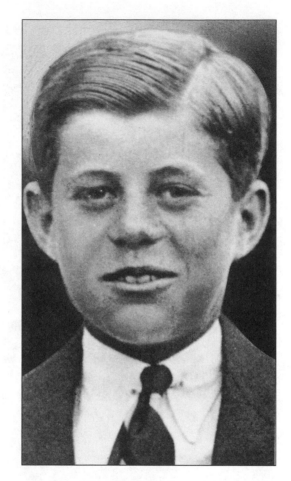

Kennedy around age ten.

JFK: A Life

JOHN KENNEDY, THE SECOND SON OF JOSEPH KENNEDY AND ROSE Fitzgerald Kennedy, was a sickly child who seemed destined to live his life in the considerable shadow of his elder brother, Joseph Jr. He was born on May 29, 1917, in an upstairs bedroom in the family's home on Beals Street in the Brookline section of Boston. Little John's arrival received little notice, compared with the great tidings that accompanied the birth of his older brother less than two years earlier. After Joseph Jr. was born, his maternal grandfather, the beloved Boston politician John "Honey Fitz" Fitzgerald, announced that the child would one day be president of the United States. He added, mischievously, that little Joseph also would attend Harvard University (like his father), letter in football and baseball while earning all possible academic honors, become a captain of industry, and perhaps, while preparing for his inevitable move to the White House, serve as mayor of Boston and governor of Massachusetts.

While Joe Jr. played the role of golden boy, young Jack struggled with some of the illnesses that would plague him for the rest of his life. In his mid teens, he was so thin doctors feared that he had leukemia. (He did not.) A simple cold sometimes led to a stay in the hospital. He complained of a constant pain in his knees, and of fatigue. Jack's medical problems were a source of great frustration for his socially and politically ambitious father, who was appointed U.S. ambassador to Great Britain in 1937. The millionaire patriarch continued to groom Joe Jr. as the family's favorite son, the boy who would be president.

For Jack, another career seemed to beckon—journalism. As a writer and reporter with first-rate connections, he could pursue his interest in public policy and foreign affairs without submitting to the rigors of campaign politics. During a grand European tour in 1937, Jack made it a point to look up the Rome correspondent of the *New York Times*, Arnaldo Cortesi, with whom he discussed the darkening clouds gathering over Europe. The trip inspired Kennedy to take his studies at Harvard more seriously, and he began to write well-received papers about public issues in his government classes. While Joseph Jr. seemed well on his way to a brilliant career in American politics, his younger brother was thinking about life as a foreign correspondent for the *New York Times*.

In a sign that he was moving closer to a career in journalism—not cops and robbers coverage, to be sure, but the sort of journalism practiced by the likes of Walter Lippman and Arthur Krock—Kennedy converted his senior honor's thesis into a book published in 1939, entitled *Why England Slept*. An analysis of Britain's appeasement of Hitler's Germany, *Why England Slept* sold well and received positive reviews on both sides of the Atlantic. The young author received some editorial assistance from the legendary Krock, a *New York Times* columnist who smoothed out some of the writing and helped Kennedy find an agent. But there is no doubt that the twenty-two-year-old Kennedy worked hard on the manuscript. Indeed, his peers at Harvard found his obsession with the project to be amusing, and annoying.

The war that Britain and other nations wished so desperately to avoid reached U.S. soil on December 7, 1941. Both Joseph Jr. and Jack had already joined the navy when Japanese warplanes attacked Pearl Harbor. As an ensign stationed at the Office of Naval Intelligence in Washington, D.C., Jack's connections to the world of journalism grew more intense—his sister, Kathleen, landed a job as a reporter with the *Washington Times-Herald* and was dating a colleague, while Jack himself began dating the newspaper's twice-married society columnist. The two couples often double-dated, in part to disguise Jack's potentially scandalous relationship with the columnist Inga Arvad, who was still married to her second husband.

As a member of the U.S. military, John F. Kennedy, the privileged son of one of the nation's most influential families, had embarked on an experience that would bond him with the sons and daughters of farmers from the Midwest, factory workers from Brooklyn, short-order cooks from the South, and police officers from the West. He was one of sixteen million Americans who put on a uniform during World War II, a shared point of reference for an entire generation. Years later, some of his most famous speeches would reflect the reference points of the GI generation: when he compared the defense of West Berlin to the siege at Bastogne, his peers—rich and poor, urban and rural—understood precisely what he meant. In his inaugural address, he spoke of a "beachhead of cooperation" that might "push back the jungle of suspicion," a literary device that required no explanation from a Harvard professor of English.

That Kennedy served in a uniform at all during the war is a tribute to his patriotism, for his health problems should have kept him in civilian clothes. The litany of his ailments is extraordinary: he suffered from spastic colitis (for which he was treated at the Mayo Clinic in the late 1930s), chronic lower back problems, and recurring stomach pains. In early 1941, he failed physical exams for admission to officers' candidate schools for both the army and the navy. Kennedy's influential father contacted a navy captain, Captain Alan Kirk, who had worked at the U.S. embassy in London when the elder Kennedy was U.S. ambassador. Kirk arranged for Jack Kennedy to see a doctor friend, who administered another physical examination. Jack Kennedy passed this one with ease and was admitted to the Office of Naval Intelligence.

In the aftermath of Pearl Harbor and America's entry into the war, Kennedy requested sea duty. After six months of combat training, he was assigned to command a motor torpedo boat—a PT boat in wartime shorthand. As commander of PT 109, his wartime service remains part of American folk memory.

On the night of August 1, 1943, PT 109 was in the Blackett Strait near New Georgia, searching for a Japanese convoy. Fourteen other PT boats were part of the mission. The boats were small and quick, but they were no match for the enemy ships for which they were searching. The PT boats found their targets in the dark of night and attacked.

The assault was poorly coordinated, and in the ensuing chaos, a huge Japanese destroyer sliced through the dark waters and slammed into PT 109. Two crew members were killed instantly, and the surviving eleven, including Kennedy, were cast into the sea.

With several survivors accounted for and holding on to the boat's hull, Kennedy swam to the rescue of three other crew members, including one, Pat McMahon, who was badly burned. Other crew members swam to the rescue of other survivors, until all eleven were holding on to the hull. But after nine hours, the hull began to sink. Kennedy ordered the men to swim for land. McMahon, however, was too hurt to swim. Kennedy put the ties of McMahon's life jacket in his teeth and towed his comrade for five hours until they found a small bit of land called Bird Island, or Plum Pudding Island. An exhausted Kennedy then swam an hour into the strait, hoping to flag down a U.S. ship. He failed, but later carved a message into the husk of a coconut and asked a native to bring it to the nearest Allied base. Finally, after a seven-day ordeal, the crew of PT 109 was rescued. And John Kennedy was a war hero.

In 1941, Kennedy's old ailments—the ailments that ought to have kept him out of the war—forced his return to the United States. His back, his colon, and his stomach all received medical attention, leaving navy doctors to conclude that he was unfit for further service.

Meanwhile, thousands of miles away, Joseph Kennedy Jr. had compiled an impressive war record of his own. He flew more than two dozen antisubmarine missions over the English Channel and was eligible for leave. He refused. He volunteered to pilot a huge Navy Liberator airplane loaded with twenty-two thousand pounds of explosives, which were to be dropped on a missile site on the coast of Belgium.

On August 12, Joe Kennedy's plane exploded above the English Channel. The favorite son, the Kennedy who was destined to be president, was dead.

The effect of Joseph Jr.'s death was, of course, profound. The Kennedys now had another bond with so many of their fellow citizens from different backgrounds and regions. They had lost a son. The blue star that hung in their window was changed to a gold one, signifying loss. To help him cope with his grief, Jack turned to words—he put together a privately published book, *As We Remember Joe*, filled with written reminiscences of the fallen son and brother.

Joe's death meant that Jack had become the favorite son, and the plans that had been put into place for Joe would now be adapted for the second born. But even as politics beckoned, Jack Kennedy did not lose his interest in a profession that dealt in words, not deeds. While recuperating from back surgery after his return from the war, Kennedy wrote a long magazine article that called on the U.S. to avoid a postwar arms race with the Soviet Union.

"Democracy sleeps fitfully in an armed camp," he wrote. The piece was rejected by several magazines, including *The Atlantic Monthly* and *Reader's Digest*, and was never published.

Despite that setback, Kennedy's writing career moved forward when the *Chicago Herald-American* hired him to cover the United Nations conference in San Francisco in 1945, as the war in Europe drew to a close. While the Hearst-owned newspaper probably would not have hired Kennedy were it not for his considerable connections, the job was not a make-work position for a dilettante. Kennedy wrote seventeen stories (at two hundred and fifty dollars apiece) for the newspaper, analyzing East-West tensions that had been simmering during the war against Nazi Germany. While the record shows that Kennedy carried out his assignment like a professional, there is also evidence that he did not consider himself quite the ink-stained wretch. One night, he called back to Chicago to report, simply, that he would not be filing that night as scheduled. There was, after all, a party to attend.

Inevitably, of course, John Kennedy put aside his interest in journalism in favor of campaign politics and public service. It was time to execute the plan that had been laid out for Joe Jr., but would now be carried out by Jack. He ran for Congress in 1946, a scrawny rich kid clumsily mixing it up with voters in a blue-collar district in Boston. He was not a natural. In fact, his entrance into the rough and tumble of Massachusetts politics surprised one of his old school friends, who was convinced that Kennedy would be either a teacher or a writer. His temperament seemed better suited to either profession, as his performance on the campaign trail showed. His speaking style was forced and wooden, his voice tight and tense. He seemed ill at ease, a far cry from the style of his maternal grandfather, Honey Fitz Fitzgerald, who loved the personal contact of the campaign trail.

John Fitzgerald Kennedy, on the other hand, was not a back-slapper. In fact, he hated that part of the job. It is fair to say he was a good deal more comfortable dictating articles to a secretary than he was in shaking hands with strangers at a campaign rally.

He eventually learned these skills, and became adept enough to run and win a statewide campaign in 1952, when he captured a seat in the U.S. Senate. But even then, his interest in words and ideas continued, leading to the publication of his Pulitzer Prize-winning book, *Profiles in Courage*, published in 1956. The book profiled eight U.S. senators who had defied public opinion

and partisan pressure to act according to their consciences and their percep-
tion of the public good. Their stories of political courage appealed to
Kennedy, a man who valued physical and intellectual courage.

Questions were raised almost immediately about Kennedy's exact involvement in writing the book, and those questions continue to confront historians
and biographers. Even at the time, many people believed that future presidential speechwriter Theodore Sorensen, already a Kennedy aide, did most if not
all of the writing. Most likely, the book was a collective effort, with Kennedy
himself making an important contribution, although perhaps not enough to
insist, as he did, that he was indeed the book's author.

The book raised Kennedy's own profile (leading some critics to complain
that the senator ought to show less profile and more courage) in the midst of
the 1956 presidential campaign. The press could not get enough of the young
senator from Massachusetts, especially after his marriage in 1953 to the beautiful Jacqueline Bouvier, the daughter of a privileged Catholic family who
worked as a society photographer for the *Washington Times-Herald*. The press
saw a lovely bride and a vigorous politician on the make. Jack and Jackie added
a dose of glamour to a capital in the throes of Joseph McCarthy's excesses and
Eisenhower-era grayness, the perfect antidote to the sober 1950s.

In reality, however, the marriage was a good deal less than perfect. John
Kennedy was a womanizer when he was single, and he saw no reason to
change his habits when he married. Nevertheless, he did recognize that Jackie
was unlike most of the other women he knew, however fleetingly. Kennedy's
longtime friend, Lem Billings, once noted that Jackie interested her husband,
"which was not true of many women."

With a wife at his side, Senator Kennedy was prepared to take the next
steps toward the White House. At least he believed he was prepared, but in
1956 he learned otherwise. When Democratic presidential nominee Adlai
Stevenson declared that he would abide by the Democratic Convention's
choice for vice president, Kennedy put his name in the running. But he was
outmaneuvered and outmuscled by the more experienced Senator Estes
Kefauver, who won the nomination on the second ballot—the last time it
would require more than a single ballot to nominate a candidate for national
office. Defeat allowed Kennedy a moment in the national spotlight as he conceded the vice-presidential race in a speech asking the convention to make
Kefauver's nomination unanimous.

Kennedy returned to the Senate with his sights set on reelection in 1958 and on the presidential nomination in 1960. Some of his speeches during these years hinted at themes that would become familiar to Americans in the early 1960s. At his alma mater, Harvard, in 1956, Kennedy spoke about the role of intellectuals in public service, calling for greater cooperation between men and women of ideas, and the men and women who implement policy. "I would urge that our political parties and our universities recognize the need for greater understanding between politicians and intellectuals," he said. "We do not need scholars or politicians like Lord John Russell, of whom Queen Victoria remarked, 'He would be a better man if he knew a third subject—but he was interested in nothing but the constitution of 1688 and himself.' What we need are men who can ride easily over broad fields of knowledge and recognize the mutual dependence of our two worlds."

He also continued to write, and contributed an essay to the distinguished policy journal *Foreign Affairs* in 1957. Entitled "A Democrat Looks at Foreign Policy," Kennedy called on Washington to pay greater attention to independence movements in the developing world. In advocating a "new realism" in foreign policy, he sought to place the U.S. on the side of nations struggling against the remnants of European imperialism. In this piece, as with other Kennedy speeches and articles, the emphasis was on detached analysis, rather than partisan polemics.

As he prepared to announce his candidacy for president in 1960, John Kennedy had found his voice, and found the words to express his ideals and his vision. In the coming years, he would summon the English language as it had not been summoned, at least by a political leader, since Winston Churchill had marshaled together words and phrases to inspire his countrymen and the world during the Battle of Britain in 1940.

He would go on to become the first president of the television age. He and Jacqueline were attractive and glamorous, providing the nation and the world with a host of indelible images. And yet, John Kennedy used words, not visuals, to marshal his arguments and inspire his fellow citizens as president.

Political partisans in the United States have been arguing for nearly half a century over the proper ownership of John Kennedy's words. Skeptics and iconoclasts often note that Kennedy's most famous speeches, his best-remembered phrases, were the work of others, principally his brilliant aide, Theodore Sorensen, and other writers, like Richard Goodwin. Others insist with equal passion that Kennedy's imprint was on every important speech, even if he did not actually put the words on paper himself. This argument was at the center of two recent books focusing on one of Kennedy's best-remembered speeches, his inaugural address. One author, Thurston Clarke, concluded that Kennedy had more input into the speech than most people realize. However, the other author, Richard J. Tofel, concluded that the work was primarily Sorensen's.

What is significant about this debate is that it is taking place at all. It is a testament to the power of John Kennedy's speeches that historians continue to pore through them, searching for insight into a politician who served as president for only a thousand days.

As long as the public remains fascinated with John Kennedy, as long as phrases from his speeches remain part of folk memory in the U.S. and elsewhere, there will be debate over the true and proper origin of the words attributed to him. Such an argument will only add to the evidence that Kennedy's words mattered, and that few world leaders since have spoken to us, have challenged us, and have inspired us, in quite the same way.

Congressional candidate Kennedy casts his vote in 1946. On the left is his grandmother Josephine Fitzgerald, and on the right his grandfather John Francis "Honey Fitz" Fitzgerald.

After losing the fight for the 1956 vice-presidential nomination, John Kennedy prepares to address the Democratic National Convention.

Senator Kennedy and Jacqueline Bouvier become husband and wife on Sept. 12, 1953, in a traditional Roman Catholic ceremony.

PART ONE:

The Pre-Presidential Speeches

JFK and Senator Hubert Humphrey (far right).

Introduction

J OHN KENNEDY ANNOUNCED HIS CANDIDACY FOR THE PRESIDENCY ON January 2, 1960—late by modern standards. But he had begun laying the groundwork for years—decades, when one includes the years his father spent preparing for this moment.

Speculation about a Kennedy presidential bid began in the late 1950s, even before he was reelected to a second term in the Senate in 1958. He demurred when asked about his intentions, but his schedule and his public profile spoke volumes. In the age just before television showed its power to turn regional politicians into national figures, Kennedy traveled the country to speak to local Democratic organizations and civic groups. Mass-market magazines, from *Time* to *Redbook*, ran flattering stories about the up-and-coming young senator and his beautiful wife. Would-be voters read not about the senator's voting record, but about his love of sailing. They were regaled not with critical assessments of his positions on foreign policy, but celebrations of his domestic life—his marriage to Jacqueline, their little daughter Caroline (born in November of 1957), and his remarkable brothers and sisters.

He became a celebrity before he became a candidate for president. He understood, earlier than many older political professionals and journalists, that the media age emphasized personal narrative as much as, and perhaps more than, substantial argument. And he realized intuitively that in this age of personality-based politics, presidential candidates no longer needed to wait their turn while party elders determined who was ready to become president and who was not.

Many party leaders, who took their politics more seriously than the average voter, were not susceptible to the Kennedy charm offensive. A powerful faction within the party seemed determined to resist this young man, among them Eleanor Roosevelt. She and other party liberals clung to the hope that Adlai Stevenson would mount yet another campaign, his third.

Mrs. Roosevelt carried considerable political weight, and it was clear that she was highly dubious of Kennedy, in part because of his religion. In 1958, she said that while she thought the nation was ready for a Catholic president who believed in the separation of church and state, she did not think that Kennedy was such a Catholic. This was an explosive accusation from a respected and respectable party elder. When she further criticized Kennedy for avoiding the Senate's condemnation of Joseph McCarthy in 1954, Roosevelt signaled to her fellow liberals that Kennedy would not stand up for progressive ideas.

If Stevenson were not available, the party's liberal wing was ready to rally around Minnesota senator Hubert Humphrey. As mayor of Minneapolis in 1948, Humphrey had given a rousing speech at that year's Democratic National Convention in favor of a strong civil rights plank. An energetic orator and a prairie progressive, he represented the next generation of New Dealers.

Other Democratic senators were equally eager to compete for the open presidential seat. Missouri's Stuart Symington also was a favorite with the party's liberal wing, while Senate Majority Leader Lyndon Johnson was counting on the party's traditional strength in the South.

Kennedy's opponents in 1960 were formidable: they were more mature, more experienced, and had the institutional support that Kennedy lacked.

He began assembling his campaign team in 1959, with names that would become familiar in the coming months and years: Kenneth O'Donnell and Dave Powers, two old-fashioned pols from Massachusetts; Pierre Salinger, the campaign press secretary; Theodore Sorensen, the speechwriter; Stephen Smith, who was married to the candidate's sister, Jean; and, of course, the candidate's brother, Robert, who, at the age of thirty-four, served as the campaign's manager, goad, scold, enforcer, and energizer.

By the time Kennedy made his intentions official in early 1960, his team had been working behind the scenes for months, reaching out to the state and county chairmen who still held enormous power in presidential campaigns. Now the public part of the campaign began.

From the perspective of more than forty years, one of the most striking aspects of John Kennedy's entry into the 1960 presidential campaign is how late it came—only two months before that year's New Hampshire primary. By the standards of twenty-first century U.S. politics, Kennedy's announcement was far too late to be taken seriously.

In 1960, however, presidential campaigns were still more of a sprint than a marathon. Only sixteen states had primaries—that number would double and then some by 2004. Local party officials in 1960 had a far greater voice in choosing nominees than did the rank-and-file primary voters, placing a premium on private persuasion, rather than public appearances. Remarkably, in

1960 one of the leading candidates for the Democratic presidential nomination, Lyndon Johnson, did not formally declare his candidacy until July 5—after the primaries, and only a week before the convention.

Kennedy's announcement on January 2, delivered in a Senate caucus room to a crowd of three hundred supporters and several reporters, hinted at the themes Kennedy would sound in the campaign—in essence, that the country needed to get moving again—and issued a direct challenge to some of the forces gathering against him. "I believe that any Democratic aspirant to this important office should be willing to submit to the voters his views, record, and competence in a series of primary contests," he said. That was a message for those who hoped that Adlai Stevenson would emerge once the primaries were over, the twice-fallen standard-bearer drafted into service yet again on behalf of progressive ideals.

Kennedy's youth and his religion persuaded many reporters that the senator's real goal in 1960 was not the presidency, but the vice presidency. Indeed, after finishing his announcement, Kennedy was asked if he would accept the vice-presidential nomination. He responded without equivocation: "I will not be a candidate for vice president under any circumstances and that is not subject to change."

He knew what so many did not know, that his health was problematic, to say the least, and so he believed his best and perhaps only chance for the presidency was in 1960. But even if his health problems—his chronic back pain, colitis, Addison's disease, the failure of his adrenal glands, and his reliance on an assortment of drugs and painkillers—remained manageable in the coming years, the timing would not be right. If he did not run in 1960 and another Democrat won the White House, Kennedy would have to wait until 1968. By then, he said, he would get "shoved in the background" by "fresher faces." If a Republican won, he would face the unappetizing prospect of attempting to beat an incumbent in 1964.

So, while he certainly was young enough to wait another four or eight years, he had no intention of doing so. But he had to convince the press that he was not running for president in order to be vice president, and he had to convince the Democratic Party's leadership and primary voters that he was not too young for a job that required more wisdom, experience, and judgment than ever before in the nation's history. That would take some doing— Stevenson said that the senator from Massachusetts did not "fully understand the dimensions of the foreign affairs dilemmas that are coming..."

Mrs. Roosevelt clearly agreed with that assessment, and could not resist letting Kennedy know precisely how she felt. In reply to Kennedy's complaints about some criticisms the former First Lady had directed at him, Mrs. Roosevelt sent a telegram, addressing the senator as "my dear boy" and explaining that her comments were "for your own good."

Mrs. Roosevelt's skepticism of the youthful Kennedy was shared by some of his competitors. During the bitter West Virginia primary, Humphrey referred to Kennedy as "papa's pet," advising him to "grow up and stop acting like a boy." Later on in the campaign, Lyndon Johnson passed around a joke that attacked Kennedy's youth and raised the question of JFK's rumored but unconfirmed health problems—the Texan said that his rival had just gotten good news: his pediatrician had given him a clean bill of health.

To counter these attacks, Kennedy and his aides emphasized the very issue Stevenson believed to be his weakness: foreign affairs. He was immensely more traveled than Johnson or Humphrey, and could rightly claim to be more experienced, despite his youth, on the Cold War issues that figured to dominate the campaign.

On the other hand, Kennedy used his youthful image to counter whispers about his health: his grueling schedule and vigorous demeanor seemed to belie doubts about his physical strength and abilities.

Kennedy had reason to be confident, despite the backbiting from Stevenson and Mrs. Roosevelt. In a poll of Democratic county chairmen before the primaries began, 32 percent said they believed Kennedy would be the nominee. Symington was second with 27 percent, while Johnson and Humphrey were in single digits. Stevenson was the choice of 18 percent of the chairmen.

Kennedy was wise enough to ignore those numbers. He told a reporter, "When someone says to you, 'You're doing fine,' it doesn't mean a thing."

He knew that votes, not personal sentiment, would win the nomination. And, beginning January 2, 1960, he set out to win those votes.

Former First Lady Eleanor Roosevelt
supports Kennedy after his nomination.

*Kennedy speaks to the children of miners
in impoverished West Virginia.*

CHAPTER 1

The Power of the Presidency

Address to the National Press Club
January 14, 1960

TRACK 1

L ESS THAN TWO WEEKS AFTER HE ANNOUNCED HIS CANDIDACY, Senator John Kennedy addressed the National Press Club to discuss not his campaign, but the state of the presidency.

This speech, far more than his bland announcement on January 2, set the tone for the campaign that was to follow. In front of the nation's top political reporters, the impossibly young-looking Kennedy sought to show these professional skeptics that he was a serious candidate despite the handicaps of his religion, youth, and relative inexperience.

In describing how he would use the powers of the presidency, Kennedy took aim at the man who currently held the job he wanted: Dwight David Eisenhower.

Eisenhower was sixty-nine years old in January of 1960, the oldest president in the republic's history. He was, for many cultural and social critics, the very personification of what they viewed as a gray, dull decade. For eager, young politicians, Eisenhower was a symbol of a fading generation—men and women born in the nineteenth century, the aging parents of World War II veterans who were now established adults eager to assume leadership roles in commerce, the arts, and politics.

For Senator John F. Kennedy, age forty-two, Dwight Eisenhower seemed like a perfect foil. The president looked tired and perplexed, out of touch with the generation that had landed on the beaches of Normandy and Okinawa. He was detached at a time when the country was brimming with vigor. He was old when the country was young. He was aimless when the times demanded focus.

Despite all that, he also happened to be quite popular. With personal approval ratings at 59 percent, Dwight Eisenhower—the first president constitutionally forbidden from running for a third term—was very much a formidable presence in American life in 1960. Had he been eligible to run again, he might well have won.

As historians would later concede but few contemporary observers noted, the Eisenhower years were eventful abroad and dynamic at home. During Eisenhower's term, the United States fulfilled the mandate of the American Century, assuming the role of the world's first true superpower. From Iran to the Middle East to Southeast Asia, the Eisenhower administration made it clear that America would not retreat from the role that war and destiny had thrust upon it. At home, the civil rights movement—one of the great social revolutions of the twentieth century—was gathering momentum, pushed along by the actions of individuals like Rosa Parks and institutions like the U.S. Supreme Court.

At the same time, two historically significant (and not unrelated) mass migrations were underway and together they would change the physical, political, and cultural landscape of America for generations. African Americans from the rural South were fleeing poverty and Jim Crow for the industrial cities of the North, where jobs were plentiful even if justice remained imperfect.

Meanwhile, middle-class whites were leaving the cities, in part because of the influx of southern blacks, but also because they could. The Interstate Highway System, one of the Eisenhower administration's greatest domestic accomplishments, opened up the suburbs to large-scale development. The G.I. Bill of Rights gave veterans the money to go to college or buy their first home. Postwar prosperity introduced the notion of the affluent society—two decades removed from the Great Depression, Americans were moving by the carload into the middle class. They went to college, they bought homes and cars, and they established roots in what historian Kenneth Jackson called the "crabgrass frontier."

It was not in John Kennedy's interests, as a candidate for the Democratic Party's presidential nomination in 1960, to concede the astonishing changes that had taken place during the Eisenhower years. Kennedy wished to be seen as the candidate of change, the man who would get the country moving again. So, he adopted the more conventional view of the Eisenhower years, popular among writers and academics, that the country somehow had lost its way, that its claims to greatness were threatened by inertia, disinterest, and mind-numbing conformity, and that its sense of historic purpose was floundering because of stagnant leadership in the White House.

Kennedy's candidacy, then, presented several challenges that were unrelated to what became known as the religious issue—his Catholicism. He had to persuade a content electorate that the nation needed change, and he had to attack the policies of a popular sitting president who also had won fame and the nation's gratitude as Supreme Commander of the Allied Expeditionary Force in World War II. In addition, in seeking to become the youngest presidential nominee since William Jennings Bryan in 1896, Kennedy had the burden of explaining why the party ought to choose him over his older, more established, and more experienced challengers.

On January 14 at the National Press Club in Washington, Kennedy took the first step toward addressing these challenges. The title of the speech, "The Presidency in 1960," had an intentional echo of another speech given at around this time—President Eisenhower's State of the Union address for 1960. Indeed, Kennedy clearly intended this speech to be his version of the state of the presidency, and how he would go about changing it.

Kennedy himself recognized that this seemed like an arrogant act on his part. "Not since the days of Woodrow Wilson had any candidate spoken on the presidency itself before the votes have been irrevocably cast," he said. "Let us hope that the 1960 campaign, in addition to discussing the familiar issues where our positions too often blur, will also talk about the presidency itself, as an instrument for dealing with those issues, as an office with varying roles, powers, and limitations."

By engaging in this rhetorical presumption, Kennedy sought to draw a contrast not between himself and his presumptive Republican opponents Richard Nixon and Nelson Rockefeller, but between himself and Dwight Eisenhower. "During the past eight years," he said, "we have seen one concept of the presidency at work. Our needs and hopes have been eloquently stated, but the initiative and follow-through have too often been left to others." Eisenhower saw himself as above politics, Kennedy said, while he himself preferred "the example of Abe Lincoln, who loved politics with the passion of a born practitioner."

In this speech to the nation's opinion-makers in the press, Kennedy carefully and respectfully presented himself as a man of the hour. The country "may have preferred" Eisenhower's "detached, limited concept of the presidency" in 1952 and 1956, but it now yearned for "a vigorous proponent of the national interest."

As if to address Kennedy's image as a callow youth, at least among the party's elders, the speech is filled with references to past presidents and the nation's founders. He made clear the examples he sought to follow, and the type of presidency he hoped to have. "'The president is at liberty, both in law and conscience, to be as big a man as he can.' So wrote Professor Woodrow Wilson. But President Woodrow Wilson discovered that to be a big man in the White House inevitably brings cries of dictatorship.

"So did Lincoln and Jackson and the two Roosevelts. And so may the next occupant of that office, if he is the man the times demand. But how much better it would be, in the turbulent sixties, to have a Roosevelt or a Wilson than to have another James Buchanan, cringing in the White House, afraid to move."

Here, as in so many instances, Kennedy presumed that his audience spoke the same civic language he did, so when he said that the "turbulent sixties" demanded a figure who would not be like "James Buchanan, cringing in the White House, afraid to move," he offered no further explanation. Listeners were supposed to know, and indeed ought to know, that James Buchanan, the fifteenth president of the United States who served from 1857 to 1861, avoided the hard decisions that might have prevented the Civil War.

After pronouncing what the nation required in a president in the 1960s, Kennedy set out to make sure that he would have the chance to put words into practice. That would require a combination of old fashioned deal making with political bosses who still held enormous influence over state delegations, and retail politicking in states with contested primaries.

There were not many of the latter. In fact, because there were so few truly contested primaries among the sixteen on the campaign schedule—Kennedy, for example, had no opposition in Indiana and Nebraska, and might as well have had none in New Hampshire—the stakes were huge in competitive states like Wisconsin, West Virginia, California, and Oregon.

Of all the primaries that year, West Virginia was the most anticipated. There were few Catholics there, and if Kennedy could be stopped, many figured it would happen in West Virginia. Early on in the campaign, the candidate's brother Robert and two aides asked some campaign workers in West Virginia if they were encountering any problems. One replied, "There's only one problem. He's a Catholic. That's our goddamned problem."

Most West Virginians did not realize that Kennedy was Catholic until the local press began to focus on the issue. His support in the early polls began to evaporate. Kennedy's colleague in the Senate, Hubert Humphrey of Minnesota, emerged as the favorite to beat, and possibly stop, Kennedy.

With so much at stake, Kennedy decided he had little choice but to confront the issue. He hit on a theme that he would later revisit with great success—he reminded West Virginians of his war service, and of his brother's death during the war. Nobody had asked about his religion, or his brother's, while they did their duty for their country. He told a crowd in Charleston: "I am a Catholic…does that mean I can't be president of the United States? I'm able to serve in Congress, and my brother was able to give his life, but we can't be president?"

The argument worked. So did the millions of dollars that the Kennedy campaign committed to West Virginia. Humphrey bitterly criticized the Kennedy spending spree, but there was no denying that the senator from Massachusetts worked hard for his victory. He met face-to-face with the state's coal miners, donning a hard hat and greeting men with calloused hands and black soot on their skin and clothes. He stood on tractors and talked to impoverished children who seemed to belong to another era. Postwar prosperity—the world of suburban homes and new cars and wondrous appliances—had passed by this rural, blue-collar state. He promised West Virginia that he would never forget what he saw there.

He did more than win West Virginia—he won in an unexpected landslide, taking 61 percent of the vote. Hubert Humphrey dropped out of the race.

Kennedy followed up his victory in West Virginia with wins in Maryland and Oregon, establishing himself as the clear frontrunner for the nomination. But in 1960, the era of the back-room deal had not yet been relegated to the political past. Party elders still yearned for Stevenson, especially after Humphrey dropped out of the race. Lyndon Johnson was fighting him every step of the way, and whispering about JFK's precarious health. Harry Truman called for an open convention. On July 10, the day before the convention began in Los Angeles, a reporter asked Kennedy if he believed he had the nomination wrapped up. He said no.

As the convention began, Stevenson attempted to seize the nomination from Kennedy, asking his fellow citizen of Illinois, Chicago mayor Richard J. Daley, to switch the delegation's vote from Kennedy to Stevenson. Daley, Stevenson later said, nearly threw the two-time loser out of his office. Meanwhile, Johnson continued his assaults on Kennedy, and the two men debated each other on day two of the convention in front of their respective state delegations. The following day, July 13, Eugene McCarthy, Humphrey's fellow senator from Minnesota, delivered a rousing speech formally placing Stevenson's name in nomination. The speech set off one of the last truly spontaneous demonstrations in convention history, but Kennedy was not concerned. As he watched the emotional display, he told his father that Stevenson had "everything but delegates."

He was right, of course, and after the names of Kennedy and Johnson also were placed in nomination, balloting began. Unlike today's conventions, where the outcome is decided long before the delegates assemble, there still was some doubt about whether Kennedy had enough votes—seven hundred and sixty-one—for a first-ballot victory. If he did not, there could be no telling how a second ballot might turn out.

The roll call proceeded, and while Kennedy clearly had far more votes than Johnson, his main rival, the only figure that mattered was the magical seven hundred and sixty-one. On the roll call went, as nervous aides kept a running tally. Each delegation brought Kennedy closer and, oddly, farther away, because as the chairman called on Pennsylvania and then Rhode Island and then Texas and then Utah, Kennedy gained votes but remained below the threshold.

Finally, Wyoming—the last state to be called—cast its fifteen votes for Kennedy, giving him two more than necessary.

Elsewhere in the convention hall, John Kennedy allowed himself a smile as he followed the proceedings with his brother and campaign manager, Robert. But the junior Kennedy would not allow himself even a moment of celebration—his head was bowed, and he pounded his left palm with his right hand. He knew their work was hardly done. John Kennedy needed a vice president.

Lyndon Johnson, Kennedy's main rival for the nomination at the convention, seemed to be a natural choice. He represented a large state from a vital region for Democrats, and he was a nationally known, experienced politician. But some of Kennedy's aides had assured liberal allies that JFK would never pick Johnson, a southerner presumed to be hostile to civil rights. Kennedy was confronted with the prospect of a rebellion on his left.

In the face of vocal opposition from party liberals, Kennedy sent his brother to Johnson's suite in Los Angeles on July 14 with an offer not for the vice presidency, but for the chairmanship of the Democratic National Committee. Johnson, who despised Robert Kennedy, refused to grant the emissary an interview. The offer was made through fellow Texan Sam Rayburn, who was not pleased to hear it. Back and forth negotiations through third parties continued for hours, until finally Kennedy formally offered Johnson the number two spot, and Johnson accepted. Kennedy had his reasons for sticking with the Texan: Johnson, he said, would be rendered powerless as vice president. Were he to remain in the Senate, where he was master of his domain, he was certain to be an obstacle to a Kennedy administration agenda.

That surely was the calculation of a seasoned political professional, not a callow, inexperienced, "dear boy."

At the Democratic National Convention, Kennedy tells delegates that the nation faces "a new frontier."

The new presidential nominee celebrates with his choice for vice president,
Senator Lyndon Johnson of Texas.

CHAPTER 2

The Nomination Secured

Acceptance Speech,
Democratic National Convention
July 15, 1960

TRACK 2

TWO DAYS AFTER HIS NOMINATION BECAME OFFICIAL, AND A DAY AFTER the long but ultimately successful negotiations with Lyndon Johnson, an exhausted John Kennedy prepared for his debut as the Democratic Party's candidate for president. The extreme politicking of the past few days, not to mention the campaign that preceded the convention, left Kennedy tired. But there was little time to dwell on sleep deprivation, or anything else but the vital task at hand: introducing himself to the American people as a potential president.

Kennedy's acceptance speech was given not indoors in a convention hall, but outside, in the Los Angeles Coliseum. Eighty thousand people filled the stadium's seats to await John Kennedy's appearance on a brilliant, sun-filled California evening.

As he mounted a platform and took his place behind a podium, Kennedy squinted into a fiery orange sun as it slowly slipped below the western horizon. The crowd roared for the party's new, young champion.

While the crowd's reaction no doubt buoyed him, Kennedy's performance showed the effects of the long nights leading to this moment. His delivery was not crisp. His attacks on Richard Nixon, the Republicans' nominee-presumptive, were at times ham-handed, and his recitation of the nation's ills was predictable. But for the most part, John Kennedy's debut as a presidential nominee was an extraordinary document, foreshadowing themes that would define his presidency, and, most memorably, stamping his future administration with a slogan that captured the spirit of the time: the New Frontier.

Tellingly, the first issue he chose to address was his Catholicism. Clearly, and rightly, he believed the issue had not been settled in West Virginia, and that the ghost of Al Smith—the first Catholic presidential nominee, defeated in 1928—still haunted American politics. "I hope that no American, considering the really critical issues facing this country, will waste his franchise voting either for me or against me solely on account of my religious affiliation," he said. "I am telling you now what you are entitled to know: that my decisions on any public policy will be my own—as an American, a Democrat, and a free man."

In explaining himself to a national audience for the first time as a nominee, he delivered an address littered with references to history, presidential politics, and scripture, which presumed that his listeners spoke a common language rooted in memory, shared experience, and a basic knowledge of Western history. In a sense, then, he was reaffirming what he already had stated—that while he was a Roman Catholic, he also was an American, and a free man. A century earlier, Irish Catholic immigrants had flocked to the Union Army and fought with notable courage, inspired in part by a chance to prove to a suspicious nation that Catholics could be as American as any Protestant. Similarly, in a sense, Kennedy enthusiastically drew lessons from and alluded to milestones in U.S. history, as if to prove that he spoke the same civic language, had the same civic reference points, as any other American.

It is fair to say that American politicians in the twenty-first century, regardless of party, office, or ideology, shy away from the sort of elevated rhetoric Kennedy loved, preferring instead the comfortable vacuity of popular culture where all reference points are current. But, as this speech and others would demonstrate, while John Kennedy believed he was part of a new generation, he also understood that he and his peers were part of the long and storied narrative of U.S., Anglo American, and Western civilization. He believed that Americans ought to have what he called a "sense of historic purpose," and if they did not, he was more than happy to provide it for them.

In one passage early on in the speech, he casually mentioned the last names of several long-dead and fairly obscure presidents to illustrate a point.

In his view, it was not necessary to explain who Franklin Pierce was, or Millard Fillmore or James Buchanan or William Howard Taft—any more than it would be necessary to identify Abraham Lincoln or Woodrow Wilson.

The American experience, as it was interpreted in 1960, was a common point of reference in John Kennedy's speeches, and he was singularly unafraid of assuming that his listeners knew as much as he did about history, leaders, writers, and thinkers. Today, such oratory might be decried as elitist, which it certainly was. But in 1960, that was not necessarily considered such a bad thing.

For example, in launching an attack on Richard Nixon and, at the same time, conceding the popularity of outgoing president Dwight Eisenhower, Kennedy said, "For just as historians tell us that Richard I was not fit to fill the shoes of bold Henry II—and that Richard Cromwell was not fit to wear the mantle of his uncle—they might add in future years that Richard Nixon did not measure to the footsteps of Dwight D. Eisenhower."

The point was a little nasty and nicely made, although some of Kennedy's fellow Irish Americans surely would not have been pleased to hear Richard Cromwell's uncle—Oliver Cromwell, the English antiroyalist who was one of Ireland's great villains—compared favorably with a popular U.S. president, Eisenhower. But the paragraph also is pure Kennedy, as his later speeches would show. Like Churchill, he considered himself a writer and an historian (he had, after all, won a Pulitzer Prize; Churchill did him one better by winning the Nobel Prize for literature). So he gloried in historical reference points, especially those from the Anglo American narrative, which buttressed his argument that 1960 was destined to be regarded as a turning point in U.S. history. And he clearly was not afraid of showing off his knowledge, to the point of not even bothering to identify Richard Cromwell's uncle, the famous and notorious Oliver Cromwell. But even if some listeners were a little hazy on the history of the English Commonwealth, they got the larger point. Richard Nixon was no Dwight Eisenhower.

Kennedy's allusion to some of his less illustrious predecessors was similarly based on the assumption of a common civic reference point and a shared base of knowledge. In taking a swipe at Ike—just after mentioning him in the same breath as bold Henry II and Oliver Cromwell—Kennedy turned back the pages of U.S. history to explain what he saw as the American dilemma in 1960. There may have been times in the past when the nation could move from lackluster leader to lackluster leader, he said, but this was not one of them.

"Perhaps we could better afford a Coolidge following Harding," he said. "And perhaps we could afford a Pierce following Fillmore. But after Buchanan this nation needed a Lincoln—after Taft we needed a Wilson—after Hoover we needed Franklin Roosevelt." Then, after he mentioned the name of that favorite Democratic whipping boy—Herbert Hoover—Kennedy delivered his coup de grace: "And after eight years of drugged and fitful sleep, this nation needs strong, creative Democratic leadership in the White House."

The party faithful responded with cheers, because even if they were not precisely sure of James Buchanan's failings or why it was all right for Pierce to follow Fillmore, they accepted Kennedy's contention that the Eisenhower years were sleepy and uneventful, even as the world became more dangerous.

The Los Angeles speech also featured a glimpse of some of the rhetorical devices Kennedy would use over the coming years. Perhaps the most obvious was the citation of the prophet Isaiah, called into service in this speech near its conclusion: "Recall with me the words of Isaiah," Kennedy said, complimenting his listeners on their memory of scripture. "They that wait upon the Lord shall renew their strength; they shall mount up with wings as eagles; they shall run and not be weary."

Isaiah, who lived and preached near the kingdom of Judah around 750 BC, was best known to most of Kennedy's Christian listeners as a prophet who foretold the birth of a child-redeemer. Readings from his prophesies were and remain a part of the Christmas season in many Christian churches. Christians and Jews alike were familiar with his call to turn "swords into ploughshares," his emphasis on social justice, and his insistence that rituals have no meaning unless they are accompanied by devotion and spirituality. ("'What to me is the multitude of your sacrifices,' says the Lord, 'I have had enough of burnt offerings....'")

As the official Old Testament prophet of the New Frontier, Isaiah would go on to perform yeoman work for John Kennedy in the years ahead.

The overriding theme of the speech, however, was his evocation of the New Frontier, beyond which were "the uncharted areas of science and space, unsolved problems of peace and war, unconquered pockets of ignorance and prejudice, unanswered questions of poverty and surplus." In a masterful combination of place, words, and imagery, Kennedy noted that he was facing west, just as "the pioneers of old" had looked westward to a land that "was once the last frontier." But now there was a new frontier, "the frontier of the 1960s—a

frontier of unknown opportu
and threats."

Another device that woul
Kennedy's citation of unident
always seemed to clash with his
"some would say" that "all horiz
have been won, that there is no
these people? Kennedy said he w
would return to the "some people"
tion, most memorably in Berlin in
some who say that communism is th

Drawing yet again on the Anglo
he had made a passing reference to
George, saying that "a tired nation…i   ᴗnited States, he
said, "cannot afford to be either tired

John Kennedy himself had been a tired man when he began his speech. By
its end, however, he seemed to find new energy, enough to propel him on a
journey that would take him to his, and America's, new frontier.

John F. Kennedy addressing the annual Al Smith Dinner in 1960.
At right: Francis Cardinal Spellman and Vice President Richard Nixon.

CHAPTER 3

The "So-Called Religious Issue"

Address to the Greater Houston
Ministerial Association
September 12, 1960

TRACK 3

J OHN KENNEDY'S TRIP TO HOUSTON IN 1960 WAS FILLED WITH NOT ONLY political significance, but also historical symbolism. It was in this southern city, thirty-two years earlier, that another Catholic from the Northeast received the Democratic Party's nomination for president. As delegates suffered through a Texas-style heat wave in 1928, Alfred E. Smith of New York overcame religious hostility and downright bigotry to become the first Catholic presidential nominee in U.S. history.

But even as Smith's supporters celebrated his historic victory on the convention floor in Houston, it was clear that many southern Democrats were not happy. One Texas delegate observed the Smith delegates as they paraded through the aisles: they were city dwellers, immigrants, and first-generation Americans, and many were Catholic. "I wondered where were the Americans," the delegate grumbled.

Smith was well aware of such sentiments, and he sought to reassure those who believed his ultimate loyalty was to the pope and not the republic. When a writer in the *Atlantic Monthly* charged that Smith would be forced to follow Vatican dictates as president, Smith enlisted his friend Father Francis Duffy to compose a well-reasoned reply. Even as he reaffirmed his Catholic faith,

Smith said he believed in "the absolute freedom of conscience for all men and in equality for all churches, all sects, and all beliefs...." He added that Roman Catholic "institutions" would not "interfere with the operations of the Constitution of the United States or the enforcement of the laws of the land." Indeed, there had been no such conflicts during his four terms as governor of New York, he noted.

It was all in vain. Al Smith lost in a landslide to Herbert Hoover. Smith's religion was not the only reason for his defeat—Republicans were in favor thanks to the Jazz Age's affluence and too-easy money. (In 1927, Will Rogers predicted a Democratic defeat the following year, noting that "you can't lick this prosperity thing.") Still, Smith's defeat seemed proof that the White House was open to only Anglo-Saxon Protestants. The barriers Smith shattered on behalf of Catholics, urban America, and minority groups in general, were quickly put back in place. Presidential candidates in the three decades following Smith's nomination were uniformly Protestant, with little connection to the urban, immigrant America of the twentieth century.

While John Kennedy was far removed from the immigrant experience and could hardly be described as a child of urban America, he was very much Al Smith's successor. Never mind that his family was rich and prominent, never mind that he had gone to prep school and Harvard. He was Catholic and he was Irish. His last name was Kennedy, not Roosevelt. And as he followed in Al Smith's footsteps, he learned that in some parts of the United States, things had not changed a great deal since 1928. Formidable barriers, suspicions, and prejudices would have to be confronted again. With Kennedy leading the national ticket in 1960, the candidate's staff reckoned that anti-Catholic bias might cost the Democrats 1.5 million votes—more than enough to turn the tide if the election were close, as it would be.

And so, Kennedy traveled to Houston, site of Al Smith's greatest triumph, to face the issue head-on at a meeting of Protestant ministers. He did so despite the advice of his staff and of two prominent Texans—his running mate, Lyndon Johnson, and the legendary Speaker of the House of Representatives, Sam Rayburn. "They're mostly Republicans and they're out to get you," Rayburn said.

It did not matter. Kennedy was determined to confront those who, he said, believed that he would "replace the gold in Fort Knox with a supply of holy water." His brother Bobby said that "religion is the biggest issue in the South, and in the country." The candidate believed he could not ignore the problem any longer. After his primary victory in heavily Protestant West Virginia, he had asserted that the religious issue no longer mattered. He was wrong.

It was as though Al Smith had never lived, and had never been nominated thirty-two years earlier.

In Al Smith's day, anti-Catholic propagandists suggested that the pope was preparing to set up shop in the White House, where he would destroy American liberty (which they equated with the Protestant faith, regardless of how many Catholics had given their lives to defend it). Political discussion had not evolved all that much since those days. Two months before Kennedy's trip to Houston, a Baptist minister in the Lone Star State told a large radio audience that "Roman Catholicism is not only a religion, it is a political tyranny." Another Baptist preacher, this one in Colorado, said, "Let the Romanists move out of America." A minister in Little Rock, Arkansas, declared that the country should not "turn our government over to a Catholic president who could be influenced by the pope and by the power of the Catholic hierarchy."

Al Smith would have recognized those sentiments.

Ironically, neither Smith nor Kennedy was particularly immersed in the dogma and tenets of their faith—as opposed to a later voice for Roman Catholics in the public square, Mario Cuomo. As historian Robert Slayton pointed out, Smith's friend Frances Perkins once said that Smith "never knew theology of the Roman Catholic Church, and I don't think he cared much about it." There is evidence to support Perkins' contention. In Smith's 1928 *Atlantic Monthly* article, he admitted that while he had been a "devout Catholic since childhood," he had never heard of the papal encyclicals his critics had cited as proof that he was a stooge of the Vatican.

John Kennedy, far more learned and sophisticated than Smith, was nearly as unlettered in Catholic dogma. So, just as Smith enlisted Father Duffy to advise him on matters of theology, Kennedy drafted John Cogley, a distinguished lay writer for the Catholic magazine *Commonweal*, to help him prepare for his mission to Houston.

The speech was an extraordinary gamble. Kennedy addressed not only a large group of influential and highly skeptical Protestant ministers, but also millions of other Americans who watched the speech on television. The wrong word or phrase could have handed the presidency to Richard Nixon, who was, incidentally, not a mainstream Protestant himself, but a Quaker.

Protestants, however, were not the only people with an interest in this speech. Kennedy's fellow Catholics—numbering about 36 million, and making up about 25 percent of the electorate—were sure to listen closely, too. If Kennedy seemed to distance himself from his faith, if he seemed too deferential to the people who had hounded Al Smith and who were making his own life miserable, American Catholics would have reason to question his loyalty to his faith, even as Protestants wondered about his loyalty to his country.

According to Thomas Maier's study of the Kennedy family, the candidate and his speechwriter, Theodore Sorensen, consulted the nation's leading Catholic theologian, the Reverend John Courtney Murray, in an effort to clean up any "loose wording…that would unnecessarily stir up the Catholic press." Sorensen read the speech to Father Murray over the telephone. While the extent of the priest's influence on the speech is not certain, Father Murray had long insisted that church-state separation was essential for American Catholics because they were a religious minority, and because such a division was essential in a modern democracy.

Kennedy clearly had learned to be more thoughtful in his remarks about faith and politics. A year earlier, in 1959, he had earned the ire of some Catholic newspapers when he seemed to distance himself from his faith. In an interview with *Look* magazine, he noted that he opposed federal aid to Catholic schools and the appointment of an ambassador to the Vatican. He seemed to go out of his way to show that he did not march in lockstep with the Church on political and social issues. Catholic commentators believed he went too far, and seemed entirely too eager to show that while he was a Catholic, he was not *too* Catholic.

Indeed, the question of just how Catholic Kennedy was—how much his faith meant to him, how seriously he took its rituals and strictures—remains difficult to answer. Jacqueline Kennedy took note of the irony in the attacks on her husband over his religion. "I think it's so unfair of people to be against Jack because he is a Catholic," she once famously said. "He's such a poor Catholic."

Certainly, the record shows that he was far from the Catholic ideal as a husband; then again, he was far from any person's ideal as a husband. There is no indication that he took a special interest in Church history, or much beyond the rituals he knew so well from his very religious mother, Rose. His education was avowedly secular, and his cool, ironic demeanor did little to suggest a private piety.

Thomas Maier, however, argues that Kennedy was more serious about his faith than his public image indicated. He formed a strong friendship with the archbishop of Boston, Richard Cardinal Cushing. Maier also noted that Kennedy attended Mass regularly—although in those pre-Vatican II days, "regularly" simply would not do in the eyes of orthodox Catholics. Weekly attendance was mandatory. Other friends and associates testified to Kennedy's appreciation for the sacramental side of Catholicism—its traditions and rituals—if not its dogma.

Still, whatever his private relationship with his faith, he was destined to be labeled, to his chagrin, as the Catholic candidate for president in 1960. And it was because of that label, and because of what he saw as its unfairness, that he went to Houston to settle the issue as best he could.

His speech was a masterpiece of reason, diplomacy, and perhaps a touch of defiance. Kennedy delivered it crisply, and without pausing for applause. He did not begin with formalities or references to his setting or the hospitality he had received. Instead, he attacked the issue head on from the very first sentence: he had come, he said, to address the "so-called religious issue." The phrase indicated JFK's own views—this was not a real issue. It was a "so-called" issue, a distraction from far more important business. "But because I am a Catholic...the real issues in this campaign have been obscured," he said.

From the perspective of the early twenty-first century, when Catholics have won acceptance, however grudgingly, in most of mainstream America, it is remarkable to remember that as recently as 1960, John Kennedy found himself on the defensive because of his religion.

The speech laid out the case not for John Kennedy's candidacy, but for a more tolerant America. "For while this year it may be a Catholic against whom the finger of suspicion is pointed, in other years it has been, and may someday be again, a Jew, or a Quaker, or a Unitarian, or a Baptist. It was Virginia's harassment of Baptist preachers, for example, that helped lead to Jefferson's Statute of Religious Freedom. Today I may be the victim—but tomorrow it may be you—until the whole fabric of our harmonious society is ripped at a time of great national peril."

He spoke of the signature experience of his generation—service in World War II—and noted without being maudlin that when he served in the South Pacific, nobody "suggested then that we may have 'divided loyalty,' that we did 'not believe in liberty,' or that we belonged to a disloyal group that threatened the 'freedoms for which our forefathers died.'

"And in fact this is the kind of America for which our forefathers died—whether they fled here to escape religious test oaths that denied office to members of less-favored churches—when they fought for the Constitution, the Bill of Rights, and the Virginia Statute of Religious Freedom—and when they fought at the shrine I visited today, the Alamo. For side by side with Bowie and Crockett died McCafferty and Bailey and Carey—but no one knows whether they were Catholics or not. For there was no religious test at the Alamo."

He reminded his audience that his brother Joe was killed during the war, fighting to protect not the pope, but American liberty.

"I do not speak for my church on public matters—and the church does not speak for me," he said. He cited his differences with church pronouncements on public policy, but he said pointedly that he had no intention of disavowing his faith. "But if the time should ever come—and I do not concede any conflict to be even remotely possible—when my office would require me to either violate my conscience or violate the national interest, then I would resign the office, and hope any conscientious public servant would do the same."

After finishing his remarks, he opened the floor for questions from an audience of respectable-looking middle-aged white men dressed in jackets and ties, their hair neat and trim. They had not interrupted the speech even once with applause. Kennedy had no idea how the speech was received and what kind of questions he might face.

One inquisitor asked if Kennedy would have his friend Cardinal Cushing deliver a statement to the pope containing the candidate's remarks on the separation of church and state, so that the Vatican "may officially authorize such a belief for all Roman Catholics in the United States." Kennedy, standing slightly stoop-shouldered with his hands grasping either side of the podium, replied that just as the clergy had no right to tell him what to do "in my sphere of public responsibility," he had no right to tell Cardinal Cushing to ask the Vatican "to take some action." His sincerity and his reasonableness won over the bulk of his audience. "We appreciate your forthright statement," one minister said. "May I say we have great admiration for you." As Kennedy prepared to leave, he quipped, "I am sure I have made no converts to my church." The ministers may not have been converted to Catholicism, but perhaps to Kennedy's campaign. They gave him a standing ovation.

But it would be another forty-four years—more than a decade longer than the span between Al Smith and JFK—before another Catholic was nominated for president. And even then, that Catholic candidate, John F. Kerry of Massachusetts, found himself on the defensive over the "so-called religious issue." But in an ironic twist, the people who put Kerry on the defensive were not Protestant ministers, but Roman Catholic bishops, and the issue was not the candidate's loyalty to the Constitution, but his adherence to Church doctrine.

The Kennedy family in Vatican City, 1939.

Moderator Howard K. Smith flanked by Kennedy and Nixon in the first debate.

CHAPTER 4

The First Debate

Chicago
September 26, 1960

TRACK 4

THE STORY OF JOHN KENNEDY'S FIRST DEBATE WITH RICHARD Nixon is part of American folklore. Most educated Americans know, or at least they think they know, what happened on that noteworthy evening in 1960 when two presidential nominees stood side by side for the first time in U.S. history to debate the great issues of the day.

The debate, of course, was televised on all three broadcast networks, achieving another kind of milestone—the beginning of the modern era of image-conscious, media-savvy, sound-bite politics.

As the story goes, John Kennedy won that debate because he was tan and relaxed, and Richard Nixon was pale and nervous. Many of those who watched the event on television—and some eighty million Americans did so—believed Kennedy won. Those who listened on radio, who heard only words and argument, believed Nixon was the winner. And so, style triumphed over substance, and American politics has never been the same.

While there is some truth in the popular version of that historic meeting, what happened on the night of September 26, 1960—and what did not happen—is a bit more complicated.

Perhaps the most important and forgotten fact is that the first debate was exactly that—the first debate, which was intended to focus on domestic issues. Three more followed, although none is as well remembered. Many political observers, especially those who supported Nixon, believed the first debate would be the least watched, and the final debate, the most watched. Instead, viewership declined by some twenty million by the second debate, from eighty million to sixty million, and remained at that number.

It took, literally, an act of Congress to allow television coverage of the debates. A clause in the Communications Act of 1934 required broadcasters to offer equal time to all candidates, even from obscure independent parties. Congress had to suspend the equal-time provision before the networks could proceed with a debate featuring only Kennedy and Nixon. (In the mid-1970s, federal regulators declared that debates sponsored by outside agencies were news events not bound by legislative restrictions.)

Another popular misconception has it that the Kennedy-Nixon debates created a precedent. While they were historic, the debates did not institutionalize face-to-face meetings between the major party presidential candidates. In fact, the debates between Kennedy and Nixon actually were not the first between presidential candidates. Twelve years earlier, in 1948, Republican rivals Thomas E. Dewey of New York and Harold Stassen of Minnesota debated each other in Portland, Oregon, before that state's presidential primary. And in 1956, the two leading candidates for the Democratic presidential nomination, Adlai Stevenson of Illinois and Estes Kefauver of Tennessee, debated each other in Miami before the Florida primary. Both debates were broadcast nationwide on radio. The Kennedy-Nixon debates were the first between major-party *nominees.*

And while the debates of 1960 created enormous public interest, sixteen years would pass before anything like them happened again. There were no debates during the campaigns of 1964, 1968, and 1972, and there was little in the way of public pressure to hold them. Not coincidentally, of course, Richard Nixon was the nominee in two of those three debateless elections. He had been poorly served in 1960 by agreeing to debate the lesser-known Kennedy. He made sure he did not repeat that tactical mistake in 1968 and 1972.

So it was not until 1976 that the presidential debate truly became part of the campaign season. Every campaign since has included at least one debate featuring a Democrat and a Republican, with the occasional independent. As precedents go, the one established in 1976 certainly deserves a greater place in the American memory. The debates that year offered something the Kennedy-Nixon debates did not—the spectacle of a sitting president of the United States standing side by side with his opponent.

When incumbent Gerald Ford and challenger Jimmy Carter shared a stage in Philadelphia on September 23, 1976, it was a moment literally unparalleled in American political history and a landmark in democratic politics befitting the nation's bicentennial celebrations. Until that debate, incumbent presidents had steadfastly refused to debate—or at times even acknowledge—their challengers. They did not wish to be seen on a level playing field with a mere senator or governor. But Gerald Ford ended that tradition, and today it is hard to imagine an incumbent president refusing to debate. For that reason, the Ford-Carter debates may have been more historic and more important than the better-remembered debates of 1960.

Nevertheless, there is no denying that the Kennedy-Nixon debates do retain a hold on America's memory, and have become part of the Kennedy canon. But the story behind the story begins not from the moment when Kennedy looked into the camera on September 26 and seemed so confident and so good looking, or when the camera caught a gaunt Nixon with his eyes darting about. The story actually begins in mid-August, in Greensboro, North Carolina.

During a quick campaign swing through that city, Nixon bumped his knee while getting into a car. The candidate did not make much of it at the time—it was just another bump on the rocky road to the White House. Nixon shook it off.

Twelve days later, however, even the stoic Nixon could no longer ignore the pain. The knee had become infected, and the vice president was admitted to Walter Reed Hospital. His plan to seize the initiative from Kennedy, who was tied up with a special session in the Senate, disintegrated.

Nixon remained in the hospital for two weeks, enduring daily injections of antibiotics. He had been leading in the Gallup Poll at the end of July, but by the end of August, as he lay powerless in his hospital bed, the race had become a dead heat.

Finally, he returned to the campaign on September 9, and immediately attempted to make up for lost ground. But it was too much, too soon. He contracted a fever, with his temperature soaring to 103 degrees. Nevertheless, he continued to campaign as the first debate drew near, covering twenty-five states in two weeks. On the day of the debate, he gave a speech to the carpenters union in Chicago.

By the time he arrived in the studio for the much-anticipated debate, he was exhausted, gaunt, and simply not well. He had lost ten pounds and at least one collar size, based on the shirt he wore for the debate.

The popular legend is correct: Nixon looked miserable. He refused to wear makeup, choosing instead to cover his five o'clock shadow with something called "Lazy Shave."

Kennedy, of course, looked a good deal better. But he also was better prepared, having immersed himself in dozens of "fact cards" prepared by his aides. Praise for his speech in Houston to the ministers had boosted his confidence, and while Nixon was running around Chicago on the day of the debate, Kennedy relaxed in a hotel room, cramming for possible questions and reviewing his notes.

The debate's format called for each candidate to give an opening statement focusing on domestic issues, and Kennedy understood just how important this first impression would be. He was not satisfied with the statement his writers produced, so he dictated one of his own, hours before he was due in the studio.

So the stage was set for history. The debate's moderator was Howard K. Smith of CBS, and the panel consisted of Sander Vanocur of NBC, Charles Warren of the Mutual Broadcasting System (a now-deceased giant of network radio), Stuart Novins of CBS, and Bob Fleming of ABC.

Kennedy not only looked better than Nixon did, but his opening statement—that important first impression—was a masterful piece of rhetoric. Short on specifics, replete with telling anecdotes, it was forward-looking, and it conveyed the candidate's belief that the nation could do better.

"In the election of 1960…the question is whether the world will exist half slave or half free, whether it will move in the direction of freedom, in the direction of the road that we are taking, or whether it will move in the direction of slavery…

"Therefore, I think the question before the American people is: Are we doing as much as we can do? Are we as strong as we should be? Are we as strong as we must be if we are going to maintain our independence, and if we're going to maintain and hold out the hand of friendship to those who look to us for assistance, to those who look to us for survival? I should make it very clear that I do not think we're doing enough, that I am not satisfied as an American with the progress that we are making…

"I saw cases in West Virginia, here in the United States, where children took home part of their school lunch in order to feed their families...I'm not satisfied when many of our teachers are inadequately paid...I'm not satisfied when I see men like Jimmy Hoffa, in charge of the largest union in the United States, still free...I'm not satisfied until every American enjoys his full constitutional rights...I think we can do better."

Nixon's opening statement, on the other hand, was defensive and replete with numbers that might better have been used later on, during the question and answer session.

Still, the story of the first debate is the story of appearances, one good, the other, not very good. Politics would never be quite the same.

Nixon would later write, ruefully: "It is a devastating commentary on the nature of television as a political medium that what hurt me the most in the first debate was not the substance of the encounter...but the disadvantageous contrast in our physical appearances."

The nature of television has not changed since. The nature of politics has.

Kennedy prepares for a televised address.

CHAPTER 5

The Second Debate

Washington, D.C.
October 7, 1960

TRACK 5

IN THE POPULAR TELLING OF THE 1960 ELECTION, RICHARD NIXON LOST his debate with John Kennedy because of his pallor, five o'clock shadow, and darting eyes, all of which contrasted with the tan, detached, and well-pressed Kennedy. Overlooked and nearly forgotten is the fact that the two candidates met not once, but four times. The first debate has become part of American political folklore, overshadowing the other sessions. But in the fall of 1960, with the two candidates running close in the polls, nobody counted out Richard Nixon based on his performance in that initial debate.

Frank McGee of *NBC News*, who would later become the network's anchor on the evening news, moderated the second debate, which took place in Washington. The panel consisted of Edward P. Morgan of ABC, Paul Nivens of CBS, Alvin Spivak of United Press International, and Harold Levy of *Newsday*.

Richard Nixon's health was much better than it had been in the first debate, and so—not surprisingly—was his appearance. In the eleven days between debates, he drank four milkshakes a day to regain some of the weight he had lost during his illness. And he agreed to use makeup.

From the very first question, the vice president showed that he was determined to slow the momentum Kennedy had gained thanks, in Nixon's view, to his makeup and looks. "I immediately took the offensive," Nixon later wrote.

Neither candidate gave an opening statement, taking away Kennedy's edge in extemporaneous rhetoric. And Nixon's answer to the opening question signaled that this would be a contentious session. The questioner, Nivens of CBS, noted that Kennedy had said, in essence, that the Eisenhower administration had lost Cuba. Nixon had complained more than a decade earlier that the Truman administration had lost China. Wasn't the comparison valid?

Nixon was waiting to pounce, and he did. He said he did not agree with JFK's assertion that Cuba was lost, suggesting that the Castro revolution could be short-lived. He defended the Republican record in Latin America by noting that the number of dictators in the region had been reduced, never mind Castro's rise in Cuba. And, in a brilliant gesture born of Nixon's intense preparations, he cited a passage from a book Kennedy had just published, *A Strategy of Peace*. In that book, written for the campaign, Kennedy had emphasized that the United States could not interfere in the internal affairs of neighboring nations. Nixon said Kennedy's position was correct.

This was a new Nixon—more confident, more belligerent, and more telegenic than in the previous debate.

The debate, like the campaign itself, primarily focused on Cold War issues, from national defense to international diplomacy. But UPI's Spivak inspired a discussion on the single domestic issue that would define the coming decade—civil rights. Spivak took note of both candidates' evasive statements on the subject, and then asked a pointed question. To Nixon, he said, "You have accused Senator Kennedy of avoiding the civil rights issue when he has been in the South and he has accused you of the same thing. With both North and South listening and watching, would you sum up your own intentions in the field of civil rights if you become president?"

North and South, East and West, listeners and viewers paid careful attention. For the first time in U.S. history, two presidential nominees were being asked to talk about race in a face-to-face meeting. In the past, as Spivak noted, candidates for national office could tailor their views on race—or avoid a discussion all together—depending on where they were campaigning. But now, with the entire nation tuning in, it was no longer possible to say one thing in the North, and another in the South.

Both Kennedy and Nixon, Cold Warriors to their very marrow, were immensely more comfortable talking about issues that now seem arcane—the plight of Quemoy and Matsu, two islands off Communist China, is the classic example of urgency then, trivia today. Race was an issue that both men treated gingerly, for in this closely contested election, neither man wished to alienate white southerners even as they contested for black votes.

Richard Nixon hoped to increase the black Republican vote in 1960. He had a high-profile endorsement from baseball legend Jackie Robinson, and he believed that voter registration drives led by Dr. Martin Luther King Jr. might bring in new voters with no special loyalty to or memory of Franklin Roosevelt's New Deal coalition. Under President Eisenhower, Nixon had led a federal panel designed to eliminate racial discrimination in the awarding of federal contracts, and he supported civil rights legislation in the late 1950s. Journalist Tom Wicker, covering the Nixon campaign near Atlanta, took note of the surprisingly large number of black faces in the crowd.

Kennedy, more so than Nixon, had to finesse civil rights in a way that would alienate neither the Eleanor Roosevelt-Adlai Stevenson wing of the party nor the Southern Democrats who ruled Congress. The party's liberals opposed JFK's selection of Lyndon Johnson, who was viewed as a typical white southerner hostile to the civil rights movement. But Southern Democrats opposed the civil rights plank in the party's platform.

For Kennedy, the political dilemmas of civil rights were an annoyance that tested his patience. Two months before the second debate, he had said to his aide, Harris Wofford, "Now, in five minutes, tick off the ten things that a president ought to do to clean up this goddamn civil rights mess." Wofford, who would go on to perform heroic work as a Justice Department official in the South during the Kennedy administration, said that Kennedy "was not knowledgeable" about civil rights issues, in large part because it was "alien to most of his experience" as a child of privilege who grew up in the North, attended Harvard, and traveled overseas. He had not seen the effects of Jim Crow in the South, and the issue itself did not receive intense media coverage in the 1950s. But, Wofford said, he believed Kennedy was ready to learn.

Still, it was with some caution that Kennedy, as well as Nixon, answered Spivak's query, and a follow-up question from *Newsday's* Levy about the 1957 deployment of federal troops to Little Rock, Arkansas, to enforce school desegregation and the burgeoning sit-in movement protesting segregated lunch counters.

Both candidates emphasized that civil rights was a national issue, not limited to the South. Nixon condemned outright discrimination at the lunch counter. "I have talked to Negro mothers," Nixon said. "I have heard them explain, try to explain, how they tell their children how they can go into a store and buy a loaf of bread, but then can't go into that store and sit at the counter and get a Coca-Cola. This is wrong and we have to do something about it."

Kennedy's answers sounded a theme he would return to—belatedly for some activists—as president, saying that he would "establish a moral tone" on civil rights. "There is a very strong moral basis for this concept of equality before the law," he said. "Not only equality before the law, but also equality of opportunity. We are in a very difficult time. We need all the talent we can get...We are a goldfish bowl before the world. We have to practice what we preach...I believe the president of the United States should indicate that."

In fact, moral leadership on the civil rights issues already had been established—not by the cautious, calculating candidates for president, but by Martin Luther King and his fellow civil rights leaders. Less than two weeks after the debate, King and some fifty supporters were arrested en masse in Atlanta after conducting a sit-in at a segregated restaurant. King, increasingly regarded as a dangerous man to the enforcers of segregation, was sentenced to four months in prison on the unrelated but convenient charge of operating a motor vehicle without a license.

In the ensuing political drama over King's sentence, John Kennedy called King's wife, Coretta Scott King, to express his sympathies. Richard Nixon's spokesman issued a terse "no comment" when asked about King's sentence.

Nixon's dream of winning significant black support in 1960 evaporated. King's father, Martin Luther King Sr., announced that he had decided to switch his vote from Nixon to Kennedy, because of JFK's timely call to his daughter-in-law. In a statement that revealed more than he intended, the elder King said he did not think he would ever vote for a Catholic for president. But now he would vote for Kennedy, "Catholic or whatever he is."

Upon hearing King's announcement, JFK was more bemused than overjoyed, and he, too, revealed a glimpse of his private thoughts. "Imagine Martin Luther King having a bigot for a father," he said. "Well, we all have fathers, don't we?"

Martin Luther King Jr. and Coretta Scott King.

Chinese Nationalist leader Chiang Kai-shek. Relations between the U.S. and Communist China were a feature of the third debate.

CHAPTER 6

The Third Debate

New York and Hollywood
October 13, 1960

TRACK 6

THIS WAS THE ONLY ONE OF THE FOUR KENNEDY-NIXON DEBATES IN which the candidates argued with each other but were not face-to-face. In a display of circa-1960 technology at its most advanced, Kennedy addressed Nixon, the press, and the nation from a studio in New York. Nixon did likewise from a studio three thousand miles away, in Hollywood. And the moderator and panel of reporters addressed the candidates from a third studio, so that Kennedy and Nixon saw each other and their inquisitors only on monitors installed in their respective studios.

The evening's moderator, Bill Shadel of ABC News, took pains to note that the candidates' studios were "identical in every detail of lighting, background, physical equipment, even to the paint used in decorating." There were no aides in either studio, Shadel noted.

The panel consisted of Frank McGee of NBC who had moderated the second debate, Charles Von Fremd of *CBS News*, Douglass Cater of the now-defunct *Reporter* magazine, and Roscoe Drummond of the *New York Herald Tribune*. The names of Cater and Drummond were drawn by lot from among the print reporters who covered the two candidates.

This debate featured a prolonged and at times heated discussion of

Quemoy and Matsu, the two islands off the Chinese coast that the Communists were threatening. The Chinese nationalist leader, Chiang Kai-shek, put troops on the two islands as a means of defending the anticommunist enclave on the island of Formosa, now generally referred to as Taiwan. The Communist Chinese saw the deployment, by a U.S. ally, as an unacceptable threat. The two islands were just several miles from the Chinese mainland, but more than a hundred miles from Chiang's nationalist base on Formosa.

In the previous debate, JFK hinted that the islands were not worth defending, unless a Communist attack on them was part of a general assault on U.S. allies on Formosa. The day before the third debate, Kennedy revisited that theme, using the word "trigger-happy" to describe Republicans—Nixon presumably included—who supported a more aggressive policy to protest Quemoy and Matsu.

Nixon saw his opportunity, and he took it. Several minutes into the third debate, he attacked Kennedy for his use of the phrase, and he implied that the Democrats were the party of war. "I would ask [Kennedy] to name one Republican president who led this nation into war" over the last fifty years, he said. "There were three Democratic presidents who led us into war." (Sixteen years later, vice presidential candidate Bob Dole would revisit Nixon's theme in a televised debate with Walter Mondale. Dole, a disabled World War II veteran, condemned the "Democrat wars" of the twentieth century. Nixon quickly noted that he did not mean to say that one party had a monopoly on war mongering.)

Kennedy stuck to his position, arguing that the two islands were not part of U.S. obligations to Chiang and the Chinese nationalists on Formosa. The candidates revisited the issue during the course of several answers. Years later, Nixon said that he "hit hard" on the issue of the two islands because he believed "Kennedy's willingness to surrender the islands to the Communists under threat of war was no different from submitting to blackmail." By the time Nixon wrote those words in the late 1970s, few Americans remembered the controversy. And today, the debate over the islands is as obscure as another issue raised in this session, the movement of gold from the U.S. to its trading partners around the world.

More memorable were Kennedy's flashes of wit—at one point he said, "I always have difficulty recognizing my positions when they are stated by the vice president"—and the candidates' exchanges over former president Harry Truman's salty language and the issue of Kennedy's Catholicism.

Truman loathed Nixon so deeply he gladly overcame his own suspicions about Kennedy to campaign actively for the Democratic Party ticket in 1960. In Truman's eyes, Nixon was a coconspirator with Joseph McCarthy in a campaign to smear Democrats as soft on Communists, and perhaps even crypto-Communists themselves. The 1960 campaign offered Truman a chance to avenge what he saw as unfair criticisms not only of his administration, but of people like his secretary of state, George C. Marshall, author of The Marshall Plan and the U.S. Army's chief of staff during World War II.

Truman was never one to hide behind decorous language. In the fall of 1960, he said that the sitting vice president of the United States—Nixon—the Republican Party, and the party's supporters should "go to hell." Von Fremd of CBS raised the issue during the third debate, noting that the chairman of the Republican National Committee, Thurston Morton, had demanded an apology from Kennedy for Truman's language. Kennedy gave a lighthearted answer. "Well, I must say that Mr. Truman has his methods of expressing things…Maybe it's not my style, but I really don't think there's anything I can say to President Truman that's going to cause him, at the age of seventy-six, to change his particular speaking manner. Perhaps Mrs. Truman can, but I don't think I can."

Nixon took the issue a bit more seriously. "President Eisenhower restored dignity and decency and, frankly, good language to the conduct of the presidency of the United States," he said. "And I only hope that, should I win this election, that I could approach President Eisenhower in maintaining the dignity of the office, in seeing to it that whenever any mother or father talks to his child, he can look at the man in the White House, and whatever he may think of his policies, he will say, 'Well, there is a man who maintains the kind of standards personally that I would want my child to follow.'"

Years later, Nixon's own salty language was captured on tape, and then made public, during the Watergate crisis.

Kennedy apparently was satisfied with his handling of the Truman affair, because he revisited the issue several days after the third debate, at the annual Al Smith Dinner in New York. The dinner, hosted by Francis Cardinal Spellman, honored the memory of the first Catholic candidate for president, and was made memorable by the presence of both candidates dressed in formal dress (Kennedy in a black tie, Nixon in white) and paying homage to the cardinal and to Smith. Kennedy commented on Nixon's warning against profanity in the third debate. "One of the inspiring notes that was struck in the last debate was struck by the vice president in his very moving warning to the children of the nation and the candidates against the use of profanity by presidents and ex-presidents when they are on the stump. And I know after fourteen years in the Congress with the vice president that he was very sincere in his views about the use of profanity. But I am told that a prominent Republican said to him yesterday in Jacksonsville, Florida, 'Mr. Vice President, that was a damn fine speech.' And the vice president said, 'I appreciate the compliment, but not the language.' And the Republican went on, 'Yes, sir, I liked it so much that I contributed a thousand dollars to your campaign.' And Mr. Nixon replied, 'The hell you say.'"

Kennedy added that in accordance with Nixon's condemnation of Truman's expressed desire to send the vice president and Republicans to hell, he had sent a telegram to the former president. "While I understand and sympathize with your deep motivation," Kennedy's telegram read, "I think it is important that our side try to refrain from raising the religious issue."

But the religious issue had indeed been raised, and was again in the third debate. Drummond, of the *Herald Tribune*, quoted an inflammatory statement from the inflammatory New York congressman Adam Clayton Powell Jr. that suggested that the Ku Klux Klan would support Nixon while "right-thinking Christians and Jews" would support Kennedy.

JFK's measured response and Nixon's unequivocal condemnation of religious bigotry, delivered to an audience of sixty million people, made it clear that neither side approved of religious-based appeals. And, as Nixon biographer Tom Wicker has noted, the Quaker from California steadfastly refused to raise the issue of Kennedy's religion. While Nixon's critics have said that he did just that by talking about his refusal to raise the issue, Wicker notes that Nixon did so generally in response to reporters' questions. He did not raise the issue on his own.

"It can be and has been argued that Nixon secretly inspired anti-Catholic attacks while publicly and piously denying that he was doing any such thing," Wicker wrote. "But there's no evidence for that."

The third debate, like the one before it, drew about sixty million viewers. For the fourth and final session, the candidates would speak exclusively about foreign affairs. Nixon's strategists believed this final session would show their man's strengths and expose Kennedy's weaknesses.

Kennedy and Nixon were in different cities for their third debate,
a high-tech feat for 1960s television.

The final debate, featuring an in-depth discussion of foreign policy issues.

CHAPTER 7

The Fourth Debate

New York
October 21, 1960

TRACK 7

RICHARD NIXON AND HIS AIDES AGREED THAT THIS DEBATE, RESTRICTED to foreign policy issues, would highlight John Kennedy's lack of experience on the global stage, and would enhance the vice president's image as a world leader. Where they disagreed, however, was on the timing of the debate. Nixon believed that the first debate would garner the highest audience of the debate cycle, but his aides thought viewership would start low and finish high. Nixon deferred to his advisors and agreed to a schedule in which his strong suit—foreign policy—would be discussed in the fourth and last debate.

Once again, events conspired to make these debates a misery for the vice president. He was right, and his advisors were wrong. As he later lamented, "The number of viewers [for the final three debates] stubbornly remained twenty million fewer" than the first debate, which had focused on domestic issues and, of course, Nixon's poor appearance.

The moderator of the final session was Quincy Howe of ABC—although, in a split second of anxiety at the beginning of the program, Howe identified his employer as CBS. (He quickly corrected his mistake.) The panelists were Walter Cronkite of CBS, John Chancellor of NBC, John Edwards of ABC, and Frank Singiser of the Mutual Broadcasting System. The two candidates spoke from behind podiums, placed in front of a stark, paneled wall.

Just a day before the debates, Kennedy—or, more accurately, Kennedy's campaign aides—had issued a particularly bellicose statement about Cuba. In the statement, which the candidate himself did not actually see, according to Arthur Schlesinger, Kennedy said the U.S. should assist "democratic anti-Castro forces in exile" who were working to achieve regime change in Havana. He complained that the Eisenhower administration had failed to support "these fighters for freedom."

Nixon was furious. He believed Kennedy was exploiting information he received from the CIA about just such a plan to overthrow Castro. Those plans—which would come to fruition, of sorts, in the Bay of Pigs fiasco—were top secret, but had been outlined for Kennedy, at Eisenhower's insistence, in late July.

"His statement jeopardized the project, which could succeed only if it were supported and implemented secretly," a still-bitter Nixon wrote after in his memoirs. That is a matter of debate, so to speak. In his biography of Nixon, journalist Tom Wicker pointed out that when the CIA briefed Kennedy on Cuban policy, plans for an exile-led coup still were uncertain, and Kennedy may not have learned of the secret, CIA-trained army until after the election. Wicker added, however, that Nixon's belief that Kennedy had traded on his CIA briefing was "plausible."

Whatever the case, events once again had conspired against Nixon during the debate cycle. When the two candidates argued over Cuba, Kennedy seemed tougher on Castro, while Nixon sounded defensive. The evening's first question concerned Cuba, and Nixon, by luck (or lack thereof) of the draw, was the first to reply. He found himself saying things he did not really believe, as he later conceded in his memoirs, because he felt obliged to "protect the secrecy of the planning" underway in Guatemala.

"I think that Senator Kennedy's policies and recommendations for the handling of the Castro regime are probably the most dangerously irresponsible recommendations that he's made during the course of this campaign," he said. "In effect, what Senator Kennedy recommends is that the United States Government should give help to the exiles and to those within Cuba who oppose the Castro regime...." Nixon went on to point out that the United States has five treaties with Latin America in which Washington "agreed not to intervene in the internal affairs of any other American country."

Nixon's supporters could not believe what they were hearing. Even worse from Nixon's standpoint, prominent journalists—not Nixon's favorite people—were impressed, and would go on to speak glowingly of the vice president's restraint. This was not the way to excite Republican voters.

Kennedy seized the opportunity. He argued that the Eisenhower administration's economic sanctions against Cuba were not tough enough, and that Castro's prestige in Latin America was on the rise because the administration had not provided the region with enough attention and foreign aid.

Tellingly, he did not elaborate on his campaign statement of the previous day. And, in fact, two days after the debate, he distanced himself from the tough talk about Cuba. He said he had never actually advocated direct U.S. intervention in Cuba's affairs. Instead, he simply wished that the U.S. use its moral leadership on behalf of anti-Castro Cubans.

As Tom Wicker noted, Nixon was not wrong to believe that Kennedy benefited by seeming tougher on Castro, even though he later backed away from his bellicose rhetoric. No wonder Nixon was bitter. In an astonishing irony, he was forced, or believed he was forced, to condemn as "irresponsible" the very policy he privately advocated—the training of an anti-Castro army of exiles. He later wrote that he had said so to protect the secrecy of the fledgling plan.

And so the debates came to an end—a merciful end, as far as Nixon was concerned, a triumphant end for Kennedy. The young senator from Massachusetts had held his own on substance with the slightly older incumbent vice president, a man who had been a national figure for more than a decade.

Were the debates the decisive issue? In an election as close as 1960's was, any issue that moved a few thousand voters one way or the other could have a rightful claim as *the* decisive issue. But it surely would be unfair and unwise to say that John Kennedy gained the White House because of Richard Nixon's five o'clock shadow and darting eyes. One could just as easily make the case that Kennedy won the election when Nixon hurt his knee in Greensboro, the beginning of a series of calamities that culminated in that first debate.

It is interesting to note, as Nixon did, that the Gallup Poll actually showed Kennedy losing half a percentage point from the first debate to the last. Nixon said that those who saw the debates as a turning point "overstate the case."

And yet, every election has peculiar dynamics that defy statistics and polls. Whether or not the debates were decisive, they surely were the most memorable elements of the 1960 campaign—even if so many of the issues under discussion have escaped the notice of history. The debates may not have prompted Kennedy supporters to switch their allegiance or persuaded Nixon supporters of Kennedy's charms, but they certainly contributed to the campaign's intangibles. Protestant America saw the Catholic Kennedy as a man devoid of horns and other marks of the anti-Christ. Wavering Democrats, whether in the Eleanor Roosevelt-Adlai Stevenson wing or in the Southern Congressional faction, saw no reason to sit on the sidelines and leave Kennedy to his fate. Undecided voters saw a confident, articulate candidate who espoused no dangerous or radical ideas, and who successfully exploited the desire for change after eight years of Republican rule in the White House.

If Nixon had declined to debate, would he have won? Tom Wicker suggests the possibility. He described Nixon's decision to debate Kennedy as "misbegotten"—at least from Nixon's perspective. "Whether it was Kennedy's greater physical and stylistic appeal to viewers…or the leveling effect—or both—there's no doubt that John Kennedy 'won' the debates, a crucial part of winning the presidency," Wicker writes.

One indicator of that victory was Nixon's decision to roll out his formidable reserve—President Dwight D. Eisenhower, still immensely popular. After remaining in the background, Ike hit the campaign trail for Nixon as the campaign neared its conclusion, and perhaps thanks to the public's affection for this soldier-politician, Nixon saw a last-minute surge. The last Gallup Poll before election day had Kennedy ahead by one percentage point—a virtual tie.

And a virtual tie it was on election day, at least in terms of the popular vote. John F. Kennedy garnered 49.7 percent of the popular vote; Nixon won 49.6 percent. The margin of victory was a mere 118,574 votes. Some 68.8 million people—64.5 percent of the nation's eligible voters—turned out to vote. (Voter turnout has declined ever since.)

The Electoral College vote was far more decisive, with Kennedy taking 303 votes to Nixon's 219. In a popular telling of this close election, JFK won thanks to old-fashioned voter fraud in Illinois, where the Cook County machine under Chicago mayor Richard J. Daley raided the cemeteries for Kennedy voters. In fact, however, Kennedy would have won the Electoral College vote even if Illinois's votes had gone to Nixon.

In Hyannis Port, John Kennedy went to bed at three o'clock in the morning on election night, with the contest still uncertain. He was awakened six hours later with word that he would become the thirty-fifth president of the United States.

Most historians agree that the debates helped elect JFK.

Irish ambassador Thomas J. Kiernan presents Kennedy with a bowl of shamrocks commemorating Saint Patrick's Day.

CHAPTER 8

A City Upon a Hill

*Address to the General Court of
the Commonwealth of Massachusetts*
January 9, 1961

TRACK 8

JOHN F. KENNEDY'S GREAT-GRANDPARENTS SAILED FROM IRELAND TO Boston in 1847, a year remembered in Irish and Irish American history as "Black '47." The main food supply of the poor, landless Irish farmer—the potato—had failed in 1845, and again in 1846. By 1847, hundreds of thousands were dying or leaving.

Bridget and Patrick Kennedy separately escaped death and starvation and started a new life together in the slums of East Boston. Poverty in America was harsh, but it was preferable to death in Ireland.

Before long, children began to arrive—the first members of this Kennedy family born in the United States. By the summer of 1853, Bridget and Patrick Kennedy had four children. But little John, eighteen months old, was terribly ill. The child had cholera, one of the many plagues that regularly visited the urban poor of East Boston and other cities in the mid-nineteenth century.

John Kennedy did not survive. He died in late 1855. Remarkably, though, his three siblings did not contract the disease. Often cholera could and did wipe out entire families.

Less than three years later, John's parents celebrated the arrival of another son, whom they christened Patrick Joseph but called P.J. Their joy was to be short-lived. Before the child was a year old, the family patriarch, thirty-five-year-old Patrick Kennedy, became desperately ill. He, too, had cholera. He died on November 22, 1858.

P.J. Kennedy grew up without a father. His mother did her best, as so many immigrant women did, to keep her family together by any means necessary. Eventually, P.J. opened a saloon and started a family of his own. His son, Joseph Kennedy, would become U.S. ambassador to the Court of St. James and the patriarch of one of the world's most famous families. And in January 1961, P.J. Kennedy's grandson, John F. Kennedy, became president of the United States.

When President-elect Kennedy stood before the political leaders of Massachusetts on January 9, 1961, for what he vowed would not be a farewell address to his native state, he said nothing of his family's remarkable saga. The setting, the ornate Massachusetts statehouse, would have seemed perfect for a nostalgic reminiscence, or a self-consciously humble recitation of the Kennedy family's extraordinary story. Here was a son of Massachusetts, speaking to a joint session of the commonwealth's legislature, surrounded by familiar faces, preparing to set off for the White House. There could have been no better occasion to reflect on the journey from Sumner Street in East Boston to Pennsylvania Avenue in the nation's capital, accomplished in three generations. So many of the men and women gathered to hear the president-elect saw him as not just another Massachusetts man made good—the commonwealth had shared its sons with the nation since John Adams—but as a symbol of what courageous immigrant families could achieve in America. He was more than a son of Massachusetts. He was a Catholic. His great-grandparents were poor immigrants who fled Ireland during its darkest hour. His grandfather overcame tragedy and poverty to found a business. Regardless of how one felt about the new president's politics, it was hard to deny that his was a compelling story, a story made in Massachusetts.

What's more, he was historically important. As the first Catholic president, he was the first person from outside the country's Anglo-Saxon, Protestant majority to assume the highest office in the land. His importance to Catholics and to the sons and daughters of Irish immigrants was clear. Less obvious, but compelling nevertheless, was his importance to other groups outside mainstream American culture, circa 1960. Though he was wealthy and privileged, a white male with a degree from the finishing school known as Harvard University, he was described in the *Times* of London as the first president from a member of a minority group. And so he was.

Today, when all politics is autobiography, when candidates and officeholders talk as much about their lives and their families as they do about public policy, those who continue to chip away at barriers to high public office are not shy about celebrating their achievements. But there was no such sense of triumphalism in John Kennedy's non-farewell speech to his home state.

When he compared the task of assembling a government to a notable journey across the Atlantic, the ship he cited was not the leaky vessel that brought his great-grandparents from Ireland to Boston, but the flagship *Arabella*, which brought John Winthrop and the Puritans from old England to New England. Rather than refer to the immigrant history that was more immediate and more personal for so many of his listeners, he chose imagery from the very founding of the nation, by men and women whose descendants were the proverbial blue-blood Brahmins of Beacon Hill. Their leader, Winthrop, set the standard to which Kennedy aspired. Quoting Winthrop, Kennedy said: "We must always consider...that we shall be as a city upon a hill...The eyes of all people are upon us."

The reference would later become associated with Ronald Reagan, who offered the same quotation from Winthrop in a speech in 1974. More famously, Reagan repeated the quotation throughout his presidency, including his farewell speech in 1989. Through the years, however, Reagan ad-libbed a bit by adding the adjective "shining" to Winthrop's original phrase—as in "a shining city upon a hill." Mario Cuomo, in his keynote speech at the Democratic National Convention in 1984, challenged Reagan not so much on the authenticity of the quote, but on the execution of its sentiments. "A shining city is perhaps all the president sees from the portico of the White House and the veranda of his ranch, where everyone seems to be doing well," Cuomo said. "But there's another city; there's another part to the shining city; the part where some people can't pay their mortgages, and most young people can't afford one, where students can't afford the education they need, and middle-class parents watch the dreams they hold for their children evaporate."

Undaunted by Cuomo's rhetorical counter-punch, Reagan returned to the theme in 1989, saying that "I've spoken of the shining city all my political life, but I don't know if I ever quite communicated what I saw when I said it. But in my mind it was a tall, proud city built on rocks stronger than oceans, wind-swept,

God-blessed, and teeming with people of all kinds living in harmony and peace, a city with free ports that hummed with commerce and creativity, and if there had to be city walls, the walls had doors and the doors were open to anyone with the will and the heart to get here. That's how I saw it and see it still."

When Reagan died in 2003, many eulogists said the former president's vision of America was encapsulated in that famous phrase "shining city upon a hill." Some seemed to believe the quote originated with Reagan. And few realized that Ronald Reagan was not the first president to adopt Winthrop's vision as his own.

But what, precisely, did it mean? In Kennedy's view, it meant that that "our governments, in every branch…must be as a city upon a hill, constructed and inhabited by men aware of their great trust and their great responsibilities." There is no mention of governments in Reagan's vision; there is no mention of people in Kennedy's.

It is, in any case, a historical curiosity that John Kennedy and Ronald Reagan, descendants of Gaelic-Irish immigrants and, in their own way, symbols of that more diverse America that emerged in the twentieth century, were inspired by the vision of a Puritan from England who sailed to a new world in the seventeenth century.

As he left Massachusetts in 1961, John Kennedy took on the challenge of building an administration that would match the promise of his words.

PART TWO: 1961

Kennedy is sworn in as president.

Introduction

BECAUSE HE HAD WON THE PRESIDENCY WITH ONLY A PLURALITY OF 49.7 percent of the popular vote, Kennedy saw no mandate for a Hundred Days' burst of action in either domestic or foreign affairs. Nevertheless, he believed that his victory signaled that the public was ready for a fresh start at home and abroad. Opinion surveys and the most thoughtful editorials of the day suggested that Americans were feeling a bit gloomy about the country's prospects. Unresolved racial tensions; a sluggish economy; and fears that Sputnik, the first dramatic act of the space age, demonstrated a Soviet lead over the United States in science, engineering, and missile technology raised concerns about democracy's capacity to compete with a more controlled society.

At the start of his term, Kennedy understood that a successful presidency depended on his ability to translate his New Frontier slogan into substantive gains that raised morale and made Americans more hopeful about their future. He wished to draw the strongest possible contrast between the drift of his predecessor and the promise of renewed mastery. He saw his inaugural speech as especially important. He remembered how Jefferson's and FDR's first addresses had launched their administrations on positive notes and he was determined to do the same.

His inaugural theme was sacrifice for the sake of the national well being, a call to civic duty in inspirational language, and an appeal to shared national values. "Ask not what your country can do for you—ask what you can do for your country," he declared. "Let every nation know, whether it wishes us well or ill, that we shall pay any price, bear any burden, meet any hardship, support any friend, oppose any foe to assure the survival and success of liberty." His words thrilled the country and the speech joined FDR's first as the most quoted inaugural speeches of the twentieth century. True, Roosevelt's was about the domestic crisis of the Depression and Kennedy's about the worldwide challenge of communism, but both were appeals to ordinary citizens to renew their faith in the country's institutions and its capacity to triumph over adversity.

At the beginning of March, six weeks into his term, Kennedy followed his inspiring inaugural appeal with declarations setting up a Peace Corps and asking Latin America to join him in an Alliance for Progress. The Corps represented a concrete means by which young Americans could convert national ideals into international gains—both for citizens of third world host countries and the United States in its competition with Soviet communism for hearts and minds everywhere. The Alliance was a statement of Kennedy's determination to recast America's image in the Western Hemisphere as a superpower bully and promote greater prosperity and social justice in Latin American countries that seemed all too vulnerable to socialist promises of a better life for long-suffering peasants and laborers.

Kennedy lost his administration's forward momentum in April when the invasion at Cuba's Bay of Pigs failed and embarrassed him. Privately, he was incensed at himself and his advisers for having committed themselves to such a questionable operation. For days afterward, he walked around asking, "How could I have been so stupid?" He had been warned that a hoped-for uprising by anti-Castro Cubans might not materialize, and former secretary of state Dean Acheson had given him reason to doubt the wisdom of the whole enterprise. He asked Kennedy how many troops Castro could put on the beaches to oppose the fifteen hundred invaders. Perhaps twenty-five thousand, the president replied. Acheson declared, "It doesn't take Price-Waterhouse to figure out that fifteen hundred aren't as good as twenty-five thousand." Despite strongly supporting the operation, the CIA signaled its doubts by giving the invasion the codename "Bumpy Road." Kennedy privately described the failed invasion and its aftermath as "the worst experience of my life."

In public, he bravely took full responsibility for the failure. He authorized a White House statement saying, "President Kennedy has stated from the beginning that as president, he bears sole responsibility.... The president is strongly opposed to anyone within or without the administration attempting to shift the responsibility." He quoted "an old saying that victory has a hundred fathers and defeat is an orphan." This was his defeat: "I'm the responsible officer of the government," he told the press. When he spoke to the American Society of Newspaper Editors on April 20, he did not mask his concern that the Cuban invasion had shattered trust in his commitment to better relations with Latin America. He described "a relentless struggle in every corner of the globe," and warned against complacency and a failure of nerve to meet the challenges ahead.

To bolster flagging American spirits, Kennedy spoke before a joint session of Congress at the end of May. It was an update on the current state of the union and particularly the country's challenges abroad. He reminded his audience of what a constant and difficult struggle faced the United States in its competition with communism. He listed a series of measures he hoped Congress would enact to strengthen the country, including, most dramatically, funding for a plan to land a man on the moon by the end of the decade. Apollo, as the moon mission was called, resonated with Kennedy's description of his presidency as a New Frontier devoted to heroic causes. "We choose to go to the moon in this decade," Kennedy said, "and do the other things, not because they are easy, but because they are hard; because that goal will serve to organize and measure the best of our energies and skills."

During a June meeting with Nikita Khrushchev in Vienna, Kennedy found himself on the defensive over Berlin. Khrushchev said he intended to transfer full control of East Berlin from Moscow to the East German government. Soviet frustration over the steady stream of educated East Europeans and Germans through Berlin to the West principally motivated Khrushchev's threat to give the East Germans the discretion to close routes to the city from West Germany. By the summer of 1961, Soviet pronouncements about Berlin had created a crisis about Western rights of access to the city that threatened to provoke a Soviet-American conflict.

To make clear that the Soviet threat would not intimidate the United States and that he was ready to negotiate, but not out of fear, Kennedy gave a superbly balanced address on July 25. He left no doubt that the crisis was the result of Moscow's doing. He also emphasized that he would not let the Soviets overturn America's legal rights in West Berlin. "We will at all times be ready to talk, if talk will help," he declared. "But we must also be ready to resist with force, if force is used upon us." He summed up his position by saying, "We seek peace—but we shall not surrender."

In September, when Kennedy spoke again about Soviet-American relations at the opening of the United Nations' 1961 session, he knew that Khrushchev had backed away from his Berlin threat. The construction of a wall the previous summer had alleviated Khrushchev's problem; the flow of embarrassing refugees to the West had largely been stopped. Although Kennedy's speech reiterated his determination to assure Western interests in Berlin and elsewhere, he urged Soviet understanding of the need for negotiation rather than saber rattling. "Mankind must do away with war or war will do away with mankind," he declared in the most memorable line of his speech.

After many difficult moments in the first twelve months of his presidency, Kennedy ended the year in an upbeat mood. He had survived the crises over Cuba and Berlin and looked forward to the possibility of constructive negotiations in 1962.

Delivery of the brief, memorable inaugural address.

CHAPTER 9

The Inaugural Address

Washington, D.C.
January 20, 1961

TRACK 9

THERE HAD BEEN FIFTEEN INAUGURAL ADDRESSES IN THE TWENTIETH century before 1961. Only one—President Franklin Roosevelt's speech in 1933—had found a place in the American canon of sacred political scripture. The speech's immortal line ("So, first of all, let me assert my firm belief that the only thing we have to fear is fear itself") ensured that FDR's candid and yet reassuring words would live forever in the public imagination.

John Kennedy was determined to make sure that his own inaugural address measured up not only to FDR's 1933 speech, but to Thomas Jefferson's in 1801, to both of Abraham Lincoln's, and to the wartime speeches of his hero and role model, Winston Churchill.

He succeeded. One sure measure of his success is the continuing debate over who, in the end, actually wrote the inaugural address. As previously noted, two books published in 2005 came to very different conclusions, but the debate itself—nearly half a century after the speech was delivered—is a victory for Kennedy's high hopes for his first speech as president. The debate goes on because the words have not been forgotten. They are part of what Lincoln called the "mystic chords of memory," stretching from generation to generation, remembered today by grandparents, to be recited tomorrow by schoolchildren.

The speech reflects the hours he labored over various drafts and the guidance he provided to his chief speechwriter, Theodore C. Sorensen, and others. He directed Sorensen to study Lincoln's Gettysburg Address and to find what magic lay in that piece of prose poetry. (Sorensen found that Lincoln rarely used three words when one would do.) Kennedy read and reread the speech, first for content, and then for emphasis.

In the end, Kennedy's artful use of language and his delivery ensured a place for his speech alongside some of the greatest ever given in U.S. history. It also drew a contrast between the new administration (consisting of people "born in this century") and the old. Kennedy, at forty-three years old the youngest president ever elected, had promised to get the country "moving again," and he seized every opportunity to contrast his style—his self-proclaimed "vigor"—with that of Dwight Eisenhower, at that point the oldest man who had ever held the presidency. Ike was not known for his facility with words (although, ironically, his farewell speech given just three days before Kennedy's inaugural would itself find a place in textbooks, thanks to his coining of the phrase "military-industrial complex"). Kennedy clearly understood the power of words and the importance of eloquence.

Kennedy believed that an inspiring and well-remembered speech would set the proper tone for a new president eager to summon his fellow citizens to greatness. But not by words alone did Kennedy wish to symbolize the passing of the torch of leadership. His inauguration—the pomp and the parties—would make that point as well. Dwight Eisenhower and his presidential party wore homburgs to inauguration day, 1953. John Kennedy and his party wore top hats and tails. Ike's mid-American tastes in music, culture, and even furniture were swept aside. Elegance, style, and glamour were now the order of the day. Stars like Frank Sinatra, Ethel Merman, and Gene Kelly were enlisted to perform and host glittering inaugural parties—a celebration not of gray conformity, but of Hollywood cool. In place of matronly Mamie Eisenhower was the lovely, young, and elegant Jacqueline Bouvier Kennedy, radiant on inauguration day though she was only about two months removed from a difficult childbirth. John F. Kennedy Jr. had been born in November, just after election day.

The torch had indeed been passed, and everything about inauguration day, 1961, reflected that sentiment.

It was a cold morning in Washington on that Friday, January 20. Eight inches of midwinter snow had fallen the night before, sending hundreds of

U.S. troops into the capital's streets armed with snow-removal equipment. By dawn, the storm had passed and the sky was clear. But a bright sun mocked the hopes of the thousands who would hear the new president's speech. Temperatures were in the low twenties despite abundant sunshine, and a sharp wind demanded tribute in the form of scarves and gloves.

Kennedy began his morning with a breakfast that included bacon, an act that would have constituted a breach of faith on any other Friday morning. Catholics refrained from eating meat on Friday in those days before Vatican II, but the archbishop of Washington had granted a dispensation to the capital's Catholics to commemorate the inauguration of the first Catholic president.

The inaugural address for which he had such elevated ambitions was nearly finished, save for last-minute revisions. One of those changes consisted of two words, and they were inserted after pleas from his young aide, Harris Wofford, who would become a leading advocate for civil rights in the new administration. Wofford desperately wished for some mention of the burgeoning civil rights crisis, but he was losing that battle until Kennedy agreed to insert a two-word phrase—"at home"—into a sentence about human rights violations around the world. Wofford pointed out to the president-elect that there was a human rights problem in the United States as well, and his speech ought to reflect that reality. And so, when Kennedy delivered his speech, he asserted that his administration was committed to human rights "at home" as well as around the world. The two words were inserted into one of the speech's longest sentences, one filled with several well-remembered phrases: "Let the word go forth from this time and place, to friend and foe alike, that the torch has been passed to a new generation of Americans—born in this century, tempered by war, disciplined by a hard and bitter peace, proud of our ancient heritage, and unwilling to witness or permit the slow undoing of those human rights to which this nation has always been committed, and to which we are committed today at home and around the world."

This ringing sentence, in many ways the epicenter of the inaugural address, is best remembered for the brilliant assertions in its opening phrases: "Let the word go forth...the torch has been passed." The two words inserted at the last minute were overshadowed by the ringing declarations that came before, and they were the only reference to domestic affairs in the speech. Kennedy's main interests lay elsewhere—while he had dealt with civil rights issues as a senator, in many ways he simply did not understand, as a privileged northerner, the odious effects of Jim Crow on southern blacks.

Other phrases had been polished from good to glittering in the days leading up to January 20. According to speechwriter Sorensen's book *Kennedy*, the very first sentence morphed from "We celebrate today not a victory of party but the sacrament of democracy" to the now-remembered "We observe today not a victory of party but a celebration of freedom." Another well-remembered line, which subtly suggested imagery from John Kennedy's service in the Pacific Ocean during World War II, underwent drastic changes in the editing process. The first draft of the speech contained this phrase: "And if the fruits of cooperation prove sweeter than the dregs of suspicion, let both sides join ultimately in creating a true world order—neither a Pax Americana, nor a Pax Russiana, nor even a balance of power—but a community of power." As rewritten with input from Kennedy and others, the phrase read: "And if a beachhead of cooperation can push back the jungle of suspicion, let both sides join in creating a new endeavor, not a new balance of power, but a new world of law...."

Other aspects of the speech would become familiar to Americans in the coming years. Kennedy used the phrase "let us" several times in the inaugural, as in "So let us begin anew" and "Let us never negotiate out of fear. But let us never fear to negotiate." Kennedy would return to that summons many times in future speeches.

The most famous phrase in the speech, "And so, my fellow Americans: Ask not what your country can do for you—ask what you can do for your country," was a clarion call to high purpose and national service, a summons to community, to patriotism, and to selflessness. Its baroque formula (he did not simply say: "Do not ask what your country can do for you...") added elegance to eloquence and inspired a generation of young people who would enter politics or the Peace Corps years after Kennedy's death.

In retrospect, it is almost shocking to consider that Kennedy feared his speech might be overshadowed by the words of the aging poet Robert Frost, who was invited to speak before the swearing-in of the new president. JFK wanted Frost to read not from a new poem, which might contain flights of eloquence destined to make the inaugural address look plodding and dull, but from one of his best-known works, "The Gift Outright." It was not as if Kennedy regarded "The Gift Outright" as an inferior piece. It is just that he wanted no surprises.

Frost actually had other ideas. After the noted African American contralto Marian Anderson sang the national anthem, Frost rose to read from a new work he had composed for the occasion. But the wind and sun glare played havoc with the poet's eighty-six-year-old eyes. He abandoned his effort, and so recited from memory "The Gift Outright."

Frost did not overshadow his fellow New Englander.

When it came time for his swearing-in, John Kennedy placed himself across from Chief Justice Earl Warren, protected from the cold by neither coat nor hat. The sun did nothing to warm the proceedings, but its light picked up the reddish brown of Kennedy's hair. He radiated youth and vitality.

And then he spoke, not in the hurried cadence of his early years as a politician, but in tones modulated by a voice coach. His New England accent was trimmed around the edges, and his emphasis was pitch-perfect.

"Let every nation know, whether it wishes us well or ill, that we shall pay any price, bear any burden, meet any hardship, support any friend, oppose any foe, to assure the survival and the success of liberty." That assertion served notice at home and abroad that this new generation of Americans was willing to confront communism throughout the world. But in the coming years, John Kennedy and his fellow Americans would come to realize that the price was high indeed, and the burdens heavier than they imagined on this cold day in Washington in early 1961.

But the speech, while very much a Cold War document, was by no means a rejection of compromise and coexistence. In another portion of the speech, Kennedy called on the country and the world to "begin anew—remembering on both sides that civility is not a sign of weakness, and sincerity is always subject to proof. Let us never negotiate out of fear. But let us never fear to negotiate."

And after issuing his ringing summons to bear burdens and pay the price for the survival of liberty, Kennedy suggested that Americans and their adversaries would do better to find what they had in common, rather than focus on their differences. "Let both sides explore what problems unite us instead of belaboring those problems which divide us," he said. "Let both sides seek to invoke the wonders of science instead of its terrors. Together let us explore the stars, conquer the deserts, eradicate disease, tap the ocean depths, and encourage the arts and commerce. Let both sides unite to heed in all corners of the earth the command of Isaiah—to 'undo the heavy burdens [and] let the oppressed go free.'"

The speech was less than fourteen hundred words long, about half the usual length of an inaugural address. When it was over, and the day's commemorations of freedom were finished, those words lingered.

They linger still.

A Peace Corps worker. Since the Corps' inception,
more than 160,000 Americans have passed through its ranks.

CHAPTER 10

The Peace Corps

Announcement of the Creation of the Peace Corps
Washington, D.C.
March 1, 1961

TRACK 10

IN THE FINAL WEEKS OF THE 1960 CAMPAIGN, CANDIDATE JOHN KENNEDY proposed the creation of a new institution he called the Peace Corps. During a late-night speech on October 14 at the University of Michigan (in which he referred to his alma mater, Harvard, as "the Michigan of the East"), he challenged students to think of themselves not as consumers or careerists, but as national ambassadors of good will. "How many of you who are going to be doctors are willing to spend your days in Ghana?" he asked. "Technicians or engineers, how many of you are willing to work in the Foreign Service and spend your lives traveling around the world?"

The idea was not new with Kennedy or any of his idealistic advisors. His colleague and onetime rival, Hubert Humphrey, actually had proposed the idea before the 1960 campaign, and introduced legislation in the Senate. The notion appealed to Kennedy, with its call to sacrifice and service.

Two weeks after his visit to Michigan, during a speech in San Francisco on November 2, Kennedy returned to the theme, proposing "a peace corps of talented young men and women, willing and able to serve their country...for three years as an alternative or as a supplement to peacetime selective service."

It took Kennedy only about six weeks to turn this proposal into reality. The Peace Corps would become a symbol of Kennedy's call to public service, and a vehicle for the idealism he inspired in a generation of adolescents and young adults.

But, as Kennedy made clear in his San Francisco campaign speech, his motives in establishing the Corps were not entirely devoid of national self-interest. They never were. Before addressing his proposal in the November 2 speech, he noted that the lack of a vibrant American presence in the developing world meant that many new nations were voting against U.S. interests in the United Nations.

"Today, we do not have a single American diplomat in residence in six new countries of Africa which are members of the United Nations," he said. "Of the sixteen new African countries which were admitted to the United Nations, do you know how many voted with us on the admission of Red China? None. There are only twenty-six Negroes in the six thousand of our Foreign Service officers, and yet Africa today contains one quarter of the votes in the General Assembly."

The reference to the paucity of African Americans in the Foreign Service would be seen, in today's political dialogue, as an argument for a more diverse pool of diplomats. And it was, not as an experiment in social engineering, but for purely pragmatic reasons—the U.S. stood a better chance to win the hearts and minds of African nations if our diplomats looked more like theirs.

Kennedy viewed the Peace Corps as a way of countering the shocking statistics he cited, and for other lapses in the nation's official diplomatic corps. In the San Francisco speech, he lamented the lack of linguistic skill among the country's diplomats—an ironic complaint, given his own lack of facility in anything but English. He noted that only two of the nation's nine ambassadors to Arab nations spoke Arabic (a percentage that actually might seem high today), and that even the U.S. ambassador to France did not speak French and so "could not even discuss negotiations with General de Gaulle."

But behind the Iron Curtain, young doctors, scientists, and teachers were preparing "to spend their lives abroad in the service of world communism"—and as part of that preparation, they were "studying Swahili and African customs."

Something, he said, had to be done to counter "the examples that we read of the ugly American." (A movie by that title would be released in 1963.) He cited as an example of the Peace Corps ideal Dr. Tom Dooley, whose work with the poor of Southeast Asia had made him a legend. Earlier in the year, Dooley had been given an honorary degree at the University of Notre Dame, along with

President Eisenhower and Giovanni Cardinal Montini (the patriarch of Milan and the future Pope Paul VI). Dooley received the most attention. But he died of cancer, at the age of thirty-four, two days before Kennedy's inauguration.

On March 1, 1961, six weeks after his inauguration, John Kennedy issued an executive order creating the Peace Corps. The official statement released to the press does not coincide word for word with Kennedy's verbal announcement. After reading verbatim the first few sentences, the president ad-libbed the rest of the short statement, suggesting how personally he was attached to this initiative. But both the printed statement and the president's remarks emphasized that Peace Corps volunteers would be quite the opposite of the disengaged, English-only diplomats he deplored in his San Francisco speech of November 2, 1960. He said volunteers would share the work, food, and language of the people they sought to help.

Kennedy appointed his brother-in-law, Sargent Shriver, to implement the vision. Shriver later joked that Kennedy appointed him to the post because nobody thought the Peace Corps would work, so it would be easier to fire a family member than a political ally.

In fact, the Corps did work, thanks in large measure to the energy and idealism of Shriver, who embodied the New Frontier's spirit. Popular opinion helped, too: polls showed that more than 70 percent of Americans approved of the Peace Corps. Five thousand young people volunteered for the program in its first month. Within a year, countries around the globe were clamoring for Peace Corps volunteers, and by the mid-1960s, when the Peace Corps was at its peak, some fifteen thousand personnel were in the field or in training.

Since the Corps' inception, more than one hundred and sixty thousand Americans have passed through its ranks. They have served in 135 countries, spreading the idealistic spirit of John F. Kennedy's New Frontier. For those many thousands of Americans, the Peace Corps has been a defining experience in their lives.

Today, more than forty years after Kennedy's March 1, 1961, executive order, about seven thousand young men and women are serving in the Peace Corps in about seventy nations. They do so quietly, without the kind of moral support they received from their patron and founder, John Kennedy. Still, in the aftermath of September 11, 2001, the Corps' mission seems as vital and necessary at it was on the March morning when John Kennedy told the nation's young people what they could do for their country, and for the world.

JFK visits Latin America in late 1961.

CHAPTER 11

The Alliance for Progress

Proposal of the Alliance for Progress
Washington, D.C.
March 13, 1961

TRACK 11

I N HIS INAUGURAL ADDRESS, PRESIDENT KENNEDY DELIVERED A "SPECIAL
pledge" to "our sister republics south of our border." The United States,
he said, at last would convert "good words" into "good deeds."

Less than three months later, the president invited Latin American diplomats to a glittering formal reception in the White House. With the diplomats
and their spouses seated in front of him, a chandelier dangling above him, and a
portrait of Martha Washington staring at his right shoulder, Kennedy explained
how his country would make good on its pledge. He proposed the creation of a
cooperative effort between the United States and Latin America to improve the
lives of those many millions who lived in poverty, illness, and misery south of the
Rio Grande. The program would be called the Alliance for Progress.

The speech is long on New Frontier idealism and optimism—indeed, JFK
invoked the phrase in describing the common heritage of the Americas, born,
he said, of "the endless exploration of new frontiers." His goals for the rest of
the hemisphere were no different from those he had for the United States.
Living standards, he said, could and should be raised in Latin America
through "maximum national effort"—a phrase loaded with New Frontier
vigor. But the new pan-American relationship he proposed would be more

than a huge antipoverty program. Kennedy emphasized the arts and sciences, too, as vehicles for progress on both sides of the Rio Grande. He invited the scientists of Latin America to work with their colleagues in the United States on pragmatic projects like desalinization as well as physics and astronomy. ("Together, let us explore the stars," Kennedy had said in his inaugural address.) And he noted that the United States had "much to learn" from Latin music, art, and philosophy.

At its heart, this speech is surprisingly humble and earnest in its search for common ground between the two American continents. Kennedy's citations of South American heroes like Simon Bolivar and Jose de San Martin and Benito Juarez sought to link together the American Revolution of the eighteenth century with the independence movements to the south in the nineteenth century, and illustrate the common ideals of the hemisphere. His language was respectful and unusually candid.

"As a citizen of the United States," he said, "let me be the first to admit that we North Americans have not always grasped the significance of this common mission, just as it is also true that many in your own countries have not fully understood the urgency of the need to lift people from poverty and ignorance and despair. But we must turn from these mistakes—from the failures and the misunderstandings of the past to a future full of peril, but bright with hope."

While those sentiments sounded conciliatory and selfless, this speech is very much part of the Cold War narrative of the early 1960s. Fidel Castro, though his name was unspoken, provided as much inspiration for this speech as did Simon Bolivar and the other Latin patriots Kennedy cited.

There was no region of the world untouched by the "twilight struggle," and while places like Berlin, Cuba, and Southeast Asia were the flashpoints for this conflict in the early 1960s, South and Central America were potential battlefields as well. Soviet support for what it called "wars of national liberation" and Castro's anti-American rhetoric prompted fears of Communist insurgencies far closer to home than Laos or the Congo.

The Alliance for Progress, with its emphasis on shared democratic values and its urgent call for economic development and social justice, would become a bulwark against the spread of Castro-inspired and Soviet-assisted Communist movements in this impoverished and abysmally governed region. Robert Kennedy would later define this goal candidly. If the Alliance's "reforms—social, economic, and political—are put into effect, then communism and

Castroism will collapse in South America," he predicted. But, he added, if the promise of reform and social change collapses in the face of corruption or the inertia of the status quo, then "we will have problems in South America" regardless of what might happen in Cuba or to Castro.

Still, while Cold War politics surely added a sense of urgency to this speech, there is little reason to question Kennedy's commitment to the impoverished people of the region. The Alliance for Progress was his way of not only countering the Soviet-Castro threat in Latin America, but also of acknowledging that the United States was not necessarily seen as a force for justice and progress in the region. He stated openly that the U.S. had been wrongheaded in its approach to inter-American relations in the past, but that the time had come to put aside "the failures and the misunderstandings of the past," to a future that was full of both "peril" and "hope." His listeners knew precisely who, in Kennedy's view, represented peril, and who represented hope.

As Kennedy knew, U.S. relations with its southern neighbors had been fraught with conflict and accusations of Yankee imperialism and capitalist exploitation for more than a century. In the 1930s, Franklin Roosevelt himself had tried to ameliorate that legacy with his Good Neighbor policy, which emphasized cooperation and mutually beneficial trade, rather than raw U.S. power. But the Cold War and Castro changed Washington's attitudes toward the region. Neighborliness gave way to U.S. interventionism, propping up dubious allies, and undermining hostile leaders through the 1950s. Planning for what became the Bay of Pigs fiasco began under Dwight Eisenhower. So did CIA plots to overthrow the Castro-friendly dictator of the Dominican Republic, Rafael Trujillo, who was assassinated by political opponents ten weeks after this speech.

Perhaps more than in any other region, Latin America represented many of the contradictions between Washington's rhetoric about freedom and liberty, and its support for dictatorships, as long as they were allies against communism. The Dominican Republic's Trujillo was only one of several examples. Indeed, he was a classic Cold War ally of convenience, an appalling dictator who enriched himself (he owned 70 percent of the nation's sugar cane industry) while oppressing his countrymen. But it was only when he began to align himself with Fidel Castro—suggesting the possibility of Caribbean dominoes falling to the Communists—that the U.S. no longer had any use for him. The CIA actively encouraged plots to kill him during the late 1950s.

In this speech, Kennedy reflected the changed U.S. view of its former ally, inextricably linking him to Castro. "Our Alliance for Progress is an alliance of free governments," Kennedy said, "and it must work to eliminate tyranny from a hemisphere in which it has no rightful place. Therefore, let us express our special friendship to the people of Cuba and the Dominican Republic— and the hope they will soon rejoin the society of free men, uniting with us in common effort."

A "common effort," but to what end? Kennedy believed the Alliance for Progress could be the catalyst for social change on a continent scarred by poverty and exploited by forces, local and foreign, that propped up an almost feudal oligarchy. The United States was among the foreign forces that allowed Latin America's business and political elites to perpetuate themselves even as a growing population became more desperate for basic human needs, like shelter, food, and medical care. But now Kennedy proposed that the U.S. help Latin America "complete the revolution of the Americas, to build a hemisphere where all men can hope for a suitable standard of living, and all can live out their lives in dignity and freedom."

While Kennedy's hardheaded side viewed U.S.-led social reform as a tactic in the Cold War, his speech suggested that such measures were in keeping with the admonition he delivered in his inaugural address. The Alliance for Progress was, in Kennedy's view, an example of helping people "break the bonds of mass misery" not because the Communists were doing it, but because "it is right."

Critics of Kennedy's proposal said the Alliance was a cover for U.S. business interests eager to protect their investments from the threat of nationalization, that is, government confiscation of private capital. His suggestion that "we must support all economic integration which is a genuine step toward larger markets" struck those on the left as imperial America dictating an economic system to its poor southern neighbors. But Kennedy's rhetoric was hardly that of a capitalist tool. While he clearly sought to strengthen the bonds between Latin America and the United States—in trade as well as culture and tradition—his rhetoric emphasized the need for social justice, a loaded phrase on Wall Street then and now.

To emphasize his wish that Latin America break with a past that held it back economically and politically, Kennedy introduced his topic with references to the revolutions that united both continents. "Our nations are the product of a common struggle, the revolt from colonial rule," he said. "And our people share a common heritage—the quest for the dignity and the freedom of man." Here, Kennedy was putting himself and his country on the side of the Latin American people, though not necessarily its governments. They were not always as interested as he seemed to be in the "dignity" and "freedom" of their citizens.

Millions of Latin Americans, he said, "suffer the daily degradations of poverty and hunger. They lack decent shelter [and] protection from disease. Their children are deprived of the education or the jobs which are the gateway to a better life." These are not necessarily the words of an apologist for rapacious capital, as Kennedy's later critics suggested. Indeed, these sentiments, coming from the young leader of a nation that tended to side with governments against their citizens in Latin America, were revolutionary in their own way.

The specifics in the speech demonstrated the commitment behind the words. Kennedy asked Congress for $500 million as a "first step" in fighting illiteracy, improving land use, achieving tax and land reform, and ensuring that the "benefits of increasing abundance" were "available to all."

As striking as was his call for sweeping social changes, subsidized by U.S. taxpayers, was Kennedy's use of the words "American" and "America." When he talked about "creating an American civilization where spiritual and cultural values are strengthened by an ever-broadening base of material advance," he was not referring to merely the United States. Indeed, by "American civilization," he was joining the cultures of north and south into a single civilization, diverse in language and custom, but united by ideals and values. This, too, was a rhetorical act of graciousness on his part. America—the word, the idea—was not, in John Kennedy's speech, merely another way of referring to the United States. America meant Chile and Nicaragua and Brazil and Mexico, too.

His simpatico with his immediate audience and those who would hear his speech translated and broadcast in Spanish and Portuguese and French on the Voice of America reached its zenith, or perhaps its nadir, in closing. Kennedy was not a very good student of foreign languages, as his biographers have pointed out. His lack of facility, perhaps born of disinterest, extended even to simple phonetics. For whatever reason, he just could not get the emphasis and accents correct.

So, as he neared the speech's climax, he may have winced internally as he approached several alien-looking words. "And so I say to the men and women of the Americas—to the campesino in the fields, to the obrero in the cities to the estudiante in the schools—prepare your mind and heart for the task ahead—call forth your strength and let each devote his energies to the betterment of all, so that your children and our children in this hemisphere can find an ever richer and a freer life."

After he finished, he asked speechwriter Richard Goodwin, "How was my Spanish?"

"Perfect," Goodwin said, as one would say if one were a speechwriter to the president of the United States.

"I thought you'd say that," Kennedy replied.

Regardless of Kennedy's inability to affect a rolling Spanish cadence, the speech was well received south of the border. In December 1961, Kennedy traveled to Venezuela and Colombia on a goodwill mission, and the crowds responded warmly—a startling contrast to the violence that marked Vice President Richard Nixon's visit in 1958. As he did in March, Kennedy again conceded the flaws of past U.S. Latin policy. But he also asked the region's political and economic elites to admit their failures, too.

Traveling with Colombia's president, Alberto Lleras Camargo, Kennedy was pleased by the cheering crowds. Lleras Camargo took note of the reaction and told Kennedy why he was so warmly received. "It's because they believe you are on their side," he said.

Ironically enough, another Latin American leader impressed by the Alliance for Progress was none other than Fidel Castro, whose presence in the region inspired the idea in the first place.

Castro told a journalist in 1963 that he considered the Alliance and the ideas behind it "a good idea—it marked progress of a sort." Castro understood what Kennedy was after, even if later critics did not. "The goal of the Alliance was to effect social reform which would improve the conditions of the masses in Latin America."

On November 18, 1963, John Kennedy called implementation of the Alliance "a far greater task than any we have undertaken in our history."

Stephen Smith (far right), JFK's brother-in-law,
was one of the president's top political advisors.

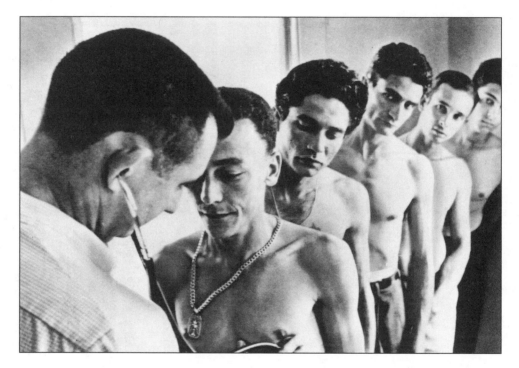

*Cuban exiles in Florida line up for medical examinations before joining an insurgent army
that hoped to bring down Fidel Castro with American help.*

CHAPTER 12

The Bay of Pigs

Speech to the American Society of Newspaper Editors
April 20, 1961

TRACK 12

White House News Conference
April 21, 1961

TRACK 13

THE COVERT PLAN TO TRAIN AN ARMY OF ANTI-CASTRO CUBAN exiles reached its climax on Monday morning, April 17, in a place called the Bay of Pigs. Months in the making, the plot was a legacy of the Eisenhower administration, and of Richard Nixon, who had fought for its implementation and then found himself arguing against it during the 1960 campaign. The CIA originated the plan, and the Joint Chiefs of Staff approved it.

Ultimately, however, John F. Kennedy implemented the plan, and John F. Kennedy had little choice but to accept blame for its failure.

Kennedy had been president for only three months when the Bay of Pigs unraveled. Americans who considered him too young and too inexperienced during the campaign suddenly had reason to believe they were right all along. He seemed indecisive, unable to stop a bad idea, unwilling to exercise judgment, unwilling to "pay any price" and "bear any burden" on behalf of liberty. For if he had been so willing, why did he not help the men trapped on a beach? And if he were unwilling to help, why did he allow the operation to proceed at all?

The invasion is commonly referred to as a fiasco, but it was far worse than that. It was, literally, a bloody, deadly disaster. It might better be referred to as a farce, save that such a description would seem to belittle the genuine courage of those zealous exiles who left their training camps filled with hope only to lose their lives in the sands of despair and futility.

The Bay of Pigs was the first of many memorable crises during John Kennedy's short-lived presidency. Because it ended so terribly, and because it reflected so poorly on the new administration, the lessons learned were never forgotten and the mistakes made were never to be repeated.

Until the Bay of Pigs, Kennedy was enjoying an extended political honeymoon. While most new presidents enjoy a warm relationship with voters, Kennedy's honeymoon was notable because he had not won a majority of the votes cast, and, indeed, had barely won at all in the popular vote. But by mid-April, public opinion polls showed him with an approval rating of 73 percent. The White House was bombarded with cards and telegrams wishing the new president well—in fact, Kennedy had to ask his fellow citizens to contain their written expressions of enthusiasm.

All the while, disaster was in the making.

In late March, Arthur Schlesinger asked Kennedy what he thought of "this damned invasion," referring to the final stages of the anti-Castro coup attempt.

"I think about it as little as possible," the president replied.

In the coming days, however, he had no choice but to think about it a great deal. Though the operation was a secret, it was not particularly well kept, at least not in Washington, Miami...and Havana. The powerful chairman of the Senate Foreign Relations Committee, William Fulbright of Arkansas, advised Kennedy against the plan, but his was a lonely voice. The coming invasion was under intense discussion during high-level White House meetings in early April. Intelligence reports indicated that oppressed Cubans would rise up and welcome the invaders.

The press learned of the invasion plans as March gave way to April. A reporter for the *New York Times*, Tad Szulc, was preparing to break a story asserting that an invasion was imminent. Kennedy called the paper's publisher, Orville Dryfoos, and tried to persuade him to kill Szulc's story.

Although it is commonly believed that Kennedy succeeded in killing the story, that is only half-true. The *Times* account reported that anti-Castro forces were being trained in Florida, but it did not report that those forces were about to go into action. Other news agencies, such as CBS and the Associated Press, did report that invasion plans were nearing completion.

At a news conference in early April, a reporter asked Kennedy how far the U.S. might go in assisting anti-Castro forces. "I want to say that there will not be, under any conditions, an intervention in Cuba by the United States armed forces," he said, adding that his administration would make sure that "there are no Americans involved in any actions inside Cuba."

On Saturday, April 15, several bombers flew from Nicaragua to carry out attacks on three airfields in Cuba. Castro's government accused the U.S. of being behind the attacks, leading Adlai Stevenson, Kennedy's ambassador to the United Nations, to issue heated and righteous denials. He was not lying—he did not know the truth. Kennedy and his aides had deliberately kept Stevenson in the dark, and then allowed him to issue denials that they knew were false.

Kennedy gave his final approval for the invasion on Sunday, April 15.

The following morning, just before five o'clock, a brigade of about fourteen hundred Cuban exiles landed on the beach at the Bay of Pigs. Kennedy was informed of the landing at 5:15 a.m., and was told that the CIA was asking for air cover from U.S. warplanes aboard the U.S.S. *Essex*, which was patrolling nearby. Kennedy refused the CIA's request—the landing would have to proceed without U.S. air support. Offering such support to the rebels would have constituted "armed intervention," and he had told the American people there would be nothing of the sort.

The invaders never had a chance. Cuba's military responded quickly to the threat—twenty thousand troops with the support of Soviet-made tanks were soon blasting away at the invasion force. Castro's air force sunk two rebel supply ships, leaving the invaders without extra ammunition. The expected uprising in the interior of the country never happened—Castro had ordered mass arrests of suspected dissidents in the days leading up to the invasion.

Pinned down on the beach, their supplies and communications system aboard the sunken ships, the rebels began to give up. Kennedy, in desperation, relented on his earlier order and allowed the deployment of a few U.S. warplanes without markings, but they arrived too late. About twelve hundred rebels surrendered. The rest were killed or wounded.

Everything had gone wrong. John Kennedy no longer seemed master of all he surveyed, coolly confident and in control of the Free World. Instead, he seemed to be all that his opponents said he was: inexperienced, immature, rash.

The political repercussions were bound to be enormous, as Kennedy immediately understood. "How could I have been so stupid," he said several times during post-invasion meetings. Not only was the invasion a failure, but also the administration had allowed Stevenson to make a fool of himself at the UN. To repair the damage and to instill a sense of national unity, the president consulted his predecessor, Eisenhower, and his recent opponent, Nixon, as well as leaders in Congress. When Kennedy contacted Nixon to invite him to the White House for a consultation, Nixon's daughter, Tricia, took the call. She left a message for her father, next to the telephone: "JFK called. I knew it! It wouldn't be long before he would get into trouble and have to call on you for help!"

Though he had been given bad advice and lousy intelligence, Kennedy realized he had nobody to blame but himself, and, in fact, would not publicly blame anybody but himself. The White House issued a statement, which read: "President Kennedy has stated from the beginning that as president he bears sole responsibility" for his administration's actions. The short statement added that Kennedy was "strongly opposed" to any attempt to "shift the responsibility" for the disaster.

Kennedy had been scheduled to give a speech to the American Society of Newspaper Editors on April 20 in Washington's Statler Hilton Hotel. Despite the disaster in Cuba on April 16, he went ahead with the plan, although the speech he gave certainly was not the one he had planned. He began by conceding the obvious: the news from Cuba, he said, "has grown worse instead of better." But if the press, or the nation, or Castro, or Moscow, were expecting apologies or self-doubt, they were very much mistaken. The speech was defiant in tone, conceding nothing to Havana or Moscow even as he reiterated his belief that "unilateral American intervention" would have been "contrary to our traditions and our international obligations." But, he warned, "our restraint is not inexhaustible."

"Should it ever appear that the inter-American doctrine of noninterference merely conceals or excuses a policy of nonaction—if the nations of this hemisphere should fail to meet their commitments against outside Communist penetration—then I want it clearly understood that this government will not hesitate in meeting its primary obligations, which are to the security of this nation. Should that time ever come, we do not intend to be lectured on 'intervention' by those whose character was stamped for all time on the bloody streets of Budapest." The reference was to the bloody Soviet suppression of a fledgling rebellion against Russian rule in Hungary in 1956. It was designed to remind his audience that the enemy was not a small Latin nation off the Florida coast, but the Soviets.

The United States, Kennedy promised, would "profit from this lesson" and would "intensify our efforts for a struggle in many ways more difficult than war, where disappointment will often accompany us."

Behind the scenes, John Kennedy said that the disaster in Cuba was the "worst experience of my life." His wife, Jacqueline, told his mother, Rose, that the president had tears in his eyes when he thought about the lives lost on the beach. But just as he masked his health problems, John Kennedy hid his bitter disappointment during this affirmative speech to the nation's top editors.

The following day, Kennedy again faced the press, although in very different circumstances. This time, the journalists were not on hand to be a mere audience, but to ask questions at a press conference in a theater-like setting in the White House. Behind a podium and in front of a backdrop that displayed a huge presidential seal, Kennedy looked like the loneliest man in the country. The room was packed with reporters sitting in the darkened chairs. All eyes were on the president, who was bathed in hot television lights, with no aide by his side to assist him.

Kennedy had no intention of giving the reporters what they wanted. Having taken responsibility for what took place, he wished to say no more, telling his staff that the controversy would go away if the administration simply refused to discuss it any further.

Kennedy opened the press conference by setting a ground rule. "I know that many of you have further questions about Cuba," he said. "I do not think that any useful national purpose would be served by my going further into the Cuban question this morning." The huge presidential seal on the wall behind him almost overshadowed the president himself—it was almost as though the White House, in its effort to squash further discussion of the disaster in Cuba, sought to intimidate the gathered reporters with this reminder of office's majesty and power.

Kennedy tried to deflect the Cuban issue by creating other news: He said the U.S. would offer the United Nations $40 million to create a global food reserve to reduce starvation. He announced that the Veterans Administration would pay a "special insurance dividend" of $250 million to five million ex-GIs.

The reporters were not interested in the president's announcements. The first question was about Kennedy's conversation the previous evening with Nixon about Cuba. Kennedy said simply that "the vice president came to the White House at my invitation, and I informed him or brought him up to date on the events of the past few days." A reporter followed up by asking Kennedy if he had supported the arming and training of Cuban exiles despite the advice of several top aides. "I think the facts of the matter involving Cuba will come out in due time," he said with obvious impatience.

A third inquisitor tried to break the mounting tension. "Mr. President," he said, "this is not a question about Cuba, it's a question about Castro." The journalists laughed, but Kennedy's resolve remained firm. He was not amused. The reporter asked if it were true that Castro has been "incapacitated"—such a rumor had been flying around Washington that morning. "I saw, I think, some reference on the ticker this morning that Mr. Castro was seeing some members of the press today, so I suppose we will have a better idea of that later on."

He would not give an inch, and the reporters stopped probing for more information. Instead, they confined their questions to more routine business—the effect of automation on agriculture, the space program, health care, and other items on JFK's domestic agenda.

But then journalist Sander Vanocur of NBC defied the unspoken truce, and returned to the issue everyone except Kennedy wished to discuss: Cuba. Perhaps to soften his approach, Vanocur did not refer explicitly to Cuba. Instead, he asked about "a certain foreign policy situation" that "has given rise to many conflicting stories." Vanocur said that administration officials had been "clamming up," and this very morning the president had said "we are not permitted to ask any further questions about this foreign policy situation." It was a direct challenge to Kennedy's post-invasion management of the crisis. Vanocur asked, "In view of the fact we are taking a propaganda lambasting around the world, why is it not useful, sir, for us to explore with you the real facts behind…our motivations?"

Kennedy, on the defensive, replied that "we have to make a judgment as to how much we can usefully say that would aid the interest of the United States." It was an argument he would elaborate on in the coming weeks. "One of the problems of a free society, a problem not met by a dictatorship, is this problem of information."

That thought led to one of Kennedy's classic quotations: "There's an old saying that victory has a hundred fathers and defeat is an orphan, and I wouldn't be surprised if information is poured into you in regard to all the recent activities." In other words, those with a vested interest in protecting themselves in the face of disaster would surely provide information that would implicate others. It was a shrewd assessment of how Washington works, especially in the aftermath of disaster.

Kennedy's handling of the Bay of Pigs crisis—that is, its aftermath—belied first impressions of a new, untested president in over his head. His already high public approval ratings soared even higher as the country rallied around their president. A Gallup Poll taken a week after the disaster showed the president with an astonishing approval rating of 83 percent. Sixty-one percent approved of Kennedy's handling of the Bay of Pigs. Even more, 65 percent, agreed with Kennedy's assertion that U.S. armed forces should not be used to oust Castro.

The president was bemused, and perhaps even bewildered, by his popularity. After all, he did not think so highly of his performance, or that of his administration as a whole. "It's like Eisenhower," he said. "The worse I do, the more popular I get."

Cuban dictator Fidel Castro.

The president golfing in Hyannis Port, Massachussets.

CHAPTER 13

The President and the Press

Address to the American Newspaper Publishers Association
April 27, 1961

TRACK 14

J OHN KENNEDY'S RELATIONSHIP WITH THE PRESS WAS A GOOD DEAL MORE
complicated than is commonly believed. Critics have charged that journalists willfully ignored what they knew or heard about the president's
private life because they did not wish to embarrass a politician they supported.
But it is also true that the press ignored the extramarital affairs of many politicians, Republican and Democrat alike. That reticence still exists today to some
extent, but the rules have changed, especially in the aftermath of the sexual
scandal that led to President Clinton's impeachment in 1998. Politicians today
could not behave the way John Kennedy did and expect that their transgres-
sions would remain unreported. In 1960, however, what went on behind the
scenes stayed behind the scenes—regardless of party or ideology.

There is no question that John Kennedy and his family received favorable
publicity, but that was less a function of politics than it was of old-fashioned
storytelling. The Kennedys were young and glamorous, with two adorable little children. The president was a legitimate war hero, and the first of his generation—the World War II GIs—to win the presidency. He was accessible, he
was quotable, and he had a special reverence for language—he was, in a
phrase, good copy.

Those qualities were almost always on display during his weekly televised press conferences, which showed off his wit, intelligence, and grasp of the issues. At a press conference in 1962, for example, a reporter took note of the pressures on the president and asked Kennedy if he would do it all over again, and if he would recommend the job to others. "Well," he said, "the answer is…to the first is yes and the second is no. I don't recommend it to others—at least for a while." On another occasion, in 1963, a reporter asked if he agreed with former president Eisenhower's suggestion that there be term limits for members of Congress. "It's the sort of proposal which I may advance in a post-presidential period, but not right now," he replied.

For John Kennedy, the televised press conference was the equivalent of Franklin Roosevelt's fireside chats. FDR seized the new medium of radio to speak directly to the American people. Kennedy used television in the same way, with journalists serving as supporting players—or, on occasion, as props. Some commentators thought Kennedy was foolish to put himself in a situation where the dynamics were beyond his control. They underestimated him. In a Gallup Poll in early 1962, an astonishing 91 percent of respondents said they had a favorable impression of his performance during those news conferences. No wonder he would tell the newspaper publishers in the Waldorf that he considered it "highly beneficial to have some twenty million Americans regularly sit in on these conferences." It was their chance, he said dryly, "to observe, if I may say so, the incisive, the intelligent, and the courteous qualities displayed by your Washington correspondents."

Kennedy's view of the men and women who covered him, and their bosses, and their publishers, was equally complicated. He had been, however briefly, one of them. In 1945, as previously noted, he had covered the United Nations conference in San Francisco for the *Chicago Herald-American*. He got a taste of what daily journalism is like, and formed relationships with important journalists like Arthur Krock of the *New York Times*.

Kennedy's father had warned him to remember that reporters were not his friends, advice Kennedy did not forget. But that did not prevent him from forming useful relationships with journalists like Krock, Ben Bradlee of *Newsweek*, and others. Many reporters knew or suspected that Kennedy was a voracious womanizer, as the public learned years after his assassination. They did not report on his personal life, which many critics (of the press, and of Kennedy) have cited as evidence of the press's pro-Kennedy bias. In fact reporters did not look into any politician's private life in the early 1960s. Even avowed enemies of Kennedy, such as Jimmy Hoffa, considered sexual indiscretions to be off-limits.

Nevertheless, Kennedy certainly did not think the press was especially supportive of him or his administration. Once, at a news conference, a reporter asked Kennedy how he thought the press was treating him. "Well," he replied, "I am reading more and enjoying it less...but I have not complained nor do I plan to make any general complaints. I read and talk to myself about it, but I don't plan to issue any general statement on the press. I think that they are doing their task...And I am doing mine. And we are going to live together for a period, and then go our separate ways."

In fact, Kennedy had complained, and would continue to complain, about press coverage. He flatly refused to allow photographers to cover his occasional excursions on the golf course (in part because he recently had hit an onlooker with an errant shot). His predecessor, Eisenhower, was more than happy to be photographed with a club in hand, but that was precisely the point. Golf was the sport of the Eisenhower era. The Kennedy era would be more active—golf did not fit the image, even though Kennedy played the game.

On a more substantial issue, Kennedy was livid over coverage of the Bay of Pigs disaster—before, during, and after. Castro, he said, did not need spies to tell him what the U.S. had been planning. "All he has to do is read our papers." And in the bitter days after the invasion collapsed, he was infuriated again when Sander Vanocur and his colleagues refused to abide by Kennedy's expressed desire to avoid discussion of Cuba. "What the hell do they want me to do...say that we took the beating of our lives? That the CIA and the Pentagon are stupid?" he raged.

In his view, coverage of the Bay of Pigs had jeopardized a covert operation against an enemy ninety miles off the Florida coast. In other words, the press had played havoc with national security. For Kennedy, this was an unacceptable abuse of the First Amendment. "We're going to have to straighten this out, and soon," he vowed.

On April 26, the nation's newspaper publishers—seventeen hundred men and women who owned and controlled the primary means by which Americans got their news in 1961—found out precisely how Kennedy intended to "straighten this out."

This speech marked Kennedy's third appearance before important figures in journalism since the Bay of Pigs. Each audience, however, was quite different: the editors whom JFK addressed on April 20 were working journalists, but they also were newsroom executives far removed from the inside world of the White House press corps. They also were mere spectators—they were not participants, as the reporters were on April 21, when they gave up trying to get the president to say something about Cuba.

The audience on April 26 was something else again. The nation's newspaper publishers were business executives charged with the financial health of their products. Some, in the tradition of William Randolph Hearst, exercised tight editorial control over the pages they owned. Others preferred to let their employees handle the news while they tended to the business of publishing or running radio stations, in which some publishers dabbled.

What most of these publishers had in common was their politics. As successful and wealthy business leaders, most publishers were Republican. In fact, three times as many newspapers endorsed Richard Nixon as supported Kennedy in 1960. Endorsements generally are dictated by publishers, not the journalists on their payroll.

Kennedy knew he was traveling into hostile territory when he entered the hotel's grand ballroom. He also knew that his message very likely would make the publishers even more wary of him. He said at the beginning of his speech that he had entitled the address "The President and the Press." But, he added, some "may suggest that this would be more naturally worded 'The President Versus the Press.' But those are not my sentiments tonight."

Oh, but they were.

Before getting to the heart of his message—that the press should exercise greater restraint on issues of national security—Kennedy could not resist teasing his audience, especially knowing the political sentiments of most of the people in the room. He said that "when a well-known diplomat from another country demanded recently that our State Department repudiate certain newspaper attacks on his colleague, it was unnecessary for us to reply that this administration was not responsible for the press, for the press had already made it clear that it was not responsible for this administration."

That was for the Nixon supporters in the room, and there were plenty of them.

The president also tied together the origins of the twilight struggle with a short, pointed history lesson from the annals of journalism.

"You may remember that in 1851 the *New York Herald Tribune* under the sponsorship and publishing of Horace Greeley, employed as its London correspondent an obscure journalist by the name of Karl Marx," Kennedy said. "We are told that foreign correspondent Marx, stone broke, and with a family ill and undernourished, constantly appealed to Greeley and managing editor Charles Dana for an increase in his munificent salary of $5 per installment, a salary which he and Engels ungratefully labeled as the 'lousiest petty bourgeois cheating.'

"But when all his financial appeals were refused, Marx looked around for other means of livelihood and fame, eventually terminating his relationship with the *Tribune* and devoting his talents full time to the cause that would bequeath the world the seeds of Leninism, Stalinism, revolution, and the Cold War. If only this capitalistic New York newspaper had treated him more kindly; if only Marx had remained a foreign correspondent, history might have been different. And I hope all publishers will bear this lesson in mind the next time they receive a poverty-stricken appeal for a small increase in the expense account from an obscure newspaper man."

Of course, those remarks crackled with characteristic Kennedy wit. But they were politically deft as well. Implicitly, Kennedy took the side of working reporters—the journalists who saw him every day in the White House— over their stingy paymasters.

If that barb did not unsettle Kennedy's audience, the rest of his text certainly did.

Kennedy argued that because the struggle with international communism was the moral equivalent of war, the press had a wartime responsibility to censor itself on issues of national security. There was little question that press coverage of the Bay of Pigs affair was very much on his mind as he broached this highly sensitive issue. He made a reference to "events of recent weeks"—events that "may have helped to illuminate" the challenge facing both the president and the press.

"This deadly challenge imposes upon our society two requirements of direct concern both to the press and to the president—two requirements that may seem almost contradictory in tone, but which must be reconciled and fulfilled if we are to meet this national peril," he said. "I refer, first, to the need for far greater public information; and, second, to the need for far greater official secrecy."

To an audience of newspaper publishers, the words "far greater official secrecy" inevitably would inspire a collective shudder. Kennedy acknowledged as much. Secrecy, he said, "is repugnant in a free and open society."

Nevertheless, Kennedy challenged his audience to reconsider its coverage of national security issues, and, in essence, to restrain itself as it would during a time of declared war. "Every newspaper now asks itself, with respect to every story: 'Is it news?'" he said. "All I suggest is that you add the question: 'Is it in the interest of the national security?'"

More than forty years later, Kennedy's concerns remain unresolved, as the White House, fighting a war on terror, battles with the press over issues of secrecy and national security.

Kennedy's main concern was about news outlets reporting on covert operations, the Cold War's equivalent of troop movements in a more traditional war. If the press censored itself when the nation was engaged in a declared war, like World War II, should it not do likewise in a struggle that Kennedy insisted was just as dangerous as any other war?

He softened this outright plea for greater secrecy with an assurance that he was not asking for suppression of dissent or a shying away from controversy. "No president should fear public scrutiny of his program," he said. "For from that scrutiny comes understanding; and from that understanding comes support or opposition. And both are necessary…

"Without debate, without criticism, no administration and no country can succeed—and no republic can survive. That is why the Athenian lawmaker Solon decreed it a crime for any citizen to shrink from controversy. And that is why our press was protected by the First Amendment—the only business in America specifically protected by the Constitution—not primarily to amuse and entertain, not to emphasize the trivial and the sentimental, not to simply 'give the public what it wants,' but to inform, to arouse, to reflect, to state our dangers and our opportunities, to indicate our crises and our choices, to lead, mold, educate, and sometimes even anger public opinion."

This sort of flattery got Kennedy nowhere. The publishers sat on their hands while the president spoke and offered only polite applause when he finished. In the following days, editorials roundly condemned JFK's fairly crude attempt to impose self-censorship on the press. Newspapers replied that dangerous times required more information, not more secrecy.

Ironically, Kennedy had reason to agree with the editorial writers. A few days after his speech, the president met with several editors who were concerned about Kennedy's criticisms of press coverage. He cited the *New York Times* and its coverage of Cuba as examples of reporting that threatened national security. But he privately conceded to the newspaper's managing editor, Turner Catledge, that if the paper had gone ahead and printed what it knew about the invasion, the White House might have been spared a disastrous mistake.

Kennedy chats with famed UPI White House reporter Helen Thomas.

Astronaut Alan Shepard is hauled from his capsule into a helicopter
after his successful space flight in 1961.

CHAPTER 14

A Man on the Moon

Special Message to Congress
on Urgent National Needs
May 25, 1961

TRACK 15

LESS THAN FOUR MONTHS AFTER JOHN KENNEDY ADDRESSED A JOINT
session of Congress to deliver his first State of the Union message, he
summoned the nation's senators and representatives to Capitol Hill
for another major address. Standing in the same place where he had delivered
his official State of the Union speech—at the Speaker's podium in the House
of Representatives chamber—he told the nation's lawmakers that he had a
special message to deliver.

"The Constitution imposes upon me the obligation to 'from time to time
give to the Congress information of the State of the Union.' While this has
traditionally been interpreted as an annual affair, this tradition has been broken in extraordinary times.

"These are extraordinary times. And we face extraordinary challenges.
Our strength as well as our convictions have imposed upon this nation the
role of leader in freedom's cause. No role in history could be more difficult or
more important."

The speech's urgency was in keeping with the rhetoric Kennedy used in
his campaign speeches and his inaugural address. America in 1961, he had said
repeatedly, faced historic challenges around the globe and at home, challenges

that required strong leadership, visionary policies, and the spirit of cooperation that had helped the United States prevail over fascism in World War II.
At a similarly critical time in its history, Great Britain had ignored the challenge of Hitlerism in Germany—a time Kennedy had witnessed firsthand
while living in Britain with his father, the ambassador, and written about in
Why England Slept. As president, John Kennedy would not allow the United
States to make a similar mistake as the Soviet Union sought to expand its
influence around the globe.

This special message, at nearly six thousand words one of Kennedy's
longest, established the new administration's priorities in greater detail than
his State of the Union speech earlier in the year. It furthered the president's
assertion that after the lethargy of the 1950s, the United States indeed was on
the move again, confidently embracing the role of liberty's champion at a time
of extraordinary peril.

But the speech had another sort of urgency. Delivered about a month
after the Bay of Pigs fiasco, it was designed to reassert Kennedy's leadership
and credibility, and to show Moscow and America's allies that the young new
president could and would rebound from a disaster born of inexperience and
foolishness.

The speech is very much a Cold War document, filled with detailed plans
for increased defense spending as well as an announcement that the president
would meet with Nikita Khrushchev for a summit meeting in Vienna later in
the spring. But it is best remembered today for a single, historic proposal.
Toward the end of the message, Kennedy put aside his previous doubts about
the importance of space travel and inextricably linked the nation's prestige to its
space program. In a sentence that history will not soon forget, Kennedy said, "I
believe this nation should commit itself to achieving the goal, before this decade
is out, of landing a man on the moon and returning him safely to earth."

The assembled senators and representatives burst into applause. Kennedy
had identified a goal that was neither Republican nor Democratic, one that
few in the crowded House of Representatives chamber would oppose. Here
was the great national challenge that so many found lacking during the
Eisenhower years. Here was the embodiment of the New Frontier.

Kennedy's astounding ambition was, in 1961, literally fantastic—a fantasy
that defiantly ignored the Soviet Union's huge head start in the space race and
America's apparent inability to keep pace. The Soviets had put a cosmonaut in

orbit already, while the best America could do was Alan Shepard's suborbital flight on May 5.

Nevertheless, Kennedy urged Congress, and the nation, to commit itself to this unlikely and highly ambitious goal. It would cost, he said, between seven and nine billion dollars, an extraordinary sum in 1961, and the equivalent of eighty billion dollars today. And it simply would not do to engage in the space race in a half-hearted fashion. "If we are to go only half way," he said, "or reduce our sights in the face of difficulty, in my judgment, it would be better not to go at all."

Kennedy's ambitions for American space travel are dealt with in chapter 20, which covers his speech at Rice University on September 12, 1962. In that address, devoted entirely to the U.S. space program, Kennedy explained why he committed the nation to such an ambitious goal, and why he believed space travel was an integral part of the country's new rendezvous with destiny.

In this special message of May 25, 1961, the space race was only one of a number of urgent issues the president wished to bring to the attention of Congress and the people, and it was not his first priority. Kennedy's primary emphasis in this speech was a subject much closer to home—what he called the great battle "for the defense of freedom." It was a battle that had to be won outright, not fought to a stalemate.

With these words, the bold phrases of his inaugural address were transformed into policy, and very expensive policy at that. It is one thing to assert that a nation will "pay any price" to "assure the survival and the success of liberty." It is quite another to present that nation with the bill, but that was John Kennedy's assignment in this special message.

He told Congress that military assistance to allies fighting communism would cost another $1.88 billion that year, not the additional $1.6 billion he requested several weeks earlier. New helicopters, armored personnel carriers, and howitzers for the U.S. Army would cost an additional $100 million. The Marine Corps would need another $60 million to pay for new recruits. Spending for civil defense would triple in the new fiscal year. A new, nuclear-powered rocket would require an additional $23 million, while $50 million was needed for satellite communications and $75 million for satellite-based weather observation. And the space program would require an additional $531 million in the next fiscal year to move toward the new goal of a man on the moon by 1969.

The president told Congress, which would have to sign off on these new expenditures, that he "did not foresee" how much his ambitious program would cost when he made his original requests three months earlier. "It is now clear," he said, that his military buildup would cost more than he anticipated. The threats he had identified earlier were more complex than he realized, including a troublesome Communist insurgency in South Vietnam. "The present crisis in Southeast Asia…the rising threat of communism in Latin America, the increased arms traffic in Africa, and all the new pressures on every nation found on the map by tracing your fingers along the borders of the Communist bloc in Asia and the Middle East, all make clear the dimension of our needs," he explained.

Kennedy acknowledged that these extra expenditures would not be painless, politically and otherwise. "It is not a pleasure for any president of the United States…to come before the Congress and ask for new appropriations which place burdens on our people," he said. But he believed his fellow Americans, mobilized to fight the spread of communism and tyranny, would respond to a call for sacrifice in the name of liberty.

Kennedy's declaration of urgent national purpose was phrased in the language of mobilization. Americans, he said, should avoid "harmful work stoppages"—strikes. They should not be "over-producing certain crops" or "spreading military secrets." He also said he hoped his fellow citizens, in an act of national selflessness, would "exercise self-restraint instead of pushing up wages or prices"—an extraordinary and perhaps even naïve assertion. During World War II, when millions of Americans were fighting on distant battlefields, wages and prices were regulated not by self-restraint, but by the Office of Price Administration. But for Kennedy, the twilight struggle superseded the more prosaic concerns of Americans who, unlike him and most of the people he knew, depended on wage income to finance their postwar dreams. Only weeks before, during the Bay of Pigs crisis, he had told Richard Nixon that it did not matter whether "the minimum wage is $1.15 or $1.25" when great issues of war and peace were at stake.

His exhortations included a plea to "serve in the Peace Corps" or other branches of public service, participate "in civil defense…pay higher postal rates…higher payroll taxes and higher teachers' salaries in order to strengthen our society." He even urged Americans to pay more attention to physical fitness, in keeping with his own highly dubious image of youthful, healthy vigor.

Kennedy's straightforward appeal for sacrifice was extraordinary at the time, when, after all, the Cold War was just that—cold. It remains striking today, in the aftermath of the first attack on American soil since Pearl Harbor. Few national leaders since Kennedy have asked Americans so directly for such specific sacrifices, even after the terrorist attacks of September 11, 2001.

Kennedy, however, insisted that a great national struggle required great national participation, through higher taxes—even higher postal rates—and a commitment to national service. "I have not asked for a single program which did not cause one or all Americans some inconvenience, or some hardship, or some sacrifice," Kennedy said. But he believed his fellow citizens would respond positively "to these new and larger demands."

Another contrast between the crisis of the early 1960s and the crisis of the early twenty-first century is Kennedy's emphasis on the nation's allies, including France. About to embark on a visit to that nation's legendary leader, Charles de Gaulle, Kennedy cited France as a symbol of "traditional and effective friendship." His talks with de Gaulle, he said, would not require "a pale unanimity—they are rather the instruments of trust and understanding over a long road."

This is not to say that Kennedy's rhetoric would sound out of place in today's debate over a very different sort of crisis. "I am here to promote the freedom doctrine," Kennedy said in this speech, using words that might have been uttered by George W. Bush forty years later.

The Kennedy Doctrine—"we are not against...any nation or any system, except as it is hostile to freedom"—would be tested not in Berlin or anywhere else in divided Europe, but in the nations and regions that make up what we today call the third world. The word "post-colonial" had not quite made its way into academia in 1961, but in this speech, Kennedy clearly had in mind the struggles of the world's emerging nations as they shook off the shackles of colonialism. This, he said, was the greatest revolution in human history. The United States, born of a rebellion against oppression, was obliged to support this revolution in the "whole southern half of the globe."

There was, of course, a Cold War calculation in Kennedy's vow of solidarity with developing countries in South America and Asia and the newly independent nations of Africa. Nikita Khrushchev portrayed the United States as the successors to European imperialists, contending that the Soviets were the true champions of these revolutionaries. He promised to help wage what he called "wars of liberation" in places like Southeast Asia.

Those wars already were underway, Kennedy said—they were unconventional wars in which the "adversaries of freedom" sought to undermine American influence by sending "arms, agitators, aid, technicians, and propaganda to every troubled area. But where fighting is required, it is usually done by others—by guerillas striking at night, by assassins striking alone." Indeed, he noted, over the past year, some four thousand civil servants had been murdered in South Vietnam.

The Soviets and their allies, however, were not the only advocates of assassination. The night before JFK delivered this speech, the State Department notified the White House of a plot to kill General Rafael Trujillo, the formerly pro-American dictator of the Dominican Republic who had begun to align himself with Castro. But U.S. disgust with Trujillo predated the Kennedy administration—Dwight Eisenhower, in one of his last acts as president, had approved a CIA plan to arm anti-Trujillo Dominicans intent on killing their dictator.

On May 31, Trujillo's opponents, armed with weapons supplied by the United States, murdered the dictator as he was driving his U.S.-made Chevrolet. The plot was executed by Dominicans, but was assisted and supplied by U.S. operatives in the region.

In his speech to the nation, Kennedy could hardly be expected to address the issue of America's own clandestine Cold War activities. But also unmentioned in this extraordinary document about the nation's urgent needs was the plight of African Americans who were trying to rid the nation of segregation and Jim Crow. Freedom Riders were challenging the status quo in the South, and as recently as four days before the speech, on May 21, white segregationists had tried to attack a church in Alabama during a talk by Dr. Martin Luther King Jr.

There was no mention of civil rights in Kennedy's long list of urgent national needs. He resisted the pleas of Harris Wofford, one of his young aides, to make a moral case against segregation and racial discrimination.

That speech would come later. At this moment in 1961, however, Kennedy had other priorities on his mind: the twilight struggle, which took precedence over everything else, including the struggle for freedom and liberty at home.

*The president, vice president, and first lady watch television coverage
of Shepard's voyage on May 5, 1961.*

Khrushchev and Kennedy meet on June 3, 1961.

CHAPTER 15

Preparing for War

*Nationwide Address
on the Berlin Crisis*
July 25, 1961

TRACK 16

O F ALL THE SPEECHES JOHN KENNEDY DELIVERED DURING HIS thousand days as president, few were as grim and frightening as this one, delivered to a national television and radio audience. It is terrifying to read or hear even today, decades removed from the president's fears—the nation's fears—that tensions over a divided city, Berlin, in a divided country, Germany, would lead to nuclear exchanges between the U.S. and the Soviet Union.

While the Cuban Missile Crisis of October 1962 is remembered as the warmest skirmish of the Cold War, the Berlin crisis of 1961 was equally fraught with peril. John Kennedy was prepared to oppose by all means possible Soviet moves to cut off American access to West Berlin, deep in the heart of Communist East Germany.

"That we cannot permit," he said.

"We are clear about what must be done—and we intend to do it. I want to talk frankly with you tonight about the first steps we shall take. These actions will require sacrifice on the part of many of our citizens. More will be required in the future. They will require, from all of us, courage and perseverance in the years to come. But if we and our allies act out of strength and unity of purpose—with calm determination and steady nerves—using restraint in our words as well as our weapons, I am hopeful that both peace and freedom will be sustained."

The president's tone and demeanor, however, seemed anything but filled with hope. Speaking from behind his desk in the White House, his face somber and tense, he told his fellow citizens to prepare for war.

Those preparations included a blunt warning—America's families ought to build fallout shelters and stock them with food and water. "In the coming months," he said on July 25, "I hope to let every citizen know what steps he can take without delay to protect his family in case of attack."

At one point during the tense months in the summer of 1961, Kennedy asked one of his aides, Red Fay, if he had built his own fallout shelter yet.

Fay laughed, thinking the president was not really serious. "I built a swimming pool," he said.

The president was not laughing. "You made a mistake," he said.

In the summer of 1961, 60 percent of Americans believed that the United States would go to war if the Soviets continued to threaten Western access to West Berlin. And in 1961, war between the U.S. and the U.S.S.R. meant total war, and total war meant nuclear war.

Behind the scenes, far out of the public's view, Kennedy was suffering through a miserable stretch of poor health, even as he deliberated over the possibility of nuclear catastrophe and the deaths of tens of millions. His chronic back problems flared up, so much so that he could not climb the stairs leading from an airport tarmac to the doorway of Air Force One, instead riding a mechanical bucket that lifted him from the ground to the airplane's door.

In mid-June, he was confined to bed as his temperature rose to 105 degrees, the result of a viral infection, according to biographer Richard Reeves. When he did get to his feet, he walked with the help of crutches—but only when out of sight of the press or any White House visitors.

All the while, he was considering how the U.S. would respond if the Soviets made a move on West Berlin.

The conflict over Berlin was both decades in the making and the immediate result of Kennedy's disastrous summit meeting with Khrushchev in Vienna in June 1961.

How Berlin came to be divided, and how it was transformed from the ruined capital of the Nazi state to a symbol of the Cold War, is rooted in controversy dating back to the spring of 1945.

On April 12 of that year, forward elements of the American Ninth Army under General William Simpson crossed the Elbe River in Germany. It was the last major topographical barrier between Anglo-American forces and Berlin, now just fifty miles away.

The Red Army, under the command of the great Russian general, Georgi Zukhov, was on the Oder River, thirty-three miles from Berlin in the other direction, to the east. But while the American position on the Elbe was merely a spearhead of some fifty thousand soldiers, the Red Army had 1.2 million on the Oder as it prepared for the war's climactic battle.

With Berlin's fall just a matter of time and the war's outcome no longer in doubt, speculation focused on which army—the Anglo-Americans or the Russians—would capture the German capital. Author Stephen Ambrose notes that in late March, Allied Supreme Commander Dwight Eisenhower declined to predict whether he or Zhukov would get to Berlin first, but he noted that the Russians were closer.

Within weeks of Ike's statement, the Americans were a lot closer, covering more than two hundred miles in two weeks. Suddenly, it seemed possible that the British and Americans might claim the capital before the Russians.

On April 14, however, the American commander on the Elbe, Simpson, received orders to pull back his troops to the western side of the river. The final American push, Eisenhower decided, would not be toward Berlin. As Ambrose writes, Ike told General George Patton that Berlin had no tactical or strategic value. Patton disagreed, as did Simpson and British Field Marshal Bernard Montgomery. Nevertheless, the American and British armies turned their attention to the north, cutting off German reserves based on Norway, and to the south, to prevent a German retreat to a strong redoubt in the Alps.

When General Simpson received his orders to pull back, he and his men were within fifty miles of Berlin. But Eisenhower explained to General George Marshall, Army chief of staff, that Simpson's troops were merely the forward elements of the U.S. push. The bulk of the army was well behind, and their supply lines were stretched to the breaking point after U.S. forces covered two hundred and fifty miles in two weeks. The Russians, on the other hand, were thirty-three miles from the city, had been preparing for two months to march toward Berlin, and were ready to move more than a million men forward. Simpson had just fifty thousand troops on the Elbe.

The Russian offensive started on April 16. Berlin fell on May 2 after a bitter battle. According to Eisenhower's critics, had the Americans and not the Russians captured the city, the postwar division of that city and indeed of Germany itself might have been averted somehow. According to this argument, the Berlin crisis that led John Kennedy to address the nation on July 25, 1961, was the result of Dwight Eisenhower's order to pull back from the Elbe on April 12, 1945.

Ambrose, however, argues convincingly that Eisenhower made the proper decision, both politically and strategically. The Soviets, he noted, were much better prepared to launch a full-scale attack on Berlin than the Americans were. What's more, the British, Americans, and Russians already had agreed to divide Germany into zones of occupation. And, in Berlin itself, the Red Army withdrew on its own accord from the American and British occupation zones within two months of the city's surrender. So, Ambrose argues, the British and Americans (and, later, the French) occupied more than half of the Nazi capital without fighting for it, as the Russians had.

By the time JFK took office, the postwar arrangement was falling apart. Soviet clients in East Germany presided over a repressive Communist government that contained an island of Western influence and power in West Berlin. Increasingly, Khrushchev said he regarded West Berlin as a bone in his throat and seemed intent on breaking the status quo.

On June 3, 1961, John Kennedy and Nikita Khrushchev met face-to-face in Vienna, Austria. After some early tense moments, the two leaders appeared to be warming up to each other over a lunch. Kennedy asked the Soviet leader about the two medals he was wearing. They were, Khrushchev noted, Lenin Peace Prizes. "I hope you get to keep them," Kennedy responded, prompting a laugh from the Russian.

Not many laughs followed. After lunch, Kennedy and Khrushchev went for a walk in a nearby garden (this was two months before his back problems would have made this walk painful, if not impossible), and observers could see the Soviet leader gesticulating and snapping at Kennedy. They were arguing over Berlin. And Kennedy found that none of his wit and charm could wear down his antagonist's defenses. "Khrushchev's presentation was brutal," recalls John C. Ausland, a member of a special Berlin task force assigned to formulate U.S. policy in the city. "He made it clear from the outset that he still wanted the allies out of Berlin."

The Vienna summit brought disagreement on a number of issues, from proposals for a treaty to end nuclear testing to a Communist insurgency in Laos. But it was over Berlin that tempers flared most dramatically.

Khrushchev, ever mindful of the twenty million Russian deaths in World War II, said he was determined to make sure that Germany remained divided. The Soviets were prepared to sign treaties with both East and West Germany to ensure that the division remain in place, and if West Germany would not sign, the Soviets and East Germans would do so on their own. And such a treaty, Khrushchev said, would abrogate the postwar agreement that allowed the U.S. and its allies access to West Berlin, one hundred and ten miles behind the Iron Curtain in East Germany.

Kennedy was unprepared for the Russian's belligerence. He later told journalist James Reston that Khrushchev "thinks because of the Bay of Pigs that I'm inexperienced. Probably thinks I'm stupid." Worst of all, the president said, the Soviet leader "thinks that I have no guts."

In a hastily arranged final meeting in Vienna, JFK reiterated that the United States was prepared to do all in its power to guarantee access to West Berlin. Khrushchev reiterated his intention to sign a treaty the following December.

"Then, Mr. Chairman," Kennedy replied, "there will be war. It will be a cold winter."

During the remainder of spring and into the summer, Kennedy prepared for the coming chill. Berlin became an obsession, far more than Cuba had been in those early months of the administration when the Bay of Pigs fiasco was being planned.

At home and abroad, politicians, journalists, and citizens wondered if the young president could live up to the words he so boldly delivered in January. Since then, he had made a botch of the Bay of Pigs and had been humiliated by the chairman of the Supreme Soviet. If he waffled on the U.S. commitment to West Berlin, his young presidency would be discredited beyond repair. "The whole position of the United States is in the balance," wrote Dean Acheson, Eisenhower's secretary of state and now a key advisor to Kennedy, although one who had little confidence in the new president.

Kennedy spent some time in Florida after his return, where he spoke with journalist Joseph Alsop about the coming confrontation over Berlin. It was no secret that the U.S. and its allies were at a severe disadvantage in conventional forces. The garrison of fifteen thousand French, British, and U.S. soldiers in West Berlin could be easily overrun in the event of a Soviet attack. The combined NATO forces in central Europe also were similarly outmanned.

The fallback position was first-use of nuclear weapons. The specter haunted Kennedy. Alsop's ensuing story in the *Saturday Review* about his interview with the president bore a headline that few at the time would have considered overly dramatic: "The Most Important Decision in U.S. History—And How the President Is Facing It."

As the president pondered his next move, Germans by the thousands fled from Soviet-controlled East Berlin, population 1.3 million, to the safety and freedom of West Berlin, population 2.3 million. The Soviets surely would not stand idly by much longer.

The president told the nation, the Soviets, and the world of his plans on July 25 during a speech from the Oval Office. The gravity of the moment, the content of the speech itself, and the hot television lights shining on him were more than enough to make Kennedy feel uncomfortable. But he was in real, physical discomfort as well. His back caused him so much pain that he had been using crutches earlier in the day, out of sight of the press corps and staff. He had been taking steroids for years for his back and other ailments, but now he increased the dosage in an effort in hopes of gaining a measure of relief. The public, of course, knew none of this.

Kennedy had prepared a multimedia presentation for the nation. He used a map to show how completely vulnerable West Berlin was to a Soviet-East German blockade. The U.S., he said, would never stand by if its adversaries sought to isolate West Berlin. Cutting off Western access to the city, he said, would doom its 2.3 million people.

Speaking to an audience with vivid memories of World War II, he reminded Americans why they were in Berlin in the first place. "We are there as a result of our victory over Nazi Germany," he said. But now, in the fast flow of twentieth century history, the very people—some of them, anyway—who had fought against the United States in that war now looked to the American people to "defend" their ability to "determine their own future and choose their own way of life."

Memories of the old war helped make his case to prepare for a new war. He noted that skeptics complained that West Berlin could not be defended if attacked. That surely was the case, but he chose to ignore reality by conjuring a memory that would resonate with his peers, who had lived through and served in World War II. "I hear it said that West Berlin is militarily untenable," he said. "And so was Bastogne." The reference was to a pivotal moment during the Battle of the Bulge, when General Anthony McAuliffe refused to surrender his outmanned garrison to the advancing Germans. (His reply to the German demand was, famously, one word: "Nuts.")

In recalling the spirit of Bastogne, Kennedy sought to rally the GI generation to the defense of a city that U.S. airplanes had reduced to rubble less than twenty years earlier.

It was not Kennedy's rhetoric that makes this speech so somber and frightening. In fact, his words were measured, even as they carried a warning to the Soviets. "We do not want to fight," he insisted, "but we have fought before…Those who threaten to unleash the forces of war on a dispute over West Berlin should recall the words of the ancient philosopher: 'A man who causes fear cannot be free from fear.'"

Kennedy's specific preparations and warnings to the American people were a good deal more ominous.

He asked Congress for an additional $3.2 billion in defense spending, increasing the army by one hundred and twenty-five thousand soldiers—to one million—the navy by twenty-nine thousand and the air force by sixty-three thousand. Reserves would be called up and ships reactivated. "And let me add that I am well aware of the fact that many American families will bear the burden of these requests," he said. "Studies or careers will be interrupted; husbands and sons will be called away; incomes in some cases will be reduced. But these are burdens which must be borne if freedom is to be defended Americans have willingly borne them before—and they will not flinch from the task now."

The most chilling part of the speech, however, was devoted to civil defense. It was one thing to talk about troop movements. It was quite another to speak to the American people bluntly about the possibility that their cities and towns might come under horrific attack—for their part in defending the capital of their former enemy.

Kennedy said he would ask Congress to appropriate an additional $200 million to identify, strengthen, and stock the nation's system of fallout shelters. "In the event of an attack, the lives of those families which are not hit in a nuclear blast and fire can still be saved—if they can be warned to take shelter and if that shelter is available," he said. "We owe that kind of insurance to our families—and to our country. In contrast to our friends in Europe, the need for this kind of protection is new to our shores. But the time to start is now."

No president had ever spoken to the American people about such a catastrophe. No president since James Madison had to confront the possibility of an invasion (save Abraham Lincoln, when the invaders were Americans from the South). And no president would again speak so gravely about attacks on American soil until the aftermath of September 11, 2001.

It is no wonder, then, that Kennedy allowed himself another candid moment at the end of his speech. "I would like to close with a personal word," he said.

"When I ran for the presidency of the United States, I knew that this country faced serious challenges, but I could not realize—nor could any man realize who does not bear the burden of this office—how heavy and constant would be those burdens.

"Three times in my lifetime our country and Europe have been involved in major wars. In each case serious misjudgments were made on both sides of the intentions of others, which brought about great devastation.

"Now, in the thermonuclear age, any misjudgment on either side about the intentions of the other could rain more devastation in several hours than has been wrought in all the wars of human history."

He promised only "long days ahead," and asked for the nation's prayers.

Less than three weeks later, on August 13, East German security officers began stringing barbed wire along the border between West and East Berlin. It was the beginning of the Berlin Wall.

The very sight of the wall would one day inspire one of John Kennedy's most memorable speeches. But in the summer of 1961, this brutal enforcement of the city's Cold War division helped ease tensions and perhaps held off the cold winter Kennedy predicted in Vienna. The exodus of refugees from east to west stopped and both sides pulled back from what seemed like an inevitable and catastrophic confrontation.

*In the spring of 1961, Kennedy's back caused him so much pain
that he had to be lifted to and from the cabin of Air Force One.*

Defense Secretary Robert McNamara (left) and Secretary of State Dean Rusk
served as advisors to JFK during the Cold War.

CHAPTER 16

A Nuclear Sword of Damocles

Address to
the UN General Assembly
September 25, 1961

TRACK 17

IN LATE SEPTEMBER 1961, *LIFE* MAGAZINE PUBLISHED AN ARTICLE WRITTEN by the president of the United States. The topic was nuclear war, or, more precisely, how Americans might survive such a conflict.

In keeping with his somber speech of July 25, John Kennedy urged Americans to prepare suitable shelters to protect them from the after-effects of a nuclear strike. The piece claimed that with proper preparation, 97 percent of the population could be saved. It was not a responsible claim, to put it mildly. Kennedy knew that, for after he returned from his tumultuous summit with Khrushchev in Vienna, he had asked the Pentagon how many Americans would die in the event of all-out nuclear war. Seventy million, he was told. The U.S. population at the time was about one hundred and forty million.

Civil defense in the fall of 1961 was among the administration's top priorities. Nuclear war seemed imminent. The president received weekly updates on civil defense preparations throughout the country, and the *Life* magazine article was part of that effort. It was written more as a letter to his fellow citizens than a piece of journalism. But while the president wished to prepare the nation for the gravity of this moment, he chose to ignore the horrifying truth—that all the fallout shelters and other preparations underway would not protect half the country.

The fall of 1961 was a terrible and frightening period for a very young administration—in age as well as in tenure. Only the Cuban Missile Crisis would rival these weeks for tension, fear, and drama. Nuclear war seemed just one mistake, one poorly drafted statement, one unguarded comment, away.

In the midst of the country's preparations for conflagration, John Kennedy flew to New York to address the opening session of the United Nations General Assembly, which was just beginning to transform itself into the true world body it is today. At the time, the last colonies of the European powers, most of them in Africa but others in Asia and the Caribbean, were just beginning to assert their independence. In 1961, 104 nations belonged to the UN General Assembly. By 2005, that number had increased to 191.

Kennedy was not sure about appearing at the UN, but tragedy intervened. About a week before the opening session, the beloved UN secretary general, Dag Hammarskjöld of Sweden, died in a plane crash in Africa. He was on a mission of mercy and peace: he was trying to bring an end to a civil war in the Congo.

In the aftermath of Hammarskjöld's death, Kennedy decided to attend the opening session after all. He had several purposes in mind. First, a carefully worded speech at the UN might help reduce the unbearable tensions of the moment. He had begun receiving private signals from Moscow that Khrushchev, too, wanted to take a step back from the abyss. At the same time, however, Kennedy also wanted to counter a Soviet-backed proposal to replace Hammarskjöld with a three-person executive.

Kennedy's speech reflected the awful tensions of the moment. After first paying tribute to the fallen UN leader, JFK turned to the role the world organization had to play in resolving the profound differences that separated the world's great powers. "Today," he said, "every inhabitant of his planet must contemplate the day when this planet may no longer be inhabitable. Every man, woman, and child lives under a nuclear sword of Damocles, hanging by the slenderest of threads, capable of being cut at any moment by accident or miscalculation or madness. The weapons of war must be abolished before they abolish us."

But even as he made the case for disarmament, Kennedy raised the specter of conflict in a place most Americans could not find on a map: South Vietnam.

Kennedy's main concern in Southeast Asia had been in Laos, which borders South Vietnam. Even before he took the oath of office, Kennedy had been monitoring events in Laos carefully. Dwight Eisenhower had told Kennedy that he believed a successful Communist-backed insurgency in Laos could lead to further Communist victories in the region. The insurgents received their most important assistance from the Communist-led regime in North Vietnam, the other half of that divided nation.

Kennedy was in office just three months when he moved one hundred and fifty U.S. Marines to the border between Laos and Thailand. More troops were stationed offshore, in navy vessels off Thailand. They seemed ready to be deployed to the border area if necessary, although the U.S. presence was more for show than anything else. Kennedy did not wish to get involved in a serious conflict in Laos. Vietnam, however, would be another story.

By the time Kennedy spoke at the UN, a shaky ceasefire was in place in Laos, and negotiations between the government and the Communist-backed rebels were underway.

So now, Kennedy's attention focused on neighboring South Vietnam. He told the UN that South Vietnam was under attack and accused insurgents of infiltrating South Vietnam via Laos. The world community, he said, must confront the question of "whether measures can be devised to protect the small and weak" from insurgent attacks.

In fact, the insurgents—the Viet Cong—were becoming bolder even as Kennedy spoke. Their announced goal was to topple the South Vietnamese government in 1961, and they seemed well on their way by the fall. The president of South Vietnam, Ngo Dinh Diem, soon was asking for more U.S. help in beating back the surging Viet Cong.

Kennedy resisted the idea of sending combat troops to Vietnam, but in late 1961, he approved a plan to send what were called "advisors" to assist the South Vietnamese army. Four hundred "advisors"—they were, in fact, U.S. troops—arrived just before Christmas. Within two weeks, that number grew to slightly more than two thousand. In theory, they were there to instruct and train the South Vietnamese army, but they carried weapons and were permitted to use them if they believed they were in danger. In the meantime, the CIA, with Kennedy's approval, began training an army of Meo tribesmen to fight the Communist rebels.

Conditions continued to worsen, and within a year of Kennedy's UN speech, the U.S. had more than eleven thousand soldiers in Vietnam. The buildup had begun. A year later, some sixteen thousand U.S. troops were in Vietnam. "We are not there to see a war lost," Kennedy said in an interview in the late summer of 1963.

It was clear even then, however, that victory was a long way off. Frustrated with the Diem regime, with events that seemed to spiral out of his control, and with press reports that were critical of the U.S. effort in Vietnam, Kennedy began considering the possibility of withdrawal.

One of the most debated questions of the Kennedy presidency is whether he would have presided over a massive expansion of the war, as his successor, Lyndon Johnson, did. It is a question without an answer, of course, but there is some suggestion that he was looking for a way out after the presidential campaign of 1964. He endorsed tentative plans to withdraw a thousand U.S. troops at the end of 1963. Privately, he was convinced that the pro-U.S. regime in South Vietnam simply could not beat the insurgents.

That regime changed violently in early November, when President Diem and his brother were overthrown in a coup and then murdered. In one of his last acts as president, Kennedy ordered a full review of U.S. policy in Vietnam. He asked for a comprehensive analysis of all possible options, including, he said, "how to get out of there."

He made that request on November 21, 1963, the day before he was murdered.

PART THREE: 1962

*Police brutality was just part of the widespread civil rights crisis
that came into the president's focus in 1962.*

Introduction

THE PRESIDENT'S HOPE THAT 1962 WOULD BE A BETTER, LESS
tumultuous year than 1961 was not to be. Kennedy's second twelve
months in office, if anything, were even more fraught with controversy and international dangers than his first.

Southeast Asia came back into focus as a danger spot, but this time it was
Vietnam rather than Laos. The loss of South Vietnam to Communist control
was a substantial concern at the start of the year. Both his judgment and his ability to act had been challenged by the Bay of Pigs disaster and the difficulties
over Berlin, including the construction of the wall symbolizing the power of the
Soviets to maintain control of Eastern Europe. As a result, Kennedy believed
that both domestic and international pressures required him to prevent a
Communist victory in Vietnam. Against his better judgment and counter to his
belief that the U.S. should not fight another land war in Asia, he increased the

number of American military advisers in Vietnam. Although he acknowledged at a February press conference that he had expanded U.S. involvement in that country's conflict, he refused to describe doing so as a prelude to an even larger commitment to fighting Saigon's war.

During the first four months of the year, Kennedy also found himself forced to resume nuclear tests in the atmosphere. In the second half of 1961, Moscow had announced a decision to end a voluntary suspension and resume nuclear testing. Kennedy's national security advisor said that "of all the Soviet provocations, it was the resumption of testing that disappointed Kennedy most." In his mind, it meant not only the spread of dangerous pollutants across the world, but also an escalation in the arms race that would cost both sides large sums of money and increase tensions that could lead to a disastrous nuclear war. After the Soviets exploded a huge fifty-megaton bomb and conducted fifty atmospheric tests in two months at the end of 1961, Kennedy believed he had no choice but to also resume testing.

In April, he reported his decision to the country in a televised address that was notable for his grim demeanor and words. By unleashing the power of the atom, he said, mankind had taken "into his mortal hands the power of self-extinction...For of all the awesome responsibilities entrusted to this office, none is more somber to contemplate than the special statutory authority to employ nuclear arms in defense of our people and freedom." He ended on a hopeful note: "It is our hope and prayer that these...deadly weapons will never have to be fired—and that our preparations for war will bring about the preservation of peace."

Domestic difficulties gave Kennedy considerable grief in 1962 as well. From the start of his presidency, he had faced questions about how to jump-start a sluggish economy. Promoting prosperity without incurring serious inflation were two sides of the same problem. Kennedy proposed an $11 billion tax cut with significant reductions in both personal and corporate tax rates. Cutting taxes, which seemed likely to increase federal budget deficits and inflation, impressed many economists as an unwise, radical solution to the country's economic problems. But in a commencement address at Yale in June, Kennedy declared, "The great enemy of the truth is very often not the lie…but the myth," the dogged attachment "to the clichés of our forebears." Although the tax cut would wait until Lyndon Johnson put it across in 1964, Kennedy's unorthodoxy proved to be an effective means of spurring forward a new round of substantial economic growth.

Checking inflation drove Kennedy into a confrontation with the steel industry that partly marked him as antibusiness. It was not true, but his refusal to let Big Steel raise prices that jeopardized the country's general price stability was as much a part of defending the national well-being as holding the Soviet Union in check. In a public appeal that forced the industry to roll back price hikes, Kennedy said he believed his fellow citizens "will find it hard, as I do, to accept a situation in which a tiny handful of steel executives, whose pursuit of private power and profit exceeds their sense of public responsibility, can show such utter contempt for the interests of 185 million Americans."

A civil rights crisis in Mississippi in September threatened to provoke widespread racial violence, embarrass the nation before the world, and give Moscow an opportunity to score propaganda points with third world countries against the United States. When James Meredith, a black air force veteran and Mississippian, tried to enroll at the state's university and Governor Ross Barnett defied a federal order to admit him, the stage was set for a showdown with the federal government. Kennedy used a national TV address to celebrate America's traditional reliance on the rule of law rather than mob violence. At the same time, however, rioters protesting Meredith's presence on the university's campus caused the deaths of two people and injuries to one hundred and sixty federal marshals trying to enforce the court's desegregation order. Although Meredith was enrolled and the crisis quickly ended, Kennedy feared that his effectiveness as a peacemaker among domestic factions had suffered a setback.

No problem weighed more heavily on Kennedy in 1962 than the Cuban Missile Crisis of October. It threatened to touch off a nuclear war Kennedy knew would cost both the United States and the Soviet Union tens of millions of lives and the whole world untold suffering. In a seventeen-minute speech in the midst of the crisis watched by a hundred million Americans, the largest TV audience at that point, Kennedy left no doubt about the gravity of the danger facing the world. He denounced Moscow for recklessly endangering peace and for lying about its action in creating a "nuclear strike capability" in Cuba. He declared that the U.S. would not tolerate the presence of these offensive weapons ninety miles from its shores. He announced a naval quarantine of Cuba to block all offensive weapons from reaching the island, and he demanded the withdrawal of those that were already in place.

Fortunately, Khrushchev retreated in the face of Kennedy's threat to use force, if necessary, to remove the danger to the United States. A secret deal made the peaceful outcome possible. Kennedy promised to remove medium-range missiles from Turkey in return for Soviet dismantling of their weapons in Cuba. The world breathed a sigh of relief, and overnight, Kennedy became a heroic leader to millions of people everywhere praising his wisdom in peacefully settling the worst Soviet-American crisis of the Cold War. Few people outside the U.S. government knew how close the world had come to a dreaded nuclear exchange. We now know that pressure on Kennedy from his military chiefs to bomb and invade Cuba would have produced Soviet retaliation likely to escalate into a full-scale conflict. Kennedy's wisdom in resisting his chiefs' insistence on military action rather than the quarantine barred the way to a nuclear holocaust.

The year 1962 ended with a strong showing for his party in the November congressional elections, his approval rating at an unprecedented 74 percent, and his selection by Americans as the most admired man in the world.

Kennedy after swimming at the home of Peter Lawford.

CHAPTER 17

A Celebrity President

Inaugural Anniversary Dinner
January 20, 1962

TRACK 18

IT IS NOT UNCOMMON FOR POLITICIANS TO ENGAGE IN SELF-PARODY, although it is usually unintentional. To commemorate the first anniversary of his inauguration, however, John Kennedy delivered a speech that included an intentional parody of the words he had spoken the previous year. A taste for self-mockery was very much a part of Kennedy's detached, ironic persona. When he read in *Time* magazine that his youngest brother, Ted, smiled "sardonically," he feigned outrage. "Bobby and I smile sardonically," he said. "Ted will learn how to smile sardonically in two or three years, but he doesn't know how yet."

He demonstrated that particular skill on January 20, 1962, at an inaugural anniversary dinner in a National Guard Armory in Washington, D.C. The occasion and the setting were not nearly as glamorous as the formal balls that celebrated his swearing-in, but the crowd did not lack for star power. Among those in attendance were Rosemary Clooney and Danny Thomas, a small part of the large celebrity following that Kennedy cultivated, and that cultivated him in return.

Hollywood types like Thomas and Clooney, not to mention Frank Sinatra, Marilyn Monroe, Joey Bishop, and Peter Lawford (the English actor who married JFK's sister, Patricia), saw Kennedy as one of them, a pop idol and skilled showman whose field happened to be politics, not music or the movies. His wife, of course, was among the most glamorous women in the world, with a following that put to shame most movie stars. Hollywood understood the appeal of this couple and responded with enthusiasm, and the Kennedys returned Hollywood's embrace. It was no more surprising to see a Danny Thomas or a Rosemary Clooney at a Kennedy event than it was to see a cabinet secretary. And, of course, one of the most memorable non-news events of the Kennedy years took place in May 1962, when Marilyn Monroe purred "Happy Birthday" to the president as a crowd that included Harry Belafonte, Henry Fonda, Mike Nichols, and Ella Fitzgerald looked on with fascination, amusement, and perhaps even a little embarrassment.

The audience on January 20 included another politician who had attracted his own star following, although he did not have JFK's cover-boy youth and charisma and actually detested the show business aspect of politics. In early 1945, Harry S. Truman had found himself face to face with Lauren Bacall when the young actress draped herself over an upright piano as the startled vice president played a tune in front of an audience of eight hundred servicemen. A photographer was on hand, and the nation's newspaper readers were treated to the sight of a pouty Bacall staring into Truman's eyes. The vice president, soon to be president, seemed to be having a wonderful time.

As sultry moments go, it was not on the scale of Marilyn Monroe's birthday serenade of JFK, but it did not please Truman's wife, Bess. The woman known in the Truman household as "the boss" ordered her husband to stop playing the piano in public. Apparently she figured it was the instrument, not her husband's rakish personality, that attracted young starlets.

It was perhaps with the image of Lauren Bacall in mind that JFK began his anniversary speech by referring to Truman's piano. "I must say it is nice to have a former president who speaks well of you," he said, "and we are glad to have [President Truman] here tonight. His only request has been, since I have been president, to get his piano up from the cellar, and we have done that—and we are going to run on it."

Truman and Kennedy had a complex relationship. Truman despised Kennedy's father, and famously explained his opposition to JFK's presidential candidacy in 1960 by saying, "It's not the pope I'm afraid of, it's the pop." It was meant to provoke a laugh, but the former president was not smiling in July

1960, when he personally condemned JFK on the eve of his nomination. "Senator, are you certain that you are quite ready for the country, or that the country is ready for you?" He went on to tell Kennedy that he wanted a candidate "with the greatest possible maturity and experience." He hit Kennedy where it hurt—portraying him as too young and, unfairly, as too inexperienced.

The Kennedys were not a group to easily forget a slight, but JFK went out of his way to be gracious to the only living former president who happened to be a Democrat. Truman was invited to the Kennedy White House the day after JFK's inauguration, the first time he had been asked back since leaving in 1951. Truman's favorite piano music—selections from Liszt and Mozart—provided the evening's entertainment, and Truman himself was invited to perform.

Nevertheless, as the months and years passed, Truman was disappointed as Kennedy failed to seek out his advice.

After acknowledging his elder, JFK turned his attention to his audience, many of whom were large contributors to his party and all of whom were loyal Democratic activists. What followed was a hilarious reinterpretation of his inaugural address, redesigned as a pitch for donor dollars.

"I spoke a year ago today, to take the inaugural, and I would like to paraphrase a couple of statements I made that day by saying that we observe today not a celebration of freedom but a victory of party, for we have sworn to pay off the same party debt our forebears ran up nearly a year and three months ago.

"Our deficit will not be paid off in the next hundred days, nor will it be paid off in the first one thousand days, nor in the life of this administration. Nor perhaps in our lifetime on this planet, but let us begin—remembering that generosity is not a sign of weakness, and that ambassadors are always subject to Senate confirmation, for if the Democratic Party cannot be helped by the many who are poor, it cannot be saved by the few who are rich. So let us begin."

The appreciative audience understood that Kennedy was celebrating not only his first anniversary in office, but also the beginning of a new election cycle. Midterm elections would be held in 1962, and Kennedy—like all first-term incumbent presidents—was determined to avoid losing House and Senate seats, a fate that usually befalls the party holding the presidency. The president noted that "history is not with us...In this century only in 1934, during the period of the great preeminence of the Democratic Party, did the party in power ever win seats, let alone hold its own" in a midterm congressional election.

Going into the '62 elections, Kennedy and the Democrats had a huge advantage in Congress—the Republicans were looking at a deficit of eighty-eight seats in the House and an astonishing twenty-nine in the Senate.

Those numbers, however, did not translate into anything resembling a rubber stamp when Kennedy presented his program to Congress in 1961. Disasters in the Bay of Pigs and in Vienna had many Democrats worried about the president's leadership, and on the divisive issue of civil rights, JFK's middle course pleased neither northern liberals nor southern conservatives. The administration's agenda was adrift, even in an overwhelmingly Democratic Congress.

Things might only worsen if Republicans made substantial gains in the fall, especially if the president's own popularity began to sag. An emboldened GOP would begin to look at 1964—when many economists believed a recession would take hold—as a chance to unseat an incumbent who had barely beaten Richard Nixon in 1960.

So, with this sparkling parody of some of his most famous words, Kennedy sought to ignite some enthusiasm among his fellow Democrats. And, he concluded, "The fire from our effort can light the world."

If nothing else, the Democrats were not burned when voters went to the polls more than ten months later. JFK's party lost four House seats, but gained four seats in the U.S. Senate. Among those Democratic Senate winners was a young man from Massachusetts named Edward Kennedy who, according to the president, would soon learn the art of "smiling sardonically."

Harry Truman plays the piano at the White House.

JFK enjoys a celebratory cigar at a fundraising dinner.

CHAPTER 18

Hammering Big Steel

Statement and News Conference
April 11, 1962

TRACK 19

ALTHOUGH JOHN KENNEDY WAS FOND OF QUOTING FROM SCRIPTURE, one common Biblical phrase never made its way into the Kennedy canon: "Vengeance is mine, says the Lord." There was good reason for its absence. Just as Kennedy learned that issues of war and peace often are too important to be left in the hands of generals, he and his brother, the attorney general, believed vengeance was far too powerful to be left to the hereafter.

The steel crisis of spring 1962 offers one of the most explicit examples of the lengths to which the Kennedy White House would go to punish a foe—in this case, a foe that had committed the deadly sin of a double cross. In this conflict, John Kennedy drafted vengeance and sent it into battle, escorted by an unprecedented display of domestic power: wiretaps, tax audits, and the proverbial knock on the door at midnight.

These measures were deployed in response to a decision by the nation's largest steel companies—a monolith known as Big Steel—to raise prices by 3.5 percent, which they announced after the Kennedy administration had worked long and hard to mediate a new contract between the steel companies and the steelworkers union. The deal had been a huge victory for the White House, for it persuaded the union to accept a contract with no increase in wages, but with a dime-an-hour raise in pension contributions.

With the country emerging from recession, the Kennedy administration feared that a round of wage and price hikes in the steel industry would have a domino effect on other industries, sparking a round of high inflation. Kennedy's chief economic advisor, Walter Heller, had warned that steel was so important to the national economy that any sort of change in the status quo, from a strike to a price increase, could "upset the applecart all by itself."

The largest steel company was United States Steel, which accounted for about 25 percent of the nation's steel output. The company's power was such that the rest of the industry followed its lead in terms of prices and wages. Its chairman, Roger Blough, was one of the most powerful businessmen in the country.

Kennedy had repeatedly called for labor peace and stable prices as part of his larger demand for national sacrifice. The contract talks between the large steel companies and the powerful union put his rhetoric to the test. Would labor and capital do what was best for their country?

Days after the union did its part, the major steel companies announced that they would raise their prices. Blough came to the White House and delivered the news to Kennedy in person. The president exploded. "You have made a terrible mistake," he said. "You double-crossed me!"

From the perspective of the twenty-first century, a conflict between a president and the steel industry seems as far removed as the Civil War. Companies like United States Steel were once giants of the global economy, and steel output was considered one of the signs of a modern, vibrant manufacturing economy. Steel accounted for a half million jobs in the early 1960s, and the industry's power was such that Walter Heller estimated that 40 percent of the increase in overall prices from 1947 to 1958 could be traced to above-average increases in the price of steel.

Kennedy's hopes for a balanced budget and low inflation could have been undone by a strike or by hikes in steel prices. So the administration went out of its way to keep the peace between capital and labor, and to remind them of their higher calling to the nation at a time of, as Kennedy phrased it in his inaugural, "maximum danger."

In the Kennedy administration's view, the steelworkers union had responded to his call for selflessness and sacrifice. In late 1961, speaking at the AFL-CIO's annual convention, Kennedy had asked labor to remember that it had a "heavy responsibility" at a "most critical time" in the nation's history. Labor responded warmly to the president.

But capital did not, certainly not in Kennedy's view. Big Steel's decision to raise prices—the other big companies followed U.S. Steel's lead—contradicted everything Kennedy had wished for from the industry. The union and the president had been played for fools.

Kennedy was rarely so angry as he was with Big Steel. He said his father had always told him that businessmen were not to be trusted. "I've been screwed," he said. He was determined to get his revenge.

And so, the might of the federal government was turned on Big Steel, a scenario that would be unheard of in the changed political atmosphere forty years later, when businessmen and women are trusted implicitly by most national political leaders. Kennedy aide Arthur Goldberg made the point when he said: "This is war."

On April 11, a seething Kennedy opened a press conference with a terse phrase. "I have several announcements to make," he said. Those announcements were, in fact, a declaration of war on steel executives.

"In this serious hour in our nation's history, when we are confronted with grave crises in Berlin and Southeast Asia, when we are devoting our energies to economic recovery and stability, when we are asking reservists to leave their homes and families for months on end, and servicemen to risk their lives— and four were killed in the last two days in Vietnam—and asking union members to hold down their wage requests, at a time when restraint and sacrifice are being asked of every citizen, the American people will find it hard, as I do, to accept a situation in which a tiny handful of steel executives can show such utter contempt for the interests of 185 million Americans."

Kennedy's language was almost unbelievably strong. He described the price hike as a "wholly unjustifiable and irresponsible defiance of the public interest." Every American could expect to pay more for nearly everything as a result of Big Steel's greed. It would, he said, "increase the cost of homes, auto, appliances, and most other items for every American family. It would increase the cost of machinery and tools to every American businessman and farmer. It would seriously handicap our efforts to prevent an inflationary spiral from eating up the pensions of our older citizens, and our new gains in purchasing power." What's more, he said, the increase would add a billion dollars to the cost of national defense.

He singled out the union for praise and patriotism. Then, noting that he had tried to work with industry executives, he could not resist echoing his famous exhortation in his inaugural address. "Some time ago I asked each American to consider what he would do for his country and I asked the steel companies. In the last twenty-four hours, we had their answer."

The press, the steel industry, and the public at large were aghast. Presidents did not speak this way about big business. In New Hampshire, the poet Robert Frost was delighted. "Oh, didn't he do a good one! Didn't he show the Irish all right?" Frost, a little more than a year earlier, had advised young Kennedy to be less Harvard, and more Irish.

Polls showed that the American people stood with the president. With his fury and his popularity driving him, Kennedy ordered a series of intense measures against the steel companies, some of which were dubious at best. He told his very enthusiastic brother, the attorney general, to look into antitrust violations in Big Steel, suggesting that they were acting in collusion to force the price increase on American consumers. Small companies that were not part of the cartel and that had kept the lid on prices suddenly were awarded defense department contracts. FBI agents visited the offices of steel executives, inquiring about expense accounts and personal records. Subpoenas were issued, and some reporters who wrote about the steel industry received post-midnight phone calls from FBI agents looking for information.

Big Steel, faced with this onslaught, backed down within days. The price increase was rolled back. It was an unmitigated victory for the Kennedy administration. The president pointedly refused to bask in this triumph, saying that he harbored no ill will "against any individual [or] industry." But privately, he loved it. Others did not share his enthusiasm. An up-and-coming economist at the University of Chicago, Milton Friedman, said Kennedy's tactics against Big Steel showed "how much power for a police state resides in Washington." Two decades later, a president more sympathetic to Friedman's ideas, Ronald Reagan, would respond to an analogous challenge by firing air traffic controllers when they went on strike in defiance of federal law.

For the president, the showdown over steel made enemies of all the right people, and—with the memory of the Bay of Pigs and the fiasco in Vienna never far from his mind—showed that he was tougher than they suspected. It certainly did wonders for his humor. Some two weeks after Big Steel's surrender, Kennedy addressed members of the national press corps at its annual

Gridiron Club dinner. He delivered a parody of his "several announcements" declaration of war on steel. Citing a "wholly unjustifiable" increase of $2.50 in the price of a ticket for the event, Kennedy said with mock fury: "In this serious hour in our nation's history...when correspondents are required to leave their families for a long and lonely weekend at Palm Beach, the American people will find it hard to accept this ruthless decision..."

For John Kennedy in April of 1962, laughter surely was the best revenge.

July 4, 1962: Kennedy inspects the Liberty Bell during his visit to Philadelphia.

CHAPTER 19

A Declaration of Independence

Speech at Independence Hall, Philadelphia
July 4, 1962

TRACK 20

Fon a President imbued with a sense of history, whose speeches were filled with historical references as well as a sense of historical purpose, what better stage for a major speech than Independence Hall on the Fourth of July?

President Kennedy's speech on Independence Day, 1962, was delivered to the nation's fifty governors, among others in the audience. He spoke in front of Independence Hall, from a podium on a raised platform that was bedecked in red, white, and blue bunting in the front, and the flags of the states in the back. Behind him soared the landmark building's famous clock tower. To either side on the platform were the invited governors.

The speech of July 4, 1962, is not among the best known in the Kennedy canon, but no less an expert than Theodore Sorensen, JFK's aide and speechwriter, considered it among the president's best. Not surprisingly, given the setting, it was filled with nods to the nation's founders and the principles enunciated in the two great American documents produced in Philadelphia: the Declaration of Independence and the U.S. Constitution. It was an intimate speech, too, one given by one executive to his colleagues in the nation's statehouses—the only people who could begin to understand the burdens, duties, and loneliness of his office. "We are not permitted the luxury of irres-olution," he told the governors. "Others may confine themselves to debate, discussion, and to the ultimate luxury—free advice. Our responsibility is one of decision—for to govern is to choose."

But Kennedy was not content to leave his listeners with just another trib-ute to civic virtue, however gilded. He chose this Fourth of July to declare, in essence, an end to the global drive for independence that began in 1776, and the beginning of a new age of interdependence.

"In most of the old colonial world," he said, "the struggle for independ-ence is coming to an end. Even in areas behind the Curtain, that which Jefferson called 'the disease of liberty' still appears to be infectious. With the passing of ancient empires, today less than 2 percent of the world's population lives in territories officially termed 'dependent.' As this effort for independ-ence, inspired by the American Declaration of Independence, now approaches a successful close, a great new effort—for interdependence—is transforming the world about us. And the spirit of that new effort is the same spirit which gave birth to the American Constitution…

"[I] will say here and now, on this Day of Independence, that the United States will be ready for a Declaration of Interdependence, that we will be prepared to discuss with a united Europe the ways and means of forming a concrete Atlantic partnership, a mutually beneficial partnership between the new union emerging in Europe and the old American Union founded here 175 years ago. All this will not be completed in a year, but let the world know it is our goal."

The notion of an interdependent world was not new, and indeed had found expression in institutions like the United Nations, the North Atlantic Treaty Organization (as well as its Iron Curtain counterpart, the Warsaw Pact), the World Bank, and the fledgling experiment in Western Europe known as the Common Market. Kennedy was not putting forward an untried theory, and made no such claim. He was merely stating what few could deny in a fast-changing world: new states were emerging from collapsed empires, oceans were no defense against attack by an intercontinental ballistic missile, and human beings, ideas, and trade respected neither border nor barrier. No nation—not even the United States—was a fortress unto itself. In the early stages of World War II, German tanks and warplanes had demonstrated the folly of static defenses, like France's Maginot Line. Similarly, the technological, economic, and social advances of the postwar world made a mockery of old ideas of sovereignty.

Kennedy's embrace of the new world he saw developing in the early 1960s made him no less of an American nationalist. In this speech, he paid eloquent tribute to the American contribution to a human narrative of political independence and national aspiration. "The theory of independence is as old as man himself, and it was not invented in this hall," he said. "But it was in this hall that the theory became a practice; that the word went out to all, in Thomas Jefferson's phrase, that 'the God who gave us life, gave us liberty at the same time.'" Such a nation, he said, was bound to play a leading role in the "worldwide movement" toward political independence.

In 1962, the old order of European hegemony in Africa, the Middle East, and parts of Asia was in its death throes. A process that had begun with the collapse of the Russian, German, Ottoman, and Austro-Hungarian empires after World War I neared its conclusion with the removal of the flags of Britain, France, Belgium, and Portugal in places like Kenya, Madagascar, Burundi, and Mozambique. New nations emerged from the colonies of old: Cameroon in western Africa, Malaysia in Southeast Asia, and Trinidad and Tobago in the Caribbean. As Europe withdrew to its former boundaries, its leaders looked to create something new to replace the old imperial system. Years earlier, no less a British nationalist than Winston Churchill foresaw what he called a "United States of Europe," where old imperial rivalries would be subsumed for the greater good of Western civilization. The fledgling Common Market was the first expression of that vision.

On July 4, 1962, John Kennedy sought to encourage both of these developments—the final moves toward independence in the developing world, and the first moves toward interdependence in the old world. He saw the burgeoning membership in the United Nations General Assembly as the ultimate expression of a revolution that began in Philadelphia in 1776 and viewed the Common Market as the beginning of another sort of revolution.

The United States, he said, had nothing to fear from a united Europe, just as it had nothing to fear from those newly independent nations who looked to the ideals of America's founders for inspiration and guidance. Indeed, he said, the United States had a vital role to play in fostering the revolutionary idea of interdependence.

When John F. Kennedy was less than nine months old, President Woodrow Wilson declared that all "the peoples of this world are in effect partners" in the pursuit of peace, prosperity, and justice, "and for our own part we see very clearly that unless justice be done to others it will not be done to us." Wilson did not use the word "interdependence," but his meaning was clear. The Wilsonian vision of an increasingly connected, less isolated world led to the creation of the League of Nations, an institution doomed to failure when isolationists in the United States rallied to block American membership.

The catastrophe of World War II and Franklin Roosevelt's personal leadership changed American attitudes toward multinational organizations and institutions that superseded static ideas of sovereignty. George Washington's warning that the United States ought to avoid "entangling alliances" with the decadent, warmongering old world—a notion embraced by conservatives in the 1930s who demanded an "America first" foreign policy—had given way to the Wilsonian idea of an America fully engaged in a world made smaller by modern technology. In this Independence Day speech, John Kennedy asserted that the United States would lead the way toward interdependence, just as it had lit the torch of independence nearly two centuries earlier.

Decades before the Internet changed communications, at a time when most Americans who had telephones hesitated to call out of state let alone dial an overseas number directly, Kennedy said that just as Alexander Hamilton told New Yorkers to "think continentally," Americans must learn to "think intercontinentally."

"Acting on our own, by ourselves, we cannot establish justice throughout the world; we cannot insure its domestic tranquility, or provide for its common defense; or promote its general welfare, or secure the blessings of liberty to ourselves and our posterity," he said, consciously echoing the opening phrases of the U.S. Constitution. "But joined with other free nations, we can do this, and more."

Today, when American politicians continue to debate cross-national issues like environmental treaties and free trade agreements, Kennedy's bold declaration of interdependence still seems jarring, even though the world has become even smaller and more interdependent than it was in 1962. At the time, the thought of international terrorists striking the United States from a base camp in isolated central Asia would have seemed too outlandish even for a Hollywood thriller. The prospect of American companies moving manufacturing jobs to

Asia or South America would have been dismissed as unthinkable. And the possibility of ordering goods halfway across the globe via computer, and having them delivered the following day, would have been dismissed as the stuff of science fiction.

But it has all come to pass. The European Union that Kennedy saw as the wave of the future—a cross-national super-state of many nations, cultures, and languages—is now a reality.

However, no international organization has yet thought to issue a Declaration of Interdependence. If one does, there can be little question that John Kennedy would have been an enthusiastic signer.

The president asks Americans to "think intercontinentally."

A 1962 visit to NASA headquarters in Houston.

CHAPTER 20

Why Go to the Moon?

Address on Space Travel, Rice University
September 12, 1962

TRACK 21

EXACTLY TWO YEARS AFTER HE SPOKE TO THE HOUSTON MINISTERIAL Association as a candidate, Kennedy returned to the city as president. While the subject of his speech at Rice University was vastly different, in some ways, he was returning to a theme: breaking down barriers to progress. To the ministers in 1960, he argued that religion ought to be no bar to national public office. At Rice, he contended that the barriers of space must fall to mankind's desire for knowledge and thirst for discovery.

For John Kennedy, space travel incorporated many of the personal and political values he held dear. An amateur historian, he appreciated the importance of a moment in time when human beings would, for the first time, travel to the moon and beyond. He knew that one day historians would view the 1960s as the beginning of a new age of discovery.

He appreciated, too, the heroism and boldness of space exploration. This was something grand, the sort of adventure associated with great nations and visionary leaders. While Kennedy's New Frontier program consisted of many goals, its very name suggested bold adventures and new discoveries. Outer space *was* the new frontier.

There was more to space travel than the moon and the stars. Space also was the new frontier of armed conflict, where the Soviet Union and the United States would compete for the prestige of discovery even as they sought military advantage beyond the Earth's atmosphere. In another heroic age, the fleets of Britain and Spain had competed for control of the Atlantic Ocean. Now, the Soviets and the United States would contend with each other to see who would control space.

As president, John Kennedy regarded space exploration as inextricably linked to the twilight struggle with communism. The Soviets had a head start, thanks to their success with Sputnik, the unmanned spacecraft sent into orbit in 1957. President Eisenhower had dismissed the significance of the achievement, but Soviet leader Nikita Khrushchev said pointedly that the world knew that America had been beaten. Kennedy was determined to not only close the discovery gap, but also surpass the Soviets, and soon.

In his special message to Congress on May 25, 1961, Kennedy established a goal of sending a man to the moon "before this decade is out." No other space project, he said, would be "more impressive to mankind," and none, he warned, would be "so difficult or expensive to accomplish."

In the spring of 1961, the United States had fallen so far behind the Soviets that Kennedy's goal seemed outlandish. Just a month before Kennedy's address to Congress, on April 12, 1961, the first manned journey into outer space had taken place, and the achievement belonged not to the United States, but to the Communists in Moscow. Yuri Gagarin's orbit of 108 minutes served as another victory for the Soviets and another reminder that the U.S. was far behind.

But behind in what? For many Americans, manned space travel and a prospective journey to the moon seemed pointless. Eisenhower had said that he "couldn't care less whether a man ever reached the moon," insisting that any such journey would be a mere "stunt." And, for a short while, Ike's successor seemed to agree. As biographer Richard Reeves notes, in early 1961 Kennedy actually thought about abolishing the National Aeronautics and Space Administration. His advisor on science, Jerome Wiesner, belonged to the Eisenhower school of apathy when it came to manned space voyage. Actually, he was not simply apathetic, but against the idea—he thought such journeys should be taken by machines, computers, and instruments alone.

Kennedy seemed persuaded, and in March, he decided to withhold federal funds for NASA's Apollo Program, which was designed to land an astronaut on the moon in some unknowable future year.

But by May, Kennedy's view had changed. The Soviet success with cosmonaut Gagarin affected Kennedy as profoundly as the Sputnik success of 1957 had shaken the country. Prodding him along was his vice president, Lyndon Johnson, who had become an enthusiastic booster of the space program. Not coincidentally, of course, NASA was based in his home state of Texas. Johnson wrote a memo to Kennedy explaining why he believed the race in space was important. If nothing else, Johnson knew how to appeal to Kennedy's competitive nature. He told the president: "This country should...recognize that other nations, regardless of their appreciation of our idealistic values, will tend to align themselves with the country which they believe will be the world leader—the winner in the long run. Dramatic accomplishments in space are being increasingly identified as a major indicator of world leadership."

That was all it took for Kennedy to change his mind—that, and Wernher von Braun's assurance that the U.S. had a "sporting chance" to beat the Russians to the moon, perhaps as early as 1967.

For their part, America's pioneer astronauts—symbols of the New Frontier generation—were astonished when Kennedy issued his challenge in 1961. They believed the space program lacked the expertise and the technology for such an ambitious goal. The Soviets already had put a man in space for nearly two hours. The best the U.S. could do was Alan Shepard's suborbital flight of just fifteen minutes on May 5.

What's more, Kennedy not only wanted to go to the moon soon, he wanted to get there first—second place was no place for John Kennedy's America, or for John Kennedy himself. That would entail, he said, "a degree of dedication, organization, and discipline which have not always characterized our research and development agencies." What's more, he said, such an effort "means we cannot afford undue work stoppages, inflated costs of material or talent, wasteful interagency rivalries, or a high turnover of key personnel." And if Americans were unwilling to bear these burdens, then they ought to concede space to the Soviets. Polls indicated that JFK had a bit of salesmanship to do—58 percent of Americans believed there was little point in spending as much as $40 billion on attaining Kennedy's goal.

In the sixteen months between Kennedy's speech to Congress and his trip to Rice University, the U.S. space program showed signs of stepping up to the president's challenge. Less than three months after Shepard's flight, Virgil

"Gus" Grissom was aboard a second U.S. suborbital flight. (About two weeks later, the Soviets proved their superiority again by sending a cosmonaut into orbit for an entire day.) NASA prepared to take the next step—a manned orbit. But taking that next step proved frustrating. The mission was scrubbed ten times between December 1961 and February 1962. Finally, on February 20, Lieutenant Colonel John Glenn was propelled into space from Cape Canaveral in Florida. Kennedy joined millions of Americans in watching the liftoff of *Friendship* 7 on live television. Allowing TV coverage was a huge gamble for Kennedy. If anything had gone wrong, the blow to American morale would have been severe. But JFK wished to show the world that the U.S. did not cover up its failures as the Soviets did.

Glenn successfully orbited the earth three times and returned safely. He became an instant American hero and a poster boy for the New Frontier. Still, as Kennedy arrived at Rice University, the United States remained in second place in the space race, a fact the president conceded in his speech.

While Kennedy's special message to Congress in 1961 had established the goal of sending a man to the moon by 1969, his speech at Rice was the finest exposition of his vision and of the importance he placed on exploring this new frontier. In the months since the 1961 speech, the Kennedy administration had ramped up the nation's space program, tripling NASA's budget. "That budget now stands at $5,400 million a year—a staggering sum," Kennedy admitted, "though somewhat less than we pay for cigarettes and cigars every year." This budget increase, and the "decision last year to shift our efforts in space from low to high gear" were counted by Kennedy "as among the most important decisions that will be made during my incumbency in the office of the presidency."

But why? The question continued to be raised—just as he had raised it during his first weeks as president, and before that, as a U.S. senator in the late 1950s. He sought to answer that question at Rice.

The Texas sunshine was in his eyes as he addressed students, faculty, and guests seated in the university's football stadium. In a dark, pinstriped suit, a small glimpse of a neatly folded handkerchief in his breast pocket, Kennedy squinted into the grandstands and made his case.

As he tried to answer a simple question—why go the moon?—with references to other epic journeys of discovery, he managed to slip in a bit of characteristic Kennedy wit. "But why, some say, the moon?" he said. "Why choose this as our goal? And they may well ask why climb the highest mountain?

Why, thirty-five years ago, fly the Atlantic?" And, with a nod to his audience, he added: "Why does Rice play Texas?" Rice was a small, selective school, while the University of Texas was a huge public institution. Rice was at a disadvantage every time its players took the field, but they persisted nevertheless.

Why did they persist? Kennedy answered his own questions in language that had become familiar to America by 1962. "We choose to go to the moon," he said. "We choose to go to the moon in this decade and do the other things, not because they are easy, but because they are hard, because that goal will serve to organize and measure the best of our energies and skills, because that challenge is one that we are willing to accept, one we are unwilling to postpone, and one which we intend to win." That was why America would go to the moon. That was why Rice played Texas. And that was explanation enough, at least for the John Kennedy who savored challenges, who admired boldness, who adored physical and intellectual courage. He cited the Pilgrim voyager William Bradford, who "said that all great and honorable actions are accompanied with great difficulties, and both must be enterprised and overcome with answerable courage."

There were other reasons, too, and they revealed Kennedy's idealistic faith in his country's good intention, and his command of practical, street-level politics. "We have vowed that we shall not see space filled with weapons of mass destruction, but with instruments of knowledge and understanding," he said. For that vision to become reality, though, the United States—and not the Soviets—needed to win the race in space. Therefore, he said, "We intend to be first...to become the world's leading space-faring nation."

As Great Britain became an empire thanks to its command of the sea, the United States would take its place among the great nations in world history through its preeminence in space. For his audience in Houston, however, Kennedy had answers to that question—why?—that were not so lofty. Space travel meant jobs, and Texas-style investments with free-flowing federal dollars.

The "space effort itself, while still in its infancy, has already created a great number of new companies and tens of thousands of new jobs," he said. "Houston, your city of Houston, with its manned spacecraft center, will become the heart of a large scientific and engineering community. During the next five years, the National Aeronautics and Space Administration expects to double the number of scientists and engineers in this area, to increase its outlays for salaries and expenses to $60 million a year [and] to invest some $200 million in plant and laboratory facilities." Other NASA spending in Houston would amount to $1 billion, he noted.

Small wonder, then, that the nation's highest-ranking Texan, Vice President Johnson, was such a proponent of space travel.

But the exploration of space, and even the race to the moon, was not a jobs program. It was not an urban renewal project, nor was it merely an exercise in public relations. And it was not intended to dole out patronage, although inevitably such acts happened. Kennedy, the convert to manned space travel, saw this journey from the perspective of history.

In concluding, he recalled the words of the British explorer George Mallory, who had a simple explanation for those who wondered why he wished to climb Mount Everest. "Because it is there," he said.

"Well," Kennedy said, "space is there, and we're going to climb it, and the moon and the planets are there, and new hope and knowledge and peace are there. And, therefore, as we set sail we ask God's blessing on the most hazardous and dangerous and greatest adventure on which man has ever embarked."

And, as he said in his inaugural speech, he did not shrink from this adventure. He welcomed it.

JFK inspects a two-man capsule at NASA.

Mississippi governor Ross Barnett.

CHAPTER 21

Mississippi Burns

The Integration of the University of Mississippi
September 30, 1962

TRACK 22

MONG THE MILLIONS WHO WATCHED JOHN F. KENNEDY DELIVER HIS inaugural address in 1961 was a young African American man from Mississippi named James Meredith. The new president never talked about the plight of people like James Meredith, relegated to second-class citizenship by segregationist leaders in the South. Nevertheless, Meredith found inspiration in Kennedy's powerful call to service and sacrifice. The following day, early in the morning, James Meredith applied to the University of Mississippi, a state-funded, public institution of higher education.

Known to generations of southerners as Ole Miss, the University of Mississippi admitted white students only, and it had no intention of changing that policy. Meredith's application was rejected, but he remained undaunted. He later explained that he believed he had a "divine responsibility to break white supremacy in Mississippi." He said that breaking the color line at Ole Miss "was only the start."

Meredith filed a lawsuit against the university. The proceedings went on for months, but came to a head in September 1962—just as the administration, the nation, and the world were edging ever closer to the precipice known as the Cuban Missile Crisis. On September 10, U.S. Supreme Court Justice

Hugo Black—a native of Alabama and a onetime member of the Ku Klux Klan—ordered that the university comply with a lower court ruling that ordered Meredith to be admitted.

The Kennedy administration was not looking for a fight on this issue. But now it had little choice.

As was evident by the speech that so inspired James Meredith—Kennedy's inaugural address—the president's top priorities were foreign affairs and the Cold War. Civil rights merited not a word in the speech, although the civil rights movement was about to become the most important domestic issue of the Kennedy years.

The president was wary of civil rights, in part because of political considerations, in part because he believed the twilight struggle with communism ultimately trumped all other issues. Southern Democrats, whose support he needed, were spokesmen for the status quo, representing the fears and prejudices of their white constituencies. But even some northern Democrats were afraid of the issue, especially as midterm congressional elections approached. It was, in retrospect, evidence of a moral blind spot on Kennedy's part. He was passionate about the deprivation of liberties behind the Iron Curtain, but he seemed to regard the plight of a tenth of the nation's population as a distraction rather than an outrage.

Then again, domestic issues in general were not his top priority. He said as much to Richard Nixon after the Bay of Pigs, when he noted that fights over the minimum wage paled in comparison to foreign affairs.

So, for the first year and a half of his administration, John Kennedy had tried to avoid civil rights issues. True, he had met with Dr. Martin Luther King Jr. in the White House during the height of the Bay of Pigs disaster, but that encounter was strictly unofficial. No reporters were present. King was in Washington to meet with the president's brother Robert. After the meeting, as recounted in Richard Reeves's biography of JFK, King went to the White House to meet with presidential aide Harris Wofford. King's appearance was not on the White House calendar, but the president's aides knew the civil rights leader was coming. The aides orchestrated a plan: Kennedy was to drop by Wofford's office spontaneously, and, as luck would have it, Martin Luther King would be there. The meeting, on April 19, 1961, went according to plan. Kennedy greeted King, saying: "I've been keeping up with you and your work. My brother's been keeping me apprised of certain developments, and if you ever need me, you know the door is always open to you."

Those were fine sentiments, but as the administration moved from crisis to crisis overseas, civil rights simply did not engage Kennedy's interests, certainly not as passionately as the Cold War did.

As events unfolded in Mississippi, however, it quickly became evident that the White House could not stand aside while Meredith's lawyers and state officials hashed out a compromise. The governor, Ross Barnett, made it clear that he was not about to submit to the demands of the White House and the justice department. The governor was an avowed segregationist, but, as became evident during the confrontation, he also was looking for political cover on the issue. He had to seem firm in the face of the courts and Washington—although he secretly was talking directly with Attorney General Robert Kennedy as the drama reached its climax. One thing was certain: the state of Mississippi would not simply acknowledge defeat and throw open the gates of Ole Miss to this young black man filled with New Frontier idealism.

The power and might of the U.S. government would be required in order to desegregate the University of Mississippi. The only question was how to best express that power and might.

Kennedy did not want the town of Oxford, home to Ole Miss, to become his version of Little Rock, Arkansas, where, in 1957, federal troops were needed to protect black students during a school desegregation crisis. The ensuing images from this sickening spectacle, Kennedy believed, damaged America's image abroad and gave the Soviets a propaganda victory.

The White House wanted to avoid a repeat of that public relations disaster—actually, both the president and the attorney general were worried about more than a few damaging pictures in the world's newspapers. They feared a pitched battle between U.S. soldiers and armed civilians. "Sending in troops is a hell of a thing for the country," Robert Kennedy said. The White House hoped that local police would be the only force required to get Meredith on campus.

Through mid-September, after Justice Black's order, the Kennedy White House engaged Governor Barnett with a series of telephone calls. Publicly, Barnett was on record as saying he would not surrender to tyranny—meaning, of course, the government of the United States. Privately, however, he also was looking for a way to avoid a confrontation. Meanwhile, federal marshals tried to escort Meredith on campus, but were turned away as mobs gathered in and around Oxford. Barnett gave himself an opportunity to deny Meredith's admission in person, by appointing himself as the university's temporary registrar on one of the days when the young student tried to register for classes.

Behind the scenes, Barnett was trying to persuade the attorney general to back down. He was not aware that his telephone conversations with Robert Kennedy were being taped. At one point, Barnett told the attorney general: "I'm going to treat you with every courtesy, but I won't agree to let that boy get to Old Miss. I will never agree to that. I would rather spend the rest of my life in a penitentiary than do that." He said that Meredith—"one little boy"—was being supported "by a Communist front," by which he meant the NAACP.

At another point, he offered to relent if he were confronted in person with armed federal agents who would be told to draw their weapons. The White House was willing to go along with this stage-managed charade, but talks fell apart when Barnett said it would take more than just one agent drawing a weapon. He believed he could surrender only in the face of multiple threats, not just a single agent with a single gun.

On September 29, President Kennedy informed Governor Barnett that he, the president, had no choice but to enforce the court's order, and that he would like the governor's help in doing so. Further negotiations were inconclusive and maddening. Barnett suggested that federal agents sneak Meredith on campus on a Sunday, when few people were around. He would look the other way while Meredith was registered. The White House reluctantly agreed, but then Barnett called back to withdraw his offer. A frustrated Kennedy agreed to federalize the Mississippi National Guard, removing those troops from the governor's control.

Robert Kennedy then played the administration's trump card: the conversations between Barnett and the White House had been taped, and the administration was willing to release those tapes.

"The president is going on TV tonight," Robert Kennedy told Barnett. "He is going through with the statement [he] had with you last night. He will have to say why he called up the National Guard—that you had an agreement to permit Meredith to go to Jackson to register…"

"That won't do at all," Barnett said.

"You broke your word to him…" Kennedy said.

"Don't say that," Barnett pleaded. "Please don't mention it…I won't want the president saying I broke my word…. We will cooperate with you."

Barnett was horrified that his secret contacts with the now-hated Robert Kennedy would be made public. He backed down, although he asked RFK's permission to "raise Cain" in Jackson while federal law enforcement agents escorted Meredith to a dorm on the Oxford campus. The attorney general agreed.

So it was done. At ten o'clock that evening, September 30, President Kennedy appeared on national television. "Mr. James Meredith is now in residence on the campus of the University of Mississippi," he said. "This has been accomplished thus far without the use of National Guard or other troops. And it is to be hoped that the law enforcement officers of the state of Mississippi and the federal marshals will continue to be sufficient in the future."

That hope already had been shattered, even before the president spoke to the nation.

Minutes before Kennedy went on the air, his brother learned that two hundred Mississippi state troopers had left the campus, leaving federal agents to fend for themselves. The agents soon were forced to fire tear gas into crowds gathering outside the university's administration building, where they believed Meredith was located. (In fact, he was in a dorm.) The Battle of Ole Miss was well underway, even as Kennedy was praising "Mississippi and her University," which, he said, "are noted for their courage, for the contribution of talent and thought to the affairs of this nation... You have a great tradition to uphold, a tradition of honor and courage won on the field of battle and on the gridiron as well as the university campus. You have a new opportunity to show that you are men of patriotism and integrity. For the most effective means of upholding the law is not the state policeman or the marshals or the National Guard. It is you. It lies in your courage to accept those laws with which you disagree as well as those with which you agree. The eyes of the nation and of all the world are upon you and upon all of us, and the honor of your university and state are in the balance."

In his biography of Robert Kennedy, Arthur M. Schlesinger Jr. rightly describes the president's address as "designed for a different occasion." It assumed that, at long last, Meredith was on campus and the issue settled. But it was far from settled.

Gunfire continued on campus, and federal agents were reporting casualties. The agents—about five hundred—were vastly outnumbered. As midnight neared, rioters were preparing to charge the administration building. Two journalists were shot; one, from the French news agency Agence France-Presse, died of his wounds. A construction worker not involved in the rioting was shot through the head and killed. More than a hundred federal law enforcement officers were injured. The president ordered the National Guard to move in, along with regular U.S. Army troops based in Memphis.

The president was stunned, although he still was capable of ironic humor. "I haven't had such an interesting day since the Bay of Pigs," he said as he monitored events from the White House.

With the situation out of control, with the embattled agents running out of tear gas and still under orders not to return fire, all eyes in Washington turned to Memphis, where military police units were exchanging their batons for more lethal weapons. Hours passed before they were in the air, bound for Oxford, and still more time elapsed at the Oxford airport—the troops were under orders not to move out until all units were present and accounted for. Kennedy was beside himself. "People are dying in Oxford," he said. "This is the worst thing I've seen in forty-five years."

The army regulars finally made it to the university at four o'clock in the morning. The army's slow, by-the-book response had been a nightmare. "No wonder it's so hard to win a war," Kennedy said. He went to bed at five thirty after a long, draining night.

James Meredith attended class that morning, October 1. The Battle of Ole Miss was over, and segregation had lost. The casualty count was two dead, more than two hundred federal agents and troops wounded, and about two hundred civilians under arrest.

Polls showed that voters—at least those outside the South—were rallying around the president as if in a time of war. Which it was, for a few hours in Oxford, Mississippi.

James Meredith is escorted to class by U.S. marshals.

Khrushchev greets Castro.

CHAPTER 22

The Cuban Missile Crisis

Nationwide Address on
the Cuban Missile Crisis
October 22, 1962

TRACK 23

OR A FEW HORRIFYING DAYS IN OCTOBER 1962, THE WORLD contemplated the unthinkable. Nuclear war between the United States and the Soviet Union seemed not merely possible, but likely. Tens of millions would die; the lucky ones in an instant, the less fortunate after terrible suffering. Great cities, centers of art and commerce, would cease to exist. The survivors would envy the dead—the sentiments not of John F. Kennedy, but of Nikita Khrushchev.

The Cuban Missile Crisis is probably the best-known episode of the Kennedy years, with good reason. The mythology that surrounds those long, awful days in October 1962 is not exaggerated: it was the most dangerous period of the Cold War, the closest the United States and the Soviet Union came to hurling their weapons of mass destruction at each other.

It has been said of Winston Churchill that everything he did and all that he learned before World War II prepared him to face the crisis of 1940, when Britain stood alone against Nazi Germany. In the same sense, the lessons John Kennedy had learned during his short time as president prepared him for this moment when the fate of millions lay in his hands.

The installation of Soviet missiles on Cuba did indeed lead to a crisis, but that word hardly does justice to the epic nature of this harrowing confrontation. After all, the desegregation of Ole Miss in 1962 was a crisis. The Bay of Pigs and its aftermath was a crisis. Civil war in Laos was a crisis; Vietnam was a crisis in the making. None of these dangerous events, however, had the potential to incinerate millions and level cities in an instant.

John Kennedy's speech to the nation on October 22, 1962, was, in many ways, the culmination of other speeches—not only the defiant words of his inaugural, but also the sober, post-Vienna warnings he issued on July 25, 1961, when he in essence urged Americans to prepare for nuclear war by building shelters and creating a stronger civil defense network. He had vowed that the nation would pay any price to advance the cause of liberty; he had told the nation what that price might entail, and now he would have to prepare his fellow citizens for the unthinkable made real.

"Within the past week, unmistakable evidence has established the fact that a series of offensive missile sites is now in preparation on that imprisoned island," he said, referring, of course, to Cuba. "The purpose of these bases can be none other than to provide a nuclear strike capability against the Western Hemisphere."

The Cuban Missile Crisis began, formally at least, on the morning of October 16, when Kennedy's national security advisor, McGeorge Bundy, showed the president pictures taken over Cuba by U-2 spy planes. The photographs offered proof that the Soviets and their Cuban allies were building missile sites on the island, capable of launching a nuclear strike against the United States. Kennedy ordered an emergency meeting of his national security advisors for later that morning.

There had been rumors about missiles in Cuba for weeks. U.S. intelligence at first believed that the Soviets might be building antiaircraft missile sites, and while those missiles could be fitted with a nuclear warhead, their range—about thirty-five miles—presented little offensive threat. Khrushchev instructed one of his aides to tell Bobby Kennedy that the buildup on Cuba was strictly defensive, and the Soviet leader said as much to Kennedy's interior secretary, Stewart Udall, during the latter's visit to Russia in early September. All the while, hard intelligence was difficult to come by, since Kennedy had agreed to suspend U-2 flights over Cuba in a gesture meant to reduce tensions.

Republican critics in Congress demanded that the president act more decisively in the face of what they saw as a direct Soviet threat. Kennedy replied by insisting that aggressive U.S. action—such as a preemptive attack on Cuba—would be a mistake, in part because the buildup did not appear to compromise American national security. To make sure, however, the president ordered a resumption of U-2 flights over Cuba.

On the morning of October 16, as he viewed the pictures Bundy brought to his bedroom, John Kennedy found out that Khrushchev had misled him. The pictures showed work underway on launching sites for ballistic missiles—missiles that could easily reach Washington and other U.S. cities. The Soviets, through their Cuban clients, had embarked on a breathtaking provocation. The crisis that would surpass all other crises had begun. The president called his brother Robert and said: "We have some big trouble."

The first in a long series of extraordinary White House meetings began at 11:45 on the morning of October 16 in the Cabinet Room. Unknown to anybody in the room except the president and, perhaps, his brother, the room was bugged, at Kennedy's direction. The president hoped to have a permanent record of his administration's deliberations, and so, several months earlier, recording devices had been installed in lighting fixtures in the Cabinet Room and in Kennedy's desk in the Oval Office. Kennedy could activate or shut off the microphones as he saw fit. The taping system was a well-kept secret, becoming public only years later, when Kennedy's nemesis, Richard Nixon, installed a similar system and was brought down in part because of it.

A small number of recordings made during the missile crisis were made public in 1983. Finally, in the late 1990s, the tapes were released in their entirety. Historians Ernest R. May and Philip D. Zelikow undertook the tedious process of transcribing the recordings, which were often difficult to hear. They then published the transcripts, which became the basis for the movie *Thirteen Days*, which captured the drama and tension of the Kennedy cabinet room during the crisis.

The transcripts show Kennedy as a mature, cool decision maker, eager for information, quick with a question or a comment, and very much in charge. As he was briefed on the morning of October 16 by Sidney Graybeal, a CIA expert on ballistic missiles, Kennedy demonstrated the inquisitiveness that was a hallmark of his leadership. Graybeal was showing the president pictures of Soviet missiles as they were hauled through Moscow during a military parade. These missiles were thought to be similar to those that would be placed in Cuba.

The president interrupted Graybeal.

"Is this ready to be fired?" he asked.

"No, sir."

"How long have we got? We can't tell, can we, how long before it can be fired?"

"No, sir..."

"But what does it have to be fired from?"

"It would have to be fired from a stable, hard surface," Graybeal replied.

Other meetings featured similar exchanges, with Kennedy constantly probing for more information. As the first days of the crisis unfolded behind closed doors—Kennedy tried his best to continue with his public schedule to keep up appearances—several military options were under discussion, including a surprise air attack on the sites or an outright invasion of the island.

On October 18, in what must have been a surreal experience for both men, President Kennedy went through with a formal meeting with Soviet Foreign Minister Andrei Gromyko, during which the Russian noted that Cuba was receiving military shipments of defensive weapons. Kennedy said afterwards that he had never heard so many "barefaced lies" in such a short time.

The following day, Kennedy went to Illinois as scheduled for a campaign appearance as November's crucial midterm elections drew near.

Meanwhile, a consensus of sorts was developing around the idea of a blockade of Cuba, designed to prevent any further buildup on the island, followed by negotiations. Throughout these tense meetings, Kennedy emphasized that the Cuban crisis did not exist in a vacuum, that the other Cold War flashpoint—Berlin—was very much in play. He feared that a U.S. attack on Cuba would be answered by a Soviet assault on West Berlin, leading to nuclear war.

One vocal military man disagreed with the president and was not shy about saying so in the cabinet room. Curtis LeMay had been a decorated bomber pilot in World War II, and was now chief of staff of the air force. He told the president that a blockade and negotiation would be "a weak response" and "almost as bad" as Neville Chamberlain's actions in Munich—the moral equivalent of appeasement. Such sentiments did not endear the general to the man who so admired Winston Churchill, the antithesis of Chamberlain. Afterwards, the president complained that military officers like LeMay had "one great advantage" in giving advice. He said, "If we listen to them, and do what they want us to do, none of us will be alive later to tell them that they were wrong."

Kennedy decided on October 20 to impose a naval quarantine around Cuba. He pointedly refused to use the word "blockade," in part because it was associated with the Soviet attempt to starve out West Berlin in 1948. Two days later, he formalized the ad hoc group of advisors he had been relying on since the crisis began. For the duration of the crisis, these dozen or so men—among them, his brother Robert, Defense Secretary Robert McNamara, Secretary of State Dean Rusk, Vice President Johnson, and General Maxwell Taylor, chairman of the Joint Chiefs of Staff—would be known as the Executive Committee of the National Security Council, known informally as Ex Comm.

Later that afternoon Kennedy called together congressional leaders to brief them on the situation and on his response. The lawmakers, at least some of them, were as unimpressed as General LeMay was. They, too, used the word "weak."

As the lawmakers left, Kennedy pulled aside his onetime rival for the Democratic nomination in 1960, Senator Hubert Humphrey of Minnesota. "If I'd known the job was this tough, I wouldn't have beaten you in West Virginia," Kennedy said. Humphrey laughed, and offered his own bit of gallows humor. "I knew," he said. "And that's why I let you beat me."

The job was tough and lonely. As John Kennedy prepared to face the nation, he was alone—the time for meetings and discussion was over. He had made a decision that might lead to catastrophe unknown in human history, a decision that might very well end human history. Could he truly have imagined such burdens when he promised to bear them, no matter how weighty, for the cause of liberty? Months later, commenting on the presidency in general, he would say: "If you take the wrong course...the president bears the burden of the responsibility quite rightly. The advisers move on to new advice."

The White House had done such a good job keeping the crisis secret that nobody knew precisely what the president would be talking about on the evening of October 22. A day earlier, Kennedy heard that some newspapers were working on stories about missiles under construction in Cuba. One reporter, James Reston of the *New York Times*, was pulled off the story after the president called the *Times'* publisher, Orville Dryfoos, and asked that the paper refrain from publishing what it knew. Reston, as Richard Reeves notes in *President Kennedy*, believed that the *Times* had been wrong to censor itself before the Bay of Pigs. And now the newspaper was withholding information again.

Khrushchev certainly was well aware of what was on Kennedy's mind. An hour before the president spoke to the nation, he delivered a blunt message to the Soviet ambassador, Anatoli Dobrynin. The United States was prepared to go to war to remove the missiles from Cuba, Kennedy told Dobrynin, who immediately relayed the message to the Kremlin.

A hundred million Americans—about two-thirds of the nation's population—were watching as Kennedy began his speech at seven o'clock Eastern time. Viewers who were used to seeing their president playfully parrying with reporters during televised press conferences tuned in to find a somber-looking Kennedy staring back at them. He had hard, surprising, and chilling news to deliver.

To illustrate the dramatic and unacceptable nature of this threat, Kennedy took note of the possible targets these missiles could reach. "Each of these missiles, in short, is capable of striking Washington, D.C., the Panama Canal, Cape Canaveral, Mexico City, or any other city in the southeastern part of the United States, in Central America, or in the Caribbean area." Other sites, he added, would house missiles with even longer ranges—from "as far north as Hudson Bay, Canada, and as far south as Lima, Peru."

His recitation of potential targets is notable in that he did not focus only on U.S. cities that would be vulnerable to attack—indeed, he did not mention the nation's largest city, New York, nor any other cities in the crowded Northeast. Instead, by singling out places like Mexico City, Peru, and Canada, Kennedy subtly emphasized that the threat from Soviet missiles in Cuba was hemispheric, and not limited to just a portion of the United States. At a time when Washington was concerned about the vulnerability of South and Central America to Communist insurgencies, Kennedy's emphasis on hemispheric security issues broadened the crisis to something well beyond U.S.-Soviet relations.

In making his case for an aggressive U.S. response, Kennedy took the moral high ground that had been ceded by Khrushchev. He quoted a public Soviet statement describing the military buildup in Cuba as "designed exclusively for defensive purposes."

"That statement," he said, "was false."

He quoted another, similar assertion by Soviet Foreign Minister Gromyko. Kennedy said the foreign minister "told me in my office…and I quote him, 'training by Soviet specialists of Cuban nationals in handling defensive armaments was by no means offensive, and if it were otherwise,' Mr.

Gromyko went on, 'the Soviet government would never become involved in rendering such assistance.'

"That statement," the president said, "also was false."

As if in reply to General LeMay, who conjured images of Neville Chamberlain and Munich in describing Kennedy's decision to impose a quarantine around Cuba, the president said that the 1930s "taught us a clear lesson: aggressive conduct, if allowed to go unchecked and unchallenged, ultimately leads to war."

"This nation is opposed to war," he said. "We are also true to our word. Our unswerving objective, therefore, must be to prevent the use of these missiles against this or any other country, and to secure their withdrawal from the Western Hemisphere."

To achieve that goal, the president announced his decision to turn back all Soviet shipments of military equipment to Cuba. "All ships of any kind bound for Cuba from whatever nation or port will, if found to contain cargoes of offensive weapons, be turned back." He pointedly noted that shipments of "the necessities of life" would not be turned away. The Soviets did that in Berlin in 1948. The Americans would not behave likewise in 1962.

Kennedy did not ignore the specter of where this all might lead. He declared that "any nuclear missile launched from Cuba" against a target in North or South America would be viewed as a Soviet attack on the United States, "requiring a full retaliatory strike upon the Soviet Union."

The president personally addressed the citizens of Cuba via a special radio signal. "I speak to you as a friend," he said, "as one who knows of your deep attachment to your fatherland, as one who shares your aspirations for liberty and justice for all.… These new weapons are not in your interest. They contribute nothing to your peace and well-being. They can only undermine it. But this country has no wish to cause you to suffer or to impose any system upon you. We know that your lives and land are being used as pawns by those who deny your freedom."

In concluding this seventeen-minute-long address, Kennedy said: "Our goal is not the victory of might, but the vindication of right—not peace at the expense of freedom, but both peace and freedom, here in this hemisphere, and, we hope, around the world."

What happened over the next several days is part of the Kennedy legacy and the history of the twentieth century. Dozens of U.S. warships were posted around Cuba; the U.S. military was on alert; the nation's intercontinental bal-listic missiles, armed with nuclear warheads, were made ready for use; bombers carrying nuclear weapons were in the air; submarines with nuclear missiles gathered off Soviet shores. Meanwhile, in Moscow, Khrushchev told several American businessmen visiting the Soviet Union at the time that Soviet subs would take out U.S. surface ships if any of his ships were sunk off Cuba. Such a confrontation would easily escalate into nuclear war.

The crisis was the only subject that mattered during the last week in October, as the world waited to see what would happen when Soviet ships loaded with military hardware approached Cuba. The U.S. took its case to the United Nations, where Adlai Stevenson brilliantly laid out the American posi-tion. At one point, Kennedy noted with characteristic detachment: "It is insane that two men, sitting on opposite sides of the world, should be able to decide to bring an end to civilization."

Civilization, of course, did not come to an end. Insanity did not prevail. As Soviet ships approached Cuba, diplomacy, not war, broke out in Washington and Moscow—even as both sides prepared for conflict. The les-sons of the *Guns of August*, which explained how the world staggered into an apocalypse, had been learned, absorbed, and put into action.

The thirteen-day crisis ended on October 28, two days before U.S. war-planes were scheduled to bomb the missile sites. Khrushchev publicly agreed to dismantle the weapons. Kennedy privately agreed to dismantle missiles in Turkey. Years later, Khrushchev would write: "Kennedy was…someone we could trust…. We accepted the concession he was making and made a conces-sion of our own by withdrawing our nuclear weapons from Cuba."

Two men on opposite sides of the world found themselves capable of pre-venting an end to civilization.

A somber group of Cuban exiles watches the president's speech
as he announces the U.S. quarantine of Cuba.

PART FOUR: 1963

*President Kennedy and the first lady land at Love Field
in Dallas on November 22, 1963.*

Introduction

J OHN KENNEDY'S STANDING AT THE BEGINNING OF 1963 AS A WISE
foreign policy leader did not readily translate into effectiveness in per-
suading Congress to pass major domestic reforms. His proposals for a
big tax cut, federal aid to all levels of education, and medical insurance for sen-
iors, remained bottled up in House committees. Ironically, civil rights, an issue
he was reluctant to bring before Congress before his reelection campaign,
forced its way to the center of his attention and onto his legislative calendar.

To compensate for his substantive caution on civil rights, he gave rhetorical support to reform. In his State of the Union message, he urged that "the
right to vote...not be denied to any citizen on grounds of his race or color."
In a subsequent economic message to Congress, he declared an end to racial
and religious discrimination as tied to economic growth. In February, in celebrating the hundredth anniversary of Lincoln's Emancipation Proclamation,

he praised fighters for black rights as enlarging the freedoms of all Americans and urged the country not to rest "until the promise of equal rights for all has been fulfilled." Although he did not put a comprehensive bill before the Congress to remedy the catalogue of wrongs afflicting black Americans, he invited the Congress to take the initiative in fighting discrimination and specifically the denial of the ballot, which was so widespread across the South.

During the spring of 1963, Martin Luther King and the Southern Christian Leadership Conference (SCLC) forced Kennedy's hand. When King challenged segregation statutes in Birmingham, Alabama, the South's most segregated city, it produced public clashes between black demonstrators and law enforcement authorities that embarrassed the country before the world. A photo on the front page of the *New York Times* and on TV screens showing a dog lunging to bite a teenage boy made Kennedy "sick." At news conferences in May, JFK repeatedly asked Alabamans to halt "a spectacle which was seriously damaging the reputation of both Birmingham and the country." In a famous letter from the Birmingham jail, where he was imprisoned after participation in an April demonstration, King chided white liberals, implicitly including Kennedy, for their failure to back sympathetic words with effective deeds.

When a subsequent crisis over desegregating the University of Alabama convinced Kennedy that appeals to reason were hopeless in getting southerners to end their system of apartheid, he decided to put a major civil rights bill before Congress that would end all forms of segregation in places of public accommodation. In June, he set his request in motion with a nationally televised address that was one of the best speeches of his thousand-day presidency. It was a heartfelt appeal in behalf of a moral cause. "We are confronted primarily with a moral issue," he declared. "It is as old as the scriptures and is as clear as the American Constitution.... One hundred years of delay have passed since President Lincoln freed the slaves, yet their heirs, their grand-sons, are not fully free.... They are not yet freed from the bonds of injustice. They are not yet freed from social and economic oppression. And this nation, for all its hopes and all its boasts, will not be fully free until all its citizens are free.... Now the time has come for this nation to fulfill its promise." The civil rights bill would not be enacted until Lyndon Johnson drove Kennedy's proposal through Congress in the summer of 1964.

Along with his civil rights appeal, Kennedy's most memorable speeches of 1963 focused on foreign affairs. In June, to persuade Soviets and Americans to sign on to a limited nuclear test ban treaty, he told an audience at American University in Washington, D.C., that a nuclear war was out of the question. The speech has been fairly described as one of the great state papers of any twentieth century American president. Both sides needed to find common ground on which to rein in the building of weapons of mass destruction. He urged Americans to reexamine their attitudes toward the Soviet Union, and announced the start of arms control negotiations in Moscow.

In July, after U.S. and Soviet negotiators had reached agreement on a treaty halting atmospheric nuclear tests, Kennedy spoke to the public again about the value of such a mutual commitment. His address presented an apocalyptic vision of a world teetering on the brink of universal disaster. A nuclear war, he warned, would kill over three hundred million people everywhere in less than an hour. Quoting Khrushchev, Kennedy said, "The survivors would envy the dead." The treaty would not eliminate the dangers of a war, but it was "a shaft of light [that] cut into the darkness." It was a first major step away from war. Prompt Senate passage echoed the will of the public and reinforced Kennedy's image as a great peacemaker.

The impression of Kennedy as devoted to the defense of U.S. and Western security even as he sought accommodation with the Soviet Union was reinforced during a ten-day trip to Europe at the end of June. Spending four days each in Germany and Ireland, and two in Italy, Kennedy showed that he was an exceptionally popular world leader. In Berlin, where he said afterward, "We will never have another day like this one as long as we live," Kennedy reached the heights of his appeal as a public speaker. His speech to hundreds of thousands of Berliners stimulated almost mass hysteria. His speech was a resounding condemnation of Soviet repression contrasted with the freedom enjoyed by West Berliners. West German chancellor Konrad Adenauer was actually frightened by the crowd's reaction. As he observed his fellow Germans cheering Kennedy, he said to U.S. secretary of state Dean Rusk, "Does this mean Germany can one day have another Hitler?"

Kennedy's assassination on November 22 in Dallas, Texas, abruptly ended his presidency and his chance of establishing himself as a great or, more likely, near-great president. His death at the age of forty-six came at a time when he seemed almost certain to win reelection by a wide margin, which would have allowed him to pursue domestic reform and follow up on the challenges he issued in his speech at American University. In death, Kennedy's hold over the country's imagination only increased. Opinion surveys over the forty-plus years since his death demonstrate an uncommon public regard for him. Despite his limited time in office, Americans consistently rank him among the top four or five presidents in the country's history. His compelling rhetoric continues to inspire hope and affection that few presidents manage to sustain after leaving office.

Kennedy with civil rights leaders.

Nikita Khrushchev and Mao Zedong in a 1958 photo,
taken when their countries were on friendlier terms.

CHAPTER 23

A Vision of Peace

Commencement Speech at
American University, Washington, D.C.
June 10, 1963

TRACK 24

W HY DID THE GREAT EMPIRES OF EUROPE MOBILIZE THEIR ARMIES in August 1914, a prelude to the mass slaughter history remembers as World War I? "Ah, if only one knew," said one German diplomat, according to historian Barbara Tuchman's Pulitzer Prize-winning book, *The Guns of August.*

If only one knew—the phrase haunted John F. Kennedy, who not only read Tuchman's book, but recommended it to his aides as well. Its brilliant reconstruction of the miscommunications, misunderstandings, and false assumptions that led to catastrophe contained a not-so-subtle lesson for decision-makers in Washington in the early 1960s.

If only one knew—why did great nations hurl their armies at each other, depleting their treasuries and exhausting their resources? Was it all a simple mistake? Could millions of deaths, the collapse of empires, and untold suffering and grief been prevented if Berlin better understood London, or if Paris were speaking with Vienna? If only one knew.

In October 1962, the potential of a far greater catastrophe—nuclear war—was averted in part because of direct and back-channel communications between Washington and Moscow. And thanks to the taping system that JFK

ordered installed in the White House, history has a record of those deliberations. We know in great detail how close to the brink the world came to the
apocalypse, and that may have been Kennedy's intention, although nobody is
quite sure what led him to install the taping system. But we do know that he
wanted a clear record of the difficult decisions he made. He once said: "If this
planet is ever ravaged by nuclear war—and if the survivors of that devastation
can then endure the fire, poison, chaos, and catastrophe—I do not want one
of those survivors to ask another, 'How did it all happen?' and to receive the
incredible reply: 'Ah, if only one knew.'"

As president in the dangerous early 1960s, John Kennedy spent endless
hours thinking about the unthinkable, discussing the unspeakable—the possibility of a nuclear exchange with the Soviet Union. He knew that some politicians and military commanders spoke almost casually about a conflict that
would make the two world wars seem like skirmishes, that would wipe great
cities off the map, and that would leave a poisoned earth as its legacy.

He had told America and the world that the United States would bear any
burden in the pursuit of liberty. But the burden of endless confrontation with the
Soviet Union was heavy, indeed, heavier than John Kennedy might have imagined at his inauguration on January 20, 1961. His fellow citizens almost seemed
resigned to the possibility that the twilight struggle would result in complete
darkness: 60 percent of respondents in a March 1963 poll said they believed the
Soviet Union would launch a nuclear attack on the U.S. Some 37 percent said
they believed America and Russia could never solve their differences in peace.

Both sides were continuing to prepare for the war, testing nuclear
weapons underground and in the atmosphere. Toxic residue from atmospheric testing was beginning to show up in the world's food supply. Kennedy
once asked an aide how radioactive materials return to the earth after a
nuclear blast. In the rain, he was told. As recounted in Richard Reeves's book,
President Kennedy: Profile of Power, Kennedy looked outside an Oval Office
window. It was raining. "You mean," he said, "it's in the rain out there?" It
was, the aide told him.

The United States and the Soviets were poisoning the planet with nuclear
tests, but what was even more frightening was the prospect of more nations
developing and testing these weapons of mass destruction. Kennedy admitted
that he was "haunted" by the prospect of ten nations with nuclear arms in 1970
and perhaps as many as twenty by 1975. "I see the possibility in the 1970s of

the president of the United States having to face a world in which fifteen or twenty or twenty-five nations may have [nuclear] weapons," he said at a news conference in 1963. The reality of where the twilight struggle might lead—not to a cold war, but to a shooting war, a war that would invariably end in nuclear catastrophe—had a profound impact on his thinking, and his speeches.

In the spring of 1963, months after the near-apocalypse of the Cuban Missile Crisis, John Kennedy decided that the burden of constant confrontation with the Soviets was far too heavy for his nation and the world. What's more, the equation was about to change. The Communists in China, more hostile and more alien than Khrushchev, were on the verge of becoming a nuclear power themselves. They believed Khrushchev was too soft on capitalism, too accommodating of the United States. They wanted a more aggressive Communist front around the world and expected the Soviets to be in the forefront, that their Russian ally should not agree to compromises with the United States. An already dangerous world was becoming even more so.

On June 10, President Kennedy delivered one of the most important speeches of the era, and certainly the most important of his presidency. In it, he outlined the case not for a twilight struggle, but for peaceful coexistence. He made no promises to bear the burdens of protracted struggle. Instead, he asked Americans to assume a different sort of burden—the burden of examining their own attitude toward the Soviets, the burden of seeking accommodation and peace.

After crises in Berlin and in Cuba, after the failure to find common ground in Vienna and the forecast for a cold winter, after sitting through meetings where men spoke matter-of-factly about the deaths of millions, John Kennedy on June 10, 1963, challenged his fellow citizens to think about peace rather than about war.

This assertion was so startling that Kennedy discussed the speech's contents with only a few close advisors, not even all of them. The speech was deliberately kept away from Defense Secretary Robert McNamara and Secretary of State Dean Rusk. Their departments, he knew, would argue against any suggestion that the United States and the Soviet Union could coexist in peace, although Rusk himself seemed to believe that drastic change was necessary. The missile crisis was far too close a call. Rusk told the president that "no one who went through the missile crisis came out the same as they went in."

What became known as the "peace speech" was months in the making. Khrushchev had sent a conciliatory message to Kennedy after the missile crisis, suggesting that the time had come to halt nuclear testing. In December 1962, Kennedy learned that journalist Norman Cousins was traveling to Moscow on a private mission from Pope John XXIII, who was concerned about the fate of Catholic priests behind the Iron Curtain. Kennedy summoned Cousins, with whom he was friendly, to the White House and told him that if the Soviet leader suggested that the United States had no desire to reduce tensions, "he should be corrected on this score."

"Just get across one point," Kennedy told Cousins, according to author Richard Reeves. "The point that there's no one in either part more anxious to get an agreement on arms control than I am."

Cousins made that point, and the Soviet responded in kind. "One thing the president and I should do, right away, is to conclude a treaty outlawing testing of nuclear weapons," Khrushchev told Cousins.

Talks continued through the spring of 1963. Cousins returned to Moscow in April and prodded him about making a deal with Kennedy to ban nuclear tests. Finally, the garrulous Khrushchev said, "You want me to set all misunderstandings aside and make a fresh start? All right, I agree to make a fresh start."

Cousins urged Kennedy to do the same. "The moment is now at hand for the most important speech of your presidency," Cousins wrote. Kennedy decided to deliver it in a previously scheduled commencement address at American University, an institution in Washington, D.C., devoted to training students for public service. The university was among the first institutions of higher education in the nation's capital to voluntarily admit black students, in 1937.

Donned in dark academic robes that covered his suit and tie, his head bare while the academics on stage around him wore caps and tassels, Kennedy was very much in his element as he addressed the university's graduates—pioneers of the New Frontier.

The long text the president delivered on June 10 was not the speech of the eager cold warrior, but of a slightly graying statesman who understood the consequences of rash words and misunderstanding. Great powers had always maneuvered against their rivals to attain superiority and victory, but now, when those nations were capable of destroying the world, the rules and the game itself had changed.

While the speech will seem visionary when read and heard in the twenty-first century, Kennedy knew that he risked criticism at home from those who would see it as too conciliatory and even defeatist. He decided it was a risk worth taking.

He explained that he had come to discuss nothing less than "the most important topic on earth: world peace." He had chosen a university setting for such a speech because it was, in the words of British poet John Masefield, "a place where those who hate ignorance may strive to know, where those who perceive truth may strive to make others see."

He then made his argument. He came to speak of peace "because of the new face of war."

"Total war makes no sense in an age when great powers can maintain large and relatively invulnerable nuclear forces and refuse to surrender without resort to those forces," he said. "It makes no sense in an age when a single nuclear weapon contains almost ten times the explosive force delivered by all the Allied air forces in the Second World War. It makes no sense in an age when the deadly poisons produced by a nuclear exchange would be carried by wind and water and soil and seed to the far corners of the globe and to generations yet unborn.

"Today the expenditure of billions of dollars every year on weapons acquired for the purpose of making sure we never need to use them is essential to keeping the peace. But surely, the acquisition of such idle stockpiles—which can only destroy and never create—is not the only, much less the most efficient, means of assuring peace.

"I speak of peace, therefore, as the necessary rational end of rational men. I realize that the pursuit of peace is not as dramatic as the pursuit of war—and frequently the words of the pursuer fall on deaf ears. But we have no more urgent task."

In a nod to critics in Congress and the military, he conceded that some believed it was "useless" to talk about peace until the Soviet Union's leaders adopted a "more enlightened attitude." He hoped one day they would, and perhaps the United States might assist in the process. In the meantime, however, he had two challenges for his fellow citizens. He urged them to examine their attitudes "toward peace itself" and to "reexamine our attitude toward the Soviet Union."

Too many people, he said, believe that peace is unachievable. To that, he replied, "No problem of human destiny is beyond human beings."

More astonishing was his assertion that Americans should recognize what they had in common with the citizens of the Soviet Union. Both nations yearned for peace, and both faced annihilation in a nuclear conflict. That unique and frightening certainty bound together the men and women of Moscow and Washington, Leningrad and New York, Stalingrad and Los Angeles. Everything Americans and Russians had worked for could be destroyed in twenty-four hours. No other two peoples had that in common.

Likewise, Americans ought to remember what else they had in common with Russians, traits that had nothing to do with the Cold War and its tensions, but with their shared humanity. "We all breathe the same air," he said. "We all cherish our children's future. And we are all mortal."

So, while Americans might find communism "repugnant," Kennedy said it was important to remember that no social system or government "is so evil that its people must be considered as lacking in virtue." Here, Kennedy distinguished between an institution—a social system or a government—and human beings.

It was an argument that most Americans would have found reasonable in 1963. After all, the United States had fought and defeated Nazism and fascism in World War II, but now the people who lived under those systems—West Germans and Italians and Japanese—were staunch allies and friends. Few in 1963 would have argued that West Germans were "lacking in virtue" simply because they had lived under and supported the Nazi regime. Indeed, West Germans now were celebrated as friends of liberty, living on the front lines of the Cold War.

In fact, the World War II alliance between the Soviet Union and the United States illustrated the point—Americans in the early and mid 1940s had learned to distinguish between the Soviet system and the Russian people, just as they distinguished between Nazism and ordinary Germans.

There was no point in denying the differences between the Soviet Union and the United States, Kennedy said, "but let us also direct attention to our common interests and to the means by which those differences may be resolved. And if we cannot end now our differences, at least we can help make the world safe for diversity."

Equally important, improved communications and understanding could prevent another August 1914—this one far more deadly. With the lessons of *The Guns of August* clearly still in mind, Kennedy noted that he wished to take "first-step measures of arms control designed to limit the intensity of the arms race and to reduce the risks of accidental war."

In pursuit of those goals, the president announced that he, Khrushchev, and British prime minister Harold Macmillan had agreed to begin intense talks in Moscow designed to draft a treaty that would ban nuclear testing. In a demonstration of good will, he announced that the United States would stop testing its nuclear weapons in the atmosphere "so long as other states do not do so." Such a declaration, he noted, "is no substitute for a formal binding treaty, but I hope it will help us achieve it."

It did that, and more. Less than two weeks after the speech—which Khrushchev praised as the "best statement made by any president since Roosevelt"—the Soviets and Americans agreed to establish a direct line of communication between Moscow and Washington. The two nations signed a limited test ban treaty within months, laying the groundwork for a comprehensive test ban treaty, a landmark in easing the arms race.

Oddly, Kennedy's speech at American University attracted little notice, perhaps because so much media attention was focused on events in the American South, where Governor Wallace was on the barricades in his defense of segregation. Or perhaps, as Kennedy himself noted, "pursuit of peace is not as dramatic as the pursuit of war."

He declared that there was no issue more urgent than the pursuit of peace. He soon learned, however, that there was no shortage of urgent tasks for the president of the United States in 1963.

RFK and Lyndon Johnson meet with Martin Luther King Jr. and other civil rights activists.

CHAPTER 24

The Nation's Moral Crisis

Report to the American People on Civil Rights
June 11, 1963

TRACK 25

EVEN AS JOHN KENNEDY REMINDED AMERICANS THAT THE RUSSIANS were human beings after all, black Americans were on the march in the South, asserting their own humanity. And even as John Kennedy grappled with issues of war and peace with a foreign antagonist thousands of miles away, a potentially explosive confrontation was taking shape at home, in Tuscaloosa, Alabama.

On June 11, 1963, the day after Kennedy's speech at American University, two young African Americans were due to register for summer classes at the University of Alabama, a defiantly all-white institution. The state's new governor, a short, feisty demagogue named George Wallace, had promised to fight for segregation now and forever. The courts, however, had ruled that the two African Americans must be allowed to register.

The scenario was not entirely new for the White House or for the country. From Little Rock, Arkansas, during the Eisenhower administration to Oxford, Mississippi, in the early days of the Kennedy administration, certain images had become distressingly familiar: angry and potentially murderous white obstructionists confronting black students who were under the protection of well-armed, grim-looking federal troops. June 11, 1963, was shaping up to be another terrifying day in the battle to persuade white Americans that blacks breathed the same air as whites and had the same dreams for their children—just like Russians.

Kennedy surely had the looming crisis—not to mention the broader civil rights struggle—in mind as he delivered his historic peace speech on June 10. In concluding his remarks, he had issued one more challenge, asking Americans to examine their attitudes "toward peace and freedom here at home."

"[We] must all, in our daily lives, live up to the age-old faith that peace and freedom walk together," he said. "In too many of our cities today, the peace is not secure because the freedom is incomplete." Local governments must "provide and protect" the freedom of "all of our citizens." And those citizens must "respect the rights of all others" and "respect the law of the land." He never said the word "civil rights," never spoke of black and white Americans, but the message was clear, to white civil authorities and black civil rights leaders alike.

In Alabama, federal authorities led by Deputy Attorney General Nicholas Katzenbach prepared for a confrontation, but of what sort, they did not know. Wallace had vowed to personally block the two students from entering the state-run university. By doing so, he risked arrest. Would he put on a mere show of defiance and then back down? Or would federal authorities have to remove him by force and place him under arrest? Nobody in the Kennedy White House could predict with certainty how the day would unfold.

The president, having just finished delivering one historic speech, was now being urged to prepare another, this one to a national television audience the following day, June 11.

Speechwriter Ted Sorensen broached the subject first. The president was reluctant to do so. As ever, Kennedy was instinctively cautious on the subject of civil rights, declining thus far to introduce sweeping civil rights legislation even in the face of intransigent racism in the South. The issue was a political nightmare—with his reelection campaign looming, Kennedy did not wish to alienate the white Southern Democrats in Congress, many of whom chaired powerful committees and who could stall the president's legislative agenda. What's more, the southern states were an important Democratic constituency, although that was beginning to change.

Ultimately, though, civil rights, like many other domestic issues, seemed like a distraction from the president's first priority, foreign affairs. "Domestic policy can only defeat us," he once said. "Foreign policy can kill us."

As the president seemed to dismiss Sorensen's idea for a nationally broadcast speech on the crisis in Alabama and the civil rights movement in general, Robert Kennedy stepped in. According to Richard Reeves's biography of President Kennedy, the attorney general asserted that a presidential address would be "helpful" in setting the stage for new civil rights legislation. Public opinion would have to be mobilized and wavering members of Congress pressured. RFK added, "I don't think you can get by without it." The public had to hear about the crisis from the president himself.

On the morning of June 11, Nicholas Katzenbach brought two black students, Vivian Malone and James Hood, to the University of Alabama campus in a car. According to a plan worked out in the White House, Katzenbach left the students in the car and walked by himself toward the campus's registration building. It was not yet noon, but the temperature in Tuscaloosa already was nearly a hundred degrees.

Governor Wallace stood behind a podium in front of the door to Foster Auditorium. He wished to look defiant for the dozens of cameras on hand to record the confrontation between the state of Alabama and an emissary from the president of the United States.

Hundreds of National Guard troops were in uniform and ready to be called to the campus. But by whom? Wallace was commander in chief of the Alabama National Guard, but John Kennedy had the power to federalize them to help enforce the court order and to remove anybody who defied it. The president chose to wait on developments before removing the National Guard from Wallace's command. If the University of Alabama could be integrated without a flash of bayonet, the country could be spared another blow to its image around the world.

Katzenbach approached Wallace's position. Wallace ordered him to halt. The two faced each other in the oppressive southern heat. Katzenbach told Wallace that the president was determined to see that the two students were allowed to register, as the courts had ordered. He asked for Wallace's assurance that he would not obstruct the process.

Wallace would not give him that assurance. He read a statement condemning "this illegal and unwanted action by the central government," claiming that the "central government" was suppressing the "rights, privileges, and sovereignty of this state." Wallace chose his words carefully. He did not say "federal government." Instead, he used the loaded phrase, "central government." What totalitarian institution ran the Soviet Union? The Central Committee, of course. Wallace was playing to the cameras. His audience would not miss the message: Kennedy and his liberal friends from the northeast were acting like Communists, trampling over the rights of small governments.

Wallace played out his role as protector of the white race, and Katzenbach, as planned, retreated back to his car and brought the students to the university's dormitories. He declared them as good as registered.

In Washington, Robert Kennedy and his aides were furious as they watched Wallace's theatrics on live television. Robert Kennedy picked up a telephone and called his brother, the president, and asked him to sign an executive order to federalize the Alabama National Guard. The president did so immediately. Troops were deployed to the campus and some four hundred regular army troops were put on standby. Wallace left campus after the National Guard showed up, clearing the way for the students to register in peace. Segregation came to an end at the University of Alabama.

Kennedy decided the time had come for a national address on civil rights. He would deliver one that very night, he told his staff. The difficult decision was not made any easier by Kennedy's physical condition. Once again, despite the efforts of doctors who administered steroids and other medications to the president, Kennedy's deteriorating back was causing him agony. His famous rocking chair allowed him little relief, although he often sought comfort in a White House swimming pool where the water was heated to eighty degrees. To ease the pain, he went for a swim before delivering one of the most important speeches of his presidency.

For blacks and their white supporters, Kennedy's sudden sense of urgency on civil rights was a long time in coming. Civil rights leaders including Dr. Martin Luther King and intellectuals such as James Baldwin had been setting the agenda for what an NBC television documentary called "The American Revolution of '63." Throughout the South, blacks were confronting segregation and injustice, provoking violent responses from white citizens and local politicians and law enforcement agencies. In late May, as the president considered the political effects of introducing a new civil rights bill, he noted bitterly that "the people in the South haven't done anything about integration for a hundred years, and when an outsider intervenes, they tell him to get out, they'll take care of it themselves—which they won't."

So, the president would have to take care of it himself.

Through the afternoon and early evening of June 11, the president's speechwriters, including Sorensen, raced a deadline as they attempted to craft a speech that figured to be almost as momentous as the "peace speech" JFK had given at American University the previous day. This was to be more than an explanation of the day's events in Alabama. This speech would set the moral tone for the introduction, at last, of sweeping civil rights legislation.

Vice President Johnson had been urging the president to give such a speech for months. Johnson emphasized the importance of framing civil rights as a moral issue and promised that southerners would respond accordingly. He told Sorensen that if Kennedy traveled to the South, looked white southerners in the eye, "and [stated] the moral issue and the Christian issue, and he does it face to face, these southerners at least [would] respect his courage."

The president no longer had time for such personal persuasion. He would make the moral case, all right—a course Robert Kennedy also advocated, but would do so with the eyes of the nation on him, via television.

With an hour to go before the president's eight o'clock speech, Sorensen and his colleagues had yet to deliver a complete, polished draft. Sorensen, Robert Kennedy, and another aide, Burke Marshall, were working in the White House cabinet room when the president wandered in. He took a look at some notes and partial drafts that were piled here and there on a table. That was all the writers had, and airtime was an hour away.

Just after seven thirty, the president and his brother convened in the Oval Office by themselves, forming an outline for an extemporaneous speech if the speechwriters failed to finish in time. About five minutes before airtime, Sorensen burst in and handed Kennedy a draft. The president looked over the copy, made some changes, and prepared to face the nation.

Like the speech given only the day before, Kennedy's civil rights speech of June 11, cobbled together with such haste, transcended rhetoric to become a part of history.

Thanks to the many hours he had spent discussing the issue with his aides beforehand, Kennedy confidently departed from his text as he made the case to white America for black equality.

"The Negro baby born in America today," he said, "regardless of the section of the nation in which he is born, has about one-half as much chance of completing…high school as a white baby born in the same place on the same day, one-third as much chance of completing college, one-third as much chance of becoming a professional man, twice as much chance of becoming unemployed, about one-seventh as much chance of earning $10,000 a year, a life expectancy which is seven years shorter, and the prospects of earning only half as much.

"This is not a sectional issue…Nor is it a partisan issue…This is not even a legal or legislative issue alone. It is better to settle these matters in the courts than on the streets, and new laws are needed at every level, but law alone cannot make men see right.

"We are confronted primarily with a moral issue. It is as old as the scriptures and is as clear as the American Constitution.

"The heart of the question is whether all Americans are to be afforded equal rights and equal opportunities, whether we are going to treat our fellow Americans as we wanted to be treated. If an American, because his skin is dark, cannot eat lunch in a restaurant open to the public, if he cannot send his children to the best public school available, if he cannot vote for the public officials who will represent him, if, in short, he cannot enjoy the full and free lives which all of us want, then who among us would be content to have the color of his skin changed and stand in his place? Who among us would then be content with the counsels of patience and delay?"

John Kennedy often left moralizing to his more righteous and more religious brother, Robert. The president was a pragmatist, cool and calculating, and not entirely comfortable with public sermons and civic issues framed in terms of morality. So his use of righteous language in this speech was an indication of how strongly he felt, even if most civil rights leaders believed they had reason to question his commitment to their cause.

In an echo of the speech he had given the previous day, Kennedy called on "every American, regardless of where he lives" to "examine his conscience" on the issue of civil rights. The promise of the Emancipation Proclamation of 1863 had yet to be fulfilled in its centennial year.

The speech also reflected his previous efforts to counter anti-Catholic prejudice in 1960, and his ever-present concerns about the Cold War. "Today we are committed to a worldwide struggle to promote and protect the rights for all who wish to be free," he said. "And when Americans are sent to Vietnam or West Berlin, we do not ask for whites only. It ought to be possible, therefore, for American students of any color to attend any public institution they select without having to be backed up by troops."

In 1960, he had used his military service, and his brother Joseph's death, to argue against those who believed a Catholic was unfit for the White House. If he could be trusted to put on a uniform and risk his life for his country, who could say his religion disqualified him from the presidency? Similarly, if blacks could serve their country in the army, they could be served at lunch counters and be admitted to public institutions.

After making both a moral and a pragmatic argument, Kennedy announced how he hoped to turn his words into action. "Next week I shall ask the Congress of the United States to act, to make a commitment it has not fully made in this century to the proposition that race has no place in American life or law," he said. His proposals would include legislation that would force public accommodations—"hotels, restaurants, theaters, retail stores, and similar establishments"—to serve all customers, regardless of race. This, he conceded, "seems to me to be an elementary right. Its denial is an arbitrary indignity that no American in 1963 should have to endure, but many do."

He also pledged that the federal government would become more aggressive in ending school segregation, noting that the pace of desegregation since the Supreme Court's *Brown v. Board of Education* ruling was "very slow."

After announcing these steps, he turned again to the broader theme, and once again attempted to appeal to the nation's better angels. "We cannot say to 10 percent of the population…that your children cannot have the chance to develop whatever talents they have; that the only way that they are going to get their rights is to go into the streets and demonstrate. I think we owe them and we owe ourselves a better country than that."

Such appeals were designed not only to frame the president's legislative agenda, but also to go over the heads of Southern Democrats in Congress who, Kennedy knew, would obstruct every civil rights initiative he offered. And, in any case, he reiterated his belief that resolving the nation's moral crisis would take more than a piece of paper issued from Capitol Hill. The problem, he said, "must be solved in the homes of every American in every community across our country."

The following day, Medgar Evers, a World War II veteran and one of Mississippi's most influential civil rights leaders, was shot in the back by a white supremacist outside his home in Jackson. His three children and his wife watched helplessly as Evers bled to death.

On June 19, Kennedy sent a civil rights bill to Capitol Hill. His brother Bobby later said that the president believed the bill, so detested by Southern Democrats, would be his "political swan song."

A peaceful protest is broken up by police.

A woman on the west sector of the Berlin wall;
she had waited three hours to see East Berlin friends.

CHAPTER 25

Ich Bin Ein Berliner

Speech at the Berlin Wall
June 26, 1963

TRACK 26

H E HAD NEVER SEEN SUCH A CROWD.
They were gathered in a plaza below him in the tens of thousands—Germans, residents of Berlin, most of them with memories of the war that had devastated their nation and their city. They were cheering, screaming, for the president of the United States, leader of a nation whose troops still occupied German soil.

They saw this man, this young president, as their defender, not the leader of an occupying army. Only two years earlier, he had told his own nation and his enemies that the United States would go to war to defend freedom in West Berlin. That section of the former Nazi capital was, he said, a citadel of freedom and liberty surrounded on all sides by the encroaching forces of oppression.

Just steps away from the crowd was the ugly, hated symbol of the city's humiliation, defeat, and partition: the Berlin wall. Germans had died trying to defy it, cut down by Soviet bullets. The soldiers were there now, across the wall, unseen, unsmiling, like guards in a prison camp.

The crowd cheered John F. Kennedy not as a savior, but as a defender. The adulation was astonishing and led to one of the most memorable moments and most remembered speeches of John F. Kennedy's presidency. The words of the young president, his voice filled with authentic outrage, are familiar even to Americans with no memory of the Kennedy years. The speech's emotional tag line—Ich bin ein Berliner—has transcended politics to become part of Western popular culture.

The speech's power comes not only from the words, which author Michael Beschloss describes as "a kind of angry poetry," but from a sense that it offers an unscripted glimpse of John Kennedy's contempt for Soviet communism and the injustices the wall symbolized. Even the brilliant rhetoric of his saber-rattling inaugural sounds like posturing when compared with the white-hot indignation of the Berlin speech.

That sense of spontaneity is heightened when the Berlin speech is placed alongside Kennedy's peace speech at American University, given just sixteen days earlier. Most of Kennedy's admirers consider the peace speech the best of the Kennedy canon. Certainly, it was well-crafted, and it clearly was the product of much discussion among the administration's best and brightest. It was disciplined by a hard and bitter reality—the Soviets could not be wished away, and certainly not blown away without risk of obliterating civilization.

The Berlin speech, ragged and raw, made a shambles of diplomatic niceties. It curled its lips at those who believed that the Western democracies could work with Communists. And yet, fewer than three weeks earlier, John Kennedy himself had suggested that Americans adopt a new attitude toward the Soviet Union, that, in fact, there were ways for Americans and Soviets to work together to avoid war and increase mankind's knowledge of space and the sciences.

There can be no doubt that John Kennedy meant what he said in his peace speech. It is equally true that he meant what he said in Berlin. He understood that the American people and the Russian people needed to understand each other, and that the two nations could no longer exist at knife's edge, a crisis away from slaughtering millions.

Nevertheless, he despised Soviet communism and this dreadful but natural extension of Russian rule over Eastern Europe. Peace was necessary, but, on this day in West Berlin, so was truth.

Kennedy's trip to Germany coincided with the fifteenth anniversary of the Berlin Airlift, that early expression of Cold War conflict over that divided city. The Soviets in 1948 had denied the Allies land access to West Berlin in an attempt to force the American, British, and French occupying forces to withdraw from the former German capital. When they did, the Soviets, through their East German clients, would gain control over the entire city.

Instead, the U.S. and its allies supplied West Berlin by air. The U.S. commander in West Berlin, General Lucius Clay, became a symbol of American resolve to defend the free citizens of a city that so recently had been the target of U.S. bombers. Now, U.S. warplanes were dropping not explosives, but food and medicine.

The airlift worked; the Communist blockade of West Berlin failed. Fifteen years later, John Kennedy—whose brother, Joseph, flew bombing missions over Germany before he was killed—traveled to West Germany and West Berlin to reiterate America's support for its onetime enemy.

As he left Washington on June 22 for a four-nation European tour, Kennedy pondered another reason why his visit to Germany was so important. The West German chancellor, Konrad Adenauer, had begun to align himself with French president Charles de Gaulle on issues ranging from the Common Market to security. De Gaulle believed the future of a new Europe lay with a tacit alliance between Paris and the West German capital of Bonn. Kennedy's vision was more Anglocentric—his closest ally in Europe was British prime minister Harold Macmillan, and Kennedy saw European issues through the prism of the Washington-London special relationship.

De Gaulle had visited Germany in September 1962 and won public relations points from his country's onetime adversary by speaking several phrases in German—quite a tribute from the Gallic nationalist. Kennedy's advisors were extremely wary of this fledgling relationship. They believed de Gaulle was fanning the flames of latent German nationalism in an effort to dilute the influence of the United States and Great Britain in European affairs. A memo prepared for Kennedy emphasized that whatever the Germans thought of de Gaulle's gestures and courtship, ultimately "their only defense is...American strength and commitment."

It was up to Kennedy to remind them of that salient point.

The president arrived in Bonn on June 23 and toured that city as well as Cologne and Frankfurt. Massive crowds cheered the leader of a nation whose bombers had so recently rained death and devastation on those cities. It was wild and spontaneous and, for the most part, unexpected. Germans shouted his name as his motorcade passed.

He left West Germany and flew to West Berlin, deep inside Soviet-controlled East Germany, on June 26. His motorcade crawled through streets jammed with cheering West Berliners as he made his way to city hall, adjacent to the wall and the site of one of two speeches he was scheduled to deliver. Twice he stopped the procession, got out of his car, and climbed guard towers that looked out over the wall into gray, grim East Berlin. The glimpse of life behind the Iron Curtain repelled him. The streets on the other side, near the Brandenburg Gate, were vacant—there was none of the bustle and freedom of movement that existed on the president's side of the wall. At one stop, however, as Kennedy peered over the wall, he saw three women waving to him from their windows. A journalist traveling with Kennedy, Hugh Sidey, watched the president's reaction as he stepped down from the platform. "He looks like a man who has just glimpsed hell," Sidey said.

Kennedy had been scheduled to give a very diplomatic speech at city hall commemorating the success of the airlift and paying tribute to the spirit of West Berlin. After seeing the wall and what lay behind it, he could no longer give that speech. He showed a draft of it to General James Polke, the current U.S. commander in Berlin, who was traveling in the president's motorcade. Polke told Kennedy he thought the prepared speech was "terrible." Kennedy agreed.

During the flight to Germany, Kennedy had indicated that he had something in mind for his Berlin visit besides the almost boilerplate speech he was supposed to deliver at West Berlin's city hall. He spoke with aide Kenneth O'Donnell about "the proud boast of the Romans," and asked McGeorge Bundy to adapt the boast "I am a citizen of Rome" into German and apply it to Berlin. Kennedy, as has been noted elsewhere in this volume, was not exactly a student of foreign languages, and he wrote the phrase on an index card, spelling it phonetically. The phrasing was not precise. Kennedy probably should have said "Ich bin Berliner." The phrase "ein Berliner" was local jargon for a jelly doughnut. Nobody in the crowd seemed to notice, or care.

Now, as the president made his way into a plaza in front of West Berlin's city hall, he looked out on a delirious crowd numbering in the hundreds of thousands. The carefully prepared speech he was supposed to give was tossed aside. Instead, he delivered remarks that were decidedly not careful, tepid, diplomatic expressions. They were words that would resonate for generations to come.

"Two thousand years ago, the proudest boast was 'civis Romanus sum.' Today, in the world of freedom, the proudest boast is 'Ich bin ein Berliner.'"

The crowd erupted, and Kennedy smiled and added a comment. "I appreciate my interpreter translating my German!"

Standing near the very symbol of the Cold War's divisions and tensions—but also its compromises and realities—John Kennedy gave meaning and purpose to the twilight struggle he so eagerly pursued throughout his short, turbulent presidency. Like other leaders in hours of maximum danger, he knew he had to explain why he was willing to put lives at risk in pursuit of ideals. During the battle of Britain, Churchill told his fellow Britons that should they stand firm, their sacrifices might allow mankind "to walk in broad, sunlit uplands" rather than sink into the moors of "perverted science." At Gettysburg, Lincoln said that the sacrifices of the dead could inspire a new birth of freedom, and might ensure the survival of a nation conceived in liberty. In Berlin in 1963, President Kennedy explained why he was willing to risk war, even nuclear war, for the sake of a city that had been the capital of Nazi Germany. He explained to Berliners why America would not abandon them—freedom in America, he said, depended on continued freedom in Berlin.

"There are many people in the world who really don't understand, or say they don't, what is the great issue between the free world and the Communist world. Let them come to Berlin. And there are some who say that communism is the wave of the future. Let them come to Berlin. And there are some who say in Europe and elsewhere we can work with the Communists. Let them come to Berlin. And there are even a few who say that it is true that communism is an evil system, but it permits us to make economic progress. Lass' sie nach Berlin kommen. Let them come to Berlin."

Again, the Berliners cheered.

Then, in a single phrase that conceded the domestic problems he had left behind, he used the wall to make the case for democracy and against totalitarianism. "Freedom has many difficulties and democracy is not perfect," he said, "but we have never had to put a wall up to keep our people in, to prevent them from leaving us." The clumsy phrasing suggests spontaneity and raw emotion. The words themselves indicate how strongly he felt about the wall and all it stood for.

"While the wall is the most obvious and vivid demonstration of the failures of the Communist system for all the world to see, we take no satisfaction in it, for it is, as your mayor has said, an offense not only against history, but an offense against humanity, separating families, dividing husbands and wives and brothers and sisters, and dividing a people who wish to be joined together."

Standing near the Berlin wall, John Kennedy did not need threats to make his points. He did not have to rely on brinkmanship. He did not have to list the depredations visited on the nations of Eastern Europe. All he needed was the wall and his own outrage. The wall provided him with the moral high ground, and he was not reluctant to seize it.

In five hundred exquisitely righteous words, John Kennedy created a bond between the United States and West Berlin—and the whole of West Germany—that no successor could break, and that each respected. John Kennedy had validated the sacrifices of West Berliners, welcomed them back to the community of civilized peoples, inspired them to dream of a better future, and, indeed, declared himself to be one of them. Ich bin ein Berliner.

As he concluded, the cheers went on and on and on. West Berlin mayor Willy Brandt stepped to the podium to try to give his speech, but his countrymen would not let him start. They shouted for Kennedy to return, to deliver a roaring encore. Back home, Americans who heard the speech on radio or television would understand now why they were being asked to pay for, and perhaps die for, the freedom of a German city.

Even with interruptions, the speech took only a few minutes to deliver. But it changed the power structure in central Europe. America had outfoxed France in the battle for West Germany's heart. Kennedy reminded Berliners and all of Europe that America was their best, and indeed only, protection against Communist aggression. And Americans were reminded that nearly twenty years after the end of World War II, they still were looked upon as liberators, and that their president truly was, in the words of Richard Reeves, the prince of the world.

Kennedy gave another speech that day, but it is as forgotten as Edward Everett's endless oration at Gettysburg in 1863. During that appearance in West Berlin's Free University, the president was more measured, more diplomatic, more scripted. He said he believed in "the necessity of great powers working together to preserve the human race."

While his actions showed that he believed in that necessity, his earlier words spoke for that portion of the human race that lived behind the Berlin wall and the Iron Curtain. The reception he received was a full-throated cry of gratitude from the people he had sworn to defend. He told Adenauer that he would leave a note for future presidents who might be having a hard time. "Go to Germany," the note would read.

As he left Germany, Kennedy said, "We'll never have another day like this one as long as we live."

That magical moment of U.S. prestige and popularity was gone in an instant. Kennedy had but five months to live and the U.S. would soon forfeit its moral stature as black Americans reminded the world of democracy's imperfections and American soldiers slogged through the fields of Vietnam in support of a dubious regime.

But the words survived. Kennedy had spoken the truth, placed his contempt on record, inspired the flagging spirits of an embattled city, and ennobled the demands placed on his own country.

JFK and Eamon de Valera meet in Dublin.

CHAPTER 26

Ireland's Favorite Son

Address in Dublin to the Irish Parliament
June 28, 1963

TRACK 27

CONTRARY TO POPULAR MYTH ON BOTH SIDES OF THE ATLANTIC Ocean, John Kennedy was not the first U.S. president of Irish descent. That title belongs to Andrew Jackson, whose parents emigrated from Carrickfergus in County Antrim before the American Revolution. After Jackson, presidents with Irish blood were hardly uncommon. They included James Buchanan, William McKinley, and Woodrow Wilson.

While John Kennedy shared Irish roots with some of his predecessors, he did not share their religion. He was Roman Catholic, the traditional faith of the vast majority of Irish people. The other presidents of Irish ancestry were Protestant, most of them descended from settlers who immigrated to Ireland from England and Scotland during the Reformation. In an age when religious affiliation signified political loyalties, Protestant settlers in Ireland served as a bulwark against the native Catholics, who were assumed sympathetic with Britain's Catholic rivals, Spain and France.

Most Irish Protestants, in fact, rejected the notion that they were Irish at all. The Presbyterians called themselves Scotch Irish, while members of the established Church of Ireland were considered Anglo Irish.

So, while Andrew Jackson may have been the son of Irish immigrants, and other presidents could trace a root or two to the Emerald Isle, they did not necessarily consider themselves Irish American. The Catholic Irish, in Ireland and America, shared that view.

And then, finally, came John Kennedy. Here, at last, was an authentic Irishman, at least in the eyes of most Irish Americans—he was a Catholic who could trace his roots to New Ross in County Wexford, the great-grandson of immigrants who fled Ireland during the famine of 1845 to 1851. A million Irishmen, nearly all of them impoverished Catholics, starved to death during those years when their main food supply, the potato, failed. Two million more emigrated, including a man named Patrick Kennedy and a woman named Bridget Murphy. They met on an emigrant ship, hardly the most likely place to find companionship, never mind love. But they married five months after landing in Boston and started a family that would one day reach the White House.

Ironically enough, the young politician who captured the hearts of his fellow Irish Catholics was the son of a multimillionaire who attended prep school and Harvard University. He was, in manner, education, and style, an American aristocrat not unlike the Boston Brahmins—the Lodges and the Cabots—who looked down at the city's Irish Catholics.

John F. Kennedy and his family surely were far removed from the life and times of Alfred E. Smith, the Irish American politician from the slums of the Lower East Side who in 1928 became the first Catholic to win a major-party presidential nomination. With his working-class New York accent and rough-and-tumble background, Al Smith was the urban, ethnic everyman of the 1920s. John Kennedy, on the other hand, was rich and polished, with all the necessary paperwork required for membership in fields dominated by Anglo-Saxon Protestants. As presidential speechwriter Peggy Noonan put it in a PBS television documentary, the first Irish Catholic president seemed to be more of a WASP from Harvard.

In reality, John Kennedy was keenly aware of his Irish heritage and the incredible journey that took his family from starving and impoverished Ireland to the slums of Boston to the Court of St. James and, finally, to the White House. He visited Ireland in 1945 and met with the heroes of Ireland's fight for freedom during and after World War I. Men such as Prime Minister Eamon de Valera and onetime IRA chief of staff Richard Mulcahy were not the sort who would be welcome in the homes of the wellborn and well-bred in Boston or in London. But Kennedy found them fascinating, and he sympathized with their struggle against British rule.

He returned in 1947, when he was a thirty-year-old freshman congressman. It was, by chance, the one hundredth anniversary of a year bitterly remembered in Irish history as Black '47—when the potato crop failed so miserably that tens of thousands died that year and even more boarded emigrant ships headed for the United States.

He and his sister, Kathleen, stayed for a while in Lismore Castle in County Waterford, where they entertained in the manner of the Anglo Irish landed gentry. Kathleen Kennedy, three years younger than Jack and the widow of an English aristocrat killed during World War II, invited along some of her friends and acquaintances from Britain, including future prime minister Anthony Eden. While there is little question that young Jack felt at ease in such rarefied company, he wanted to see more of the land that his ancestors had fled ninety-eight years earlier.

So, without Kathleen—who preferred the company of her British visitors—Jack rode out to County Wexford, five hours and a world away from the pleasures of Lismore Castle. There, he tracked down a farming family living simply in a thatched roof cottage in Dunganstown, near New Ross. They were his distant cousins, and he could not help but notice that the children all looked like Kennedys.

He loved visiting the very land his ancestors had left, not because he was overly sentimental, not because he had been brought up on stories of the green land the family had left behind, and not because he romanticized the life of the New Ross Kennedys who lived in a home with an earthen floor. He loved the experience because he had discovered a part of himself, a part that somehow had survived the deracinating effects of prep school and Harvard, not to mention his father's insistence on assimilation. A decade earlier, Joseph Kennedy Sr. had told a crowd of Irish Americans in Boston that "the influence of Irish culture in this country must be recognized as on the wane." The Irish, he said, were in the process of "cultural absorption."

And yet, Joseph Kennedy privately believed that the forces of assimilation were not powerful enough for even his family to win acceptance in Protestant, Anglo America. He complained that he and his family invariably were described as Irish even though the Kennedys had been in the United States since 1849.

John Kennedy, who made it to the top, did not seem to mind.

Once Kennedy became president, a visit to Ireland would have seemed natural enough. But, as White House advisors pointed out, there was no good strategic reason for such a journey. The Irish in America supported Kennedy in huge numbers. And, from a cold geopolitical perspective, the Republic of Ireland was irrelevant to the great issues of the day. It remained in 1963 what it was in 1945, when Kennedy first visited—a small agricultural nation that kept to itself. Ireland steadfastly refused to join NATO and chose to remain neutral in Kennedy's struggle against the Soviet Union and communism.

Nevertheless, as Kennedy prepared for a state visit to Europe in mid 1963, he made it clear that he wanted Ireland on the itinerary, along with Italy, Britain, West Germany, and Berlin. Aides worried that a side trip to Ireland was politically pointless at best and frivolous at worst. There were great issues of war and peace to discuss on the continent while at home, Dr. Martin Luther King was leading nothing less than a social revolution in the South. A visit to Ireland seemed like a waste of time in the midst of great events.

But the great-grandson of famine immigrants made his intentions quite clear. "I am the president of the United States, not you," he told aide Kenny O'Donnell, one of the many skeptics in the White House. "When I say I want to go to Ireland, it means that I'm going to Ireland. Make the arrangements."

The arrangements were made. And on June 26, 1963, John Fitzgerald Kennedy, child of American privilege and great-grandson of Irish immigrants, became the first U.S. president to visit Ireland while in office. He was the ultimate "returned Yank," the not-always-affectionate phrase the Irish have for visiting Irish Americans seeking their roots.

It was a triumphant four-day celebration, with crowds that were as wildly enthusiastic as those he had left behind in Berlin. In that divided city, Kennedy had proclaimed himself a Berliner, in tribute to his courageous hosts. In Ireland, Kennedy would not need to declare himself an Irishman, for that was understood.

He returned to the cottage in Dunganstown he had visited in 1947 and met more cousins—his hostess, Mary Kennedy Ryan, introduced the president to these long-lost relatives as "cousin Jack." Mrs. Ryan was a formidable widow who, as a young woman, was a member of the IRA's women's auxiliary during the fight for independence in the early 1920s. This interesting bit of family history was not mentioned during the president's visit, as Kennedy biographer Thomas Maier wryly observes in *The Kennedys: America's Emerald Kings.*

After leaving the Kennedy cousins, his homecoming took him to Dublin, where he was the guest of honor in the home of the Irish president, Eamon de Valera, who had met the very young JFK in 1945. Dev, as he was universally known, was eighty years old and nearly blind. Beloved and controversial, he had dominated midcentury Irish politics as prime minister, and even now was active in his ceremonial post as the Republic's president. Dev had fought against the British in the failed Easter Rising of 1916 and was the head of the rebel government that won freedom for twenty-six of Ireland's thirty-two counties in 1921. He had rejected that compromise peace, which partitioned Ireland and created an entity known as Northern Ireland, and broke with his colleagues. A short but inevitably brutal civil war followed, ending in defeat for Dev and his antitreaty comrades. Eventually, Dev made his own compromise and returned to public life, dominating Irish politics and culture for decades.

Now, he welcomed John F. Kennedy, a "distinguished scion of our race," to Ireland. John Kennedy, Dev believed, was the man who might one day end the hated partition of Ireland, and so achieve one aging Irishman's dream.

On June 28, 1963, President Kennedy appeared before the Dail, the Republic of Ireland's parliament, to deliver a formal address. The Dail met in an old Georgian mansion called Leinster House, which once served as the home of the Fitzgerald family, including the great Irish patriot, Lord Edward Fitzgerald. Kennedy, who bore the middle name "Fitzgerald" in honor of his mother's family, took special delight in pointing out the connection.

"This elegant building, as you know, was once the property of the Fitzgerald family, but I have not come here to claim it," he said. "Of all the new relations I have discovered on this trip, I regret to say that no one has yet found any link between me and a great Irish patriot, Lord Edward Fitzgerald. Lord Edward, however, did not like to stay here in his family home because, as he wrote his mother, 'Leinster House does not inspire the brightest ideas.'" He and his audience exchanged knowing smiles. "That was a long time ago, however," he said to laughter.

Kennedy's lengthy speech was a brilliant, ambitious examination of the ties that bound Ireland and the United States together, of the role small nations as Ireland could and should play in global affairs, and of Ireland's long struggle for political, cultural, and economic freedom. In his opening remarks, he recalled one of the great tragedies of the U.S. Civil War, when the Irish Brigade charged Confederate defenses at Fredericksburg, Virginia, on December 13, 1862.

"One of the most brilliant stories of that day was written by a band of twelve hundred men who went into battle wearing a green sprig in their hats," he said. "They bore a proud heritage and a special courage, given to those who had long fought for the cause of freedom. I am referring, of course, to the Irish Brigade. General Robert E. Lee, the great military leader of the Southern Confederate forces, said of this group of men after the battle, 'The gallant stand which this bold brigade made on the heights of Fredericksburg is well known. Never were men so brave...'"

Only two hundred and fifty of the twelve hundred Irishmen who fought in that engagement survived.

In an unspoken nod to one of his distinctly non-Irish heroes, Kennedy faintly echoed the words of Winston Churchill when he addressed a joint session of the U.S. Congress on December 16, 1941—days after Pearl Harbor. "I cannot help reflecting that if my father had been an American and my mother British, instead of the other way around, I might have gotten here on my own," Churchill told the American legislators.

Kennedy told the Dail: "If this nation had achieved its present political and economic stature a century or so ago, my great-grandfather might never have left New Ross, and I might, if fortunate, be sitting down there with you. Of course, if your own president had never left Brooklyn, he might be standing up here instead of me." De Valera was a native of New York.

Kennedy's speech was filled with neither sentimental pap nor overblown tributes to Irish virtues. But it surely was a milestone in Irish history and an important document in the post-colonial era. Kennedy declared that because of Ireland's own history of oppression, it was well suited to act as a "protector of the weak and voice of the small." It is a role Ireland has played at the United Nations in the decades since.

As he left Ireland, he promised to return "in the springtime." He even entertained the notion that his successor might one day appoint him ambassador to Ireland, a job that Franklin Roosevelt had offered his father. He turned it down—for an ambitious, wealthy Irish American in the 1930s, only the Court of St. James would do.

For weeks after the president's return to Washington, he spoke incessantly of Ireland, and, as biographer Maier revealed, he insisted on showing his friends and family films from the trip. Maier noted that his brother Bobby once said that the trip the president insisted on—a trip that the *New Yorker* haughtily described as a "pseudo-event"—was "the happiest time of his administration."

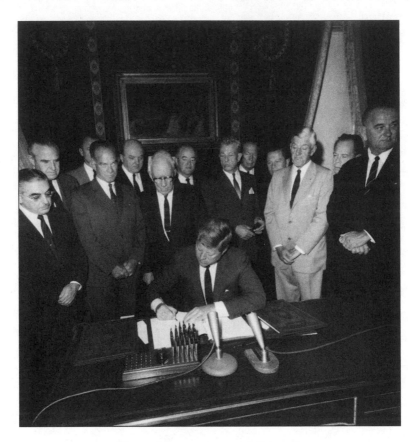

The test ban treaty is signed, July 1963.

CHAPTER 27

"A Spirit of Hope"

Address to the Nation
on the Limited Test Ban Treaty
July 26, 1963

TRACK 28

S O OFTEN WHEN JOHN KENNEDY DELIVERED A NATIONALLY televised address, the topic at hand was a crisis—in Berlin, in Cuba, in Alabama. But on July 26, 1963, Kennedy opened his speech to the nation with words of optimism. "I speak to you tonight," he said, "in a spirit of hope."

That hope came in the form of a treaty between the United States and the Soviet Union designed to halt the testing of nuclear weapons in the atmosphere. The day before the president's speech, U.S. and Soviet negotiators meeting in Moscow had put their initials on the historic agreement. Kennedy had been monitoring the talks on an hourly basis from the White House situation room.

The treaty had been years in the making and was the result of intensive public and private diplomacy involving not only Washington and Moscow, but London as well. Prime Minister Harold Macmillan, who had developed a close working friendship with Kennedy, had served as a key partner in the delicate negotiations.

For Kennedy, the treaty was an enormous personal and political victory.

"Yesterday," he said, "a shaft of light cut into the darkness. Negotiations were concluded in Moscow on a treaty to ban all nuclear tests in the atmosphere, in outer space, and under water."

Kennedy knew that not everyone in the United States—particularly hard-line anti-Communists in the U.S. Senate, where the treaty would have to be ratified, and in the armed services—would agree. So, in this speech, JFK sought to win over public opinion by emphasizing the dangers of the status quo.

"In an age when both sides [in the Cold War] have come to possess enough nuclear power to destroy the human race several times over, the world of communism and the world of free choice have been caught up in a vicious circle of conflicting ideology and interest. Each increase of tension has produced an increase of arms; each increase of arms has produced an increase in tension."

Part of that vicious circle was the testing of increasingly powerful nuclear weapons. Such tests were a regular feature of the Cold War until 1958, when both the Soviets and the U.S. voluntarily halted such tests in the face of evidence that these explosions were a dangerous environmental hazard and public relations nightmare. One of the few good outcomes of the Vienna summit in 1961 was Khrushchev's promise that the Soviets would not be the first to resume testing. But even as Khrushchev made his pledge, the Soviets were preparing to end their self-imposed moratorium on testing. On September 1, 1961, a huge nuclear blast in central Asia signaled an end to Soviet restraint. Another blast followed two days later. And when Khrushchev addressed the Communist Party Congress in October, he announced that the series of tests would finish with the detonation of a fifty-megaton hydrogen bomb—with the explosive impact of fifty million tons of TNT. But in a magnanimous gesture designed to get a laugh, he announced that while the Soviets had a one hundred megaton nuclear bomb, they would not test it "because even if we did so at the most remote site, we might knock out all our windows."

The Kennedy White House was furious. "The bastards!" Kennedy exclaimed when he heard the news. He condemned the Soviets for their "utter disregard of the desire of mankind for a decrease in the arms race." With the president's input and approval, a defense department official named Roswell Gilpatric lashed out at the Soviets in a speech in Virginia in late October. In distinctly undiplomatic language, Gilpatric emphasized American nuclear superiority and assured his audience that the U.S. could strike back at and destroy the Soviets even if they launched a surprise attack.

Two days later, the Soviets exploded a thirty-megaton nuclear weapon—the most powerful ever tested. The Cold War once again was on the verge of boiling over.

On March 2, 1962, Kennedy announced that the U.S. would reply in kind. And on April 25, nighttime turned into day on Christmas Island in the Pacific Ocean as the U.S. detonated a nuclear device above ground for the first time since the 1958 moratorium. A correspondent for *Life* magazine noted that the sky over the Pacific turned "terribly blood red. It was as if someone had poured a bucket of blood on the sky." The Christmas Island test was to be the first of forty over the next six months.

These horrifying tests were inflicting incalculable damage to the earth's environment and to human beings exposed to the tests' radioactive fallout.

Talk of a formal ban on nuclear tests dated back to the Eisenhower administration, and the issue had been raised periodically since Kennedy took office. The issue gained momentum in the spring of 1963, as Kennedy and Khrushchev moved away from the politics of confrontation. The president's June 10 speech at American University, described in chapter 23, helped set the stage for his words of hope on July 26.

The test ban treaty was an arms control agreement for the nuclear age, or so Kennedy hoped. It was designed not only to slow down the arms race between the Soviets and the West, but also to prevent nuclear proliferation worldwide. Nations that signed the treaty would be less likely to develop nuclear weapons of their own, because they would have signed on to a ban against all but underground testing.

As was the case with his American University speech, Kennedy's words of hope on July 26 were quite a contrast with his words of that January day in 1961 when he talked of a long twilight struggle against communism. Since then, both Kennedy and Khrushchev had stared into the ghoulish face of nuclear annihilation. They knew how close to the brink they had been, and how easily they might make the same journey again. Both considered the test ban treaty a major accomplishment in easing the tensions that threatened the lives of hundreds of millions.

Lurking in the background of the test ban talks were the Chinese Communists, whose militancy and fanaticism helped achieve the unlikely result of bringing together the Soviets and the Americans. Neither wished to see China armed with nuclear weapons; in fact, negotiators from both sides spoke of sharing intelligence on China's nuclear program, and perhaps even a joint assault on China to preempt its nuclear program.

The Chinese accused Khrushchev of being soft on capitalism, of caving in far too readily to Kennedy and the Western alliance. The Soviets, in mid-1963, launched a rhetorical offensive against the Chinese as they prepared for a successful conclusion to the test ban talks. The Soviet newspaper *Pravda* accused the Chinese of being far too cavalier about nuclear warfare. In essence, *Pravda* claimed, the Chinese were prepared to accept the slaughter of millions in pursuit of their goals.

Even as he was negotiating the treaty with Kennedy's envoy, Averell Harriman, Khrushchev lashed out at his fellow Communists. "What do they want? They say one should start a revolution, a war, and on the corpses and the ruins, a more prosperous society will be created. And who would remain in this prosperous society? The living would envy the dead."

In a sign of just how much the world was changing, John Kennedy would quote those sentiments—the words of one Communist chastising his supposed comrades—in explaining to the American people why a test ban treaty was so important.

"A war today or tomorrow, if it led to nuclear war, would not be like any war in history," he said. "A full-scale nuclear exchange, lasting less than sixty minutes, with the weapons now in existence, could wipe out more than three hundred million Americans, Europeans, and Russians, as well as untold numbers elsewhere. And the survivors, as Chairman Khrushchev warned the Communist Chinese, 'the survivors would envy the dead.' For they would inherit a world so devastated by explosions and poison and fire that today we cannot even conceive of its horrors. So let us try to turn the world away from war. Let us make the most of this opportunity, and every opportunity, to reduce tension, to slow down the perilous nuclear arms race, and to check the world's slide toward final annihilation."

While the treaty was not a peace agreement, while it would not put an end to East-West tensions, Kennedy said, it would "symbolize the end of one era and the beginning of another," an era where negotiation might replace brinksmanship.

Those who signed the treaty—the Soviets, Americans, British, and anyone else who cared to join—pledged that they would not conduct nuclear tests in the atmosphere, in outer space, or under the oceans. (The French, in keeping with their insistence on deciding for themselves what was best for France, said they would not sign the treaty.) Underground testing was not covered, and the treaty did not require on-site inspections or monitoring by an international agency.

Still, however flawed, Kennedy held out the hope that the agreement would not only ease tensions, but would prevent future anxieties. Soon, he said, nuclear weapons could be "in the hands of countries large and small, stable and unstable, responsible and irresponsible, scattered throughout the world." The world's nuclear powers—the U.S., the Soviet Union, the British, and the French—had a "great obligation" to "prevent the spread of nuclear weapons, to persuade other countries not to test…or produce such weapons."

Those would prove to be false hopes, as perhaps Kennedy knew even on that day in 1963, when only four nations possessed nuclear weapons. The president's fears of proliferation would come true, and then some. In the early years of the twenty-first century, the Soviet Union is no more, but the specter of nuclear catastrophe has not dissolved. Yesterday's China is today's Iran or North Korea—regimes considered indifferent to the ghastly possibilities of a nuclear explosion. Even more frightening is the possibility of a nuclear strike launched by a suicidal terrorist, acting on orders from a fanatic living in a cave.

The world has not quite turned out as Kennedy suggested it might in 1963. Still, his reasoning was not flawed. In quoting a maxim from the nation then considered the greatest threat to world peace, he said: "No one can be certain what the future will bring. No one can say whether the time has come for an easing of the struggle. But history and our own conscience will judge us harsher if we do not now make every effort to test our hopes by action, and this is the place to begin. According to the ancient Chinese proverb, 'A journey of a thousand miles must begin with a single step.' My fellow Americans, let us take that first step."

In the following weeks, the president traveled the country to rally public opinion behind the treaty, which might have been bogged down in political posturing as both parties prepared for the 1964 elections.

Kennedy's arguments carried the day. The Senate overwhelmingly approved the treaty in September, and Kennedy signed it on October 7.

CBS journalist Walter Cronkite interviews Kennedy at Cape Cod.

CHAPTER 28

"The Clouds Have Lifted"

Address to
the United Nations General Assembly
September 20, 1963

TRACK 29

THE ARC OF PRESIDENT KENNEDY'S COLD WAR ORATORY BEGINS with his inaugural address, with its emphasis on the burdens of a twilight struggle, and ends with this speech two months before his death. This speech is a continuation of the historic American University address, and a further movement away from those words that inflamed tensions and had helped put into motion events that so nearly spun out of control in the aftermath of the Vienna summit and during the Cuban Missile Crisis. Kennedy himself noted in the very beginning of this speech that the world has changed a great deal since he first spoke to the General Assembly three years earlier, on September 25, 1961. Then, the president spoke of the "nuclear sword of Damocles, hanging by the slenderest of threads."

On this occasion, the thread that held Damocles' sword seemed a good deal sturdier than it did in 1961. And the chances of accident or miscalculation—and perhaps even madness—had been reduced, perhaps only slightly, but enough so that the president could speak of a "pause" in the Cold War.

"Today the clouds have lifted a little so that new rays of hope can break through," Kennedy told the General Assembly, returning to the language he used when he announced agreement on the test ban treaty—"a shaft of light" that "cut into the darkness." But, he warned, "The world has not escaped from the darkness." The issue for the Soviets, for Americans, and for all people was just how much darkness they could tolerate, and just how much light were they willing to let in.

In this, his last major foreign policy speech to an international audience, John Kennedy showed, as he did at American University, how willing he was to step away from the brink of catastrophe, how much the close brushes with the unimaginable had changed him and the way he chose his words.

Like Robert Frost, John Kennedy was acquainted with the night. Those bonds were formed in his personal life—the deaths of his brother Joseph and sister Kathleen, his own wartime experience on PT 109, his constant battles with poor health—and during his tenure as president, when the fraying thread that held Damocles' sword seemed a moment away from breaking.

In this speech, John Kennedy sought to hasten the nation and the world past those darkest hours just before dawn. His first words to the General Assembly were: "We meet again in the quest for peace." That quest now animated his rhetoric and his thoughts.

"The world has not escaped darkness," he said. "The long shadows of conflict and crisis envelop us still. But we meet today in an atmosphere of rising hope, and a moment of comparative calm. My presence here today is not a sign of crisis, but of confidence. I am not here to report on a new threat to the peace or new signs of war. I have come to salute the United Nations and to show the support of the American people for your daily deliberations."

In his first speech as president, John Kennedy had said: "Let us never negotiate out of fear, but let us never fear to negotiate." With the test ban treaty, he had demonstrated to the United Nations and the world that the United States could indeed talk with the Soviets. The gulf between West and East, Communist and capitalist, was not as vast as even he might have led people to believe, and that this beachhead of cooperation might, in fact, push back the jungle of suspicion.

After nearly three years in office, John Kennedy was fulfilling the more optimistic visions of his inaugural. Without overlooking the differences that would continue to divide the free world and the Communist world, Kennedy asserted that both superpowers shared special responsibilities in the world and that those responsibilities required "our two nations to concentrate less on our differences."

A moment of cooperation, of recognition of each side's humanity, seemed at hand.

If, Kennedy said at the UN, "we can stretch this pause [in the Cold War] into a period of cooperation—if both sides can now gain new confidence and experience in concrete collaborations for peace—if we can now be as bold and farsighted in the control of deadly weapons as we have been in their creation—then surely this first small step can be the start of a long and fruitful journey."

A year before, in his speech at Rice University, John Kennedy had outlined his vision for putting an American on the moon by the end of the decade, inextricably linking space travel to Cold War competition. The space program, as Lyndon Johnson had told him, was a way to win prestige, a way to show off Yankee know-how, a way to persuade the nonaligned that the U.S. would prevail over the Soviets.

In this speech, Kennedy suggested that this signature issue of the New Frontier was a prospective avenue of further cooperation between the two adversaries. "Space offers no problems of sovereignty.... Why, therefore, should man's first flight to the moon be a matter of national competition?" he asked. "Why should the United States and the Soviet Union, in preparing for such expeditions, become involved in immense duplication of research, construction, and expenditure?"

This was an extraordinary gesture on Kennedy's part. Intensely competitive, he had insisted that the race to the moon was worth the effort only if the United States were committed to being first, to winning. Now, he was conceding—he was offering—his adversaries a tie.

Still, he was hardly declaring an end to the greater contest between nations, interests, and ideologies. That contest, he told the UN, would continue—"the contest between those who see a monolithic world and those who believe in diversity." And, he said, he welcomed that contest.

But that contest was worth fighting only if it improved the chances for peace and made life better for all mankind. He closed with another classical reference of the sort that few American politicians forty years later would dare make for fear of being labeled an elitist. The test ban treaty, he said, would "not secure freedom for all.

"But it can be a lever, and Archimedes, in explaining the principles of the lever, was said to have declared to his friends: 'Give me a place where I can stand—and I shall move the world.' My fellow inhabitants of this planet: Let us take our stand here in this assembly of nations."

The unveiling of the **Mona Lisa** *at the White House.*

CHAPTER 29

The Arts and Politics

Remarks at Amherst College
October 26, 1963

TRACK 30

T HE COLLEGE CAMPUS WAS THE SETTING FOR MANY OF KENNEDY'S memorable speeches. At Rice University in Houston, he exhorted the nation to reach for the stars. At American University, he challenged Americans to rethink their attitudes toward the Soviets.

In late October 1963, the president traveled to Amherst College, a small liberal arts institution in his native state of Massachusetts, to pay tribute to Robert Frost. The bard of the New Frontier, Frost had died the previous January at the age of eighty-eight. Amherst College invited Kennedy, who had done so much to raise Frost's profile, to join in a celebration of the poet's life and work.

The young president and the elderly writer surely were not intimate friends, but neither were they mere acquaintances, as Frost's starring role on inauguration day demonstrated. In the evening of his life, with his finest work done and part of the American canon, Frost enjoyed the honors and attention that came with White House patronage. His ten-day visit to Moscow in September 1962—just a month before the Cuban Missile Crisis—made headlines in newspapers across the country. Indeed, Frost received the attention not of an artist, but of a private diplomat, somebody who spoke with the advice and consent of the president. He was invited to Khrushchev's private residence and engaged in talk not of poetry, but of Cold War politics. Upon returning, the weary poet told the waiting press corps that Khrushchev judged Americans as "too liberal to fight."

Frost's comment enraged Kennedy, who was dealing with Republican criticism that he was too weak and too inexperienced to deal with the wily Soviet leader. "Why did Frost say that?" he demanded to know. The answer, of course, was that Robert Frost was a poet and not a politician or a diplomat. He was giving a candid assessment of what he believed Khrushchev was thinking. But such an explanation would not have assuaged Kennedy, who saw Frost's remarks as giving aid and comfort to his political enemies.

During a news conference in mid-September, a reporter asked Kennedy if Frost had carried a personal message from Khrushchev to the president. JFK noted that he had not yet met with Frost after the poet's return from Moscow. In fact, he never did. Frost died about four months later, on January 23, without having briefed Kennedy on his trip. It was not for lack of trying on the poet's part—even as death approached, Frost talked of arranging a meeting with Kennedy to talk about Khrushchev. But Kennedy's annoyance with the old man had not abated. JFK biographer Richard Reeves noted that a dying Frost received goodwill messages from Robert Kennedy, the pope, and even from Khrushchev, but not from the White House.

Kennedy's wrath softened with the poet's death and the passage of time. His tribute to Frost at Amherst was heartfelt and poignant, especially considering the fate that awaited Kennedy four weeks later. Speaking of the poet, the president said, "His sense of the human tragedy fortified him against self-deception and easy consolation. 'I have been,' he wrote, 'one acquainted with the night.' And because he knew the midnight as well as the high noon, because he understood the ordeal as well as the triumph of the human spirit, he gave his age strength with which to overcome despair."

Kennedy's tribute to Frost included this memorable line: "A nation reveals itself not only by the men it produces but also by the men it honors, the men it remembers." Kennedy noted that national heroes generally are "men of large accomplishments," political leaders and generals and explorers. But, he argued, Robert Frost, a writer, was a hero, too, for his contribution "not to our size but to our spirit, not to our political beliefs but to our insight, not to our self-esteem but to our self-comprehension."

This speech was not, however, a mere eulogy to a fallen poet, but a larger tribute to the role of art and culture in the life of a great nation. And it is this larger purpose that gives the speech a place in the Kennedy canon.

Culture and the arts were as much a part of the Kennedy mystique as athletic vigor and intellectual vitality. Certainly, the president's wife, Jacqueline, was at home with high culture in all its forms. The *New York Times* dubbed her "the unofficial Minister of Culture" in the Kennedy administration. Jackie Kennedy's style and elegance endeared her not only to so many Americans, male and female alike, but also to Europeans who had grown accustomed to stereotyping Americans as powerful but not especially cultured. The French in particular enjoyed a love affair with the first lady, who spoke their language and was an unabashed Francophile. The president himself understood that while he was president of the most powerful nation on earth and leader of the free world, in France he took second billing to his wife. During a trip there in 1961, he opened a press briefing in Paris with the following words: "I do not think it altogether inappropriate to introduce myself to this audience. I am the man who accompanied Jacqueline Kennedy to Paris, and I have enjoyed it."

While Jacqueline Kennedy's husband had a better ear for popular music than for classic symphonies, he certainly did use the power and glamour of the White House to bring attention to composers, musicians, writers, and artists. And from the earliest days of his administration, Kennedy lobbied for construction of a national arts center in Washington, an institution that would one day bear his name—the Kennedy Center for the Performing Arts.

One of the enduring images of the Kennedy years is that of Pablo Casals playing the cello at a White House state dinner for the governor of Puerto Rico, Luis Muñoz-Marin. The president, dressed in white tie, and his wife, in a sleeveless gown, seemed the very picture of elegant, sophisticated, confident postwar America. The event was broadcast live on two radio networks, NBC and ABC, on November 13, 1961. But the Casals performance was only one of many glittering evenings in the Kennedy White House. The National Symphony Orchestra entertained the Kennedys and their guests at a state dinner at Mount Vernon on July 11, 1961. Igor Stravinsky, the Russian composer, was a guest of the White House on January 19, 1962. The composer said that the president and his wife were "nice kids."

John Kennedy also presided over the unveiling of the *Mona Lisa* when it was brought to Washington from France and exhibited at the National

Gallery of Art in January 1963. He used the occasion to examine the values and purpose of Western civilization, as personified by Leonardo da Vinci's enigmatic portrait. "We citizens of nations unborn at the time of its creation are among the inheritors and protectors of the ideals which gave it birth," he said of the *Mona Lisa*.

In his speech at Amherst, he asserted that an artist's "fidelity" to the truth could strengthen "the fiber of our national life."

"The artist, however faithful to his personal vision of reality, becomes the last champion of the individual mind and sensibility against an intrusive society and an officious state," Kennedy said. "The great artist is thus a solitary figure. He has, as Frost said, a lover's quarrel with the world. In pursuing his perceptions of reality, he must often sail against the currents of his time. This is not a popular role. If Robert Frost was much honored in his lifetime, it was because a good many preferred to ignore his darker truths."

"If art is to nourish the roots of our culture, society must set the artist free to follow his vision wherever it takes him," the president said. And, with the Cold War contest never far from his thoughts, he added, in a clear reference to Soviet-sponsored art, "We must never forget that art is not a form of propaganda; it is a form of truth."

Pearl S. Buck, the president, the first lady, and Robert Frost.

The president and first lady leave Fort Worth,
on their way to Dallas, on November 22, 1963.

CHAPTER 30

Watchmen on the Walls
of Freedom

Remarks at the Aerospace Medical Center
November 21, 1963

TRACK 31

I N THE FALL OF 1963, JOHN KENNEDY WAS BEING PULLED IN TWO DIRECTIONS
—his reelection campaign was beginning to take shape even as events
halfway around the globe, in South Vietnam, demanded his attention.

While the president was about to enter the reelection cycle as a clear
favorite to win a second term, there was some cause for concern. At least one
national poll, Gallup, showed Kennedy's popularity had declined sharply in
1963. According to Gallup, 59 percent of Americans approved of the president's performance—not bad, but not the 76 percent approval rating he
received at the beginning of the year.

There would be a challenge to Kennedy's right in the 1964 primaries,
from the voice of white backlash in the South—Alabama's governor, George
Wallace. While Wallace had no chance of blocking Kennedy's renomination,
the governor's presence in a few primary states threatened to stir the resent-
ments of southern Democrats who despised the president—and his attorney
general—for their role in desegregating Ole Miss and the University of
Alabama. Then again, Wallace's anticipated role as the voice of white
Southern reaction might help Kennedy with those northern liberals who
believed the administration was not moving quickly enough on civil rights.

With Wallace on the attack, northern liberals would have little choice but to rally around Kennedy despite their misgivings.

Even with his dip in popularity, Kennedy was polling well against one of the leading candidates for the Republican nomination, Arizona senator Barry Goldwater. Kennedy had a sixteen-point lead over his possible challenger, according to one poll. As election year neared, the Kennedy White House sought ways of "helping" the Republicans choose Goldwater, considered to be the weakest of the possible GOP challengers. "Don't waste any chance to praise Barry," the president instructed his advisors. "Build him up a little."

Other possible Republican candidates were of greater concern. Michigan had just elected George Romney, a onetime president of the American Motors Corp., as its new governor, and the ever-watchful Kennedy team took careful notice. Though Romney was a newcomer to politics, Kennedy's advisors recognized that his record in business would serve him well. Besides, Dwight Eisenhower had won the presidency in 1952 despite his lack of political experience, and businessman Wendell Wilkie, another novice, had run a vigorous race against Franklin Roosevelt in 1940. So the Kennedys saw no reason to write off the newcomer from Michigan.

Another potential candidate, New York governor Nelson Rockefeller, had worried Kennedy earlier in 1963. But by the fall, Rockefeller was a divorced man with a new wife, and in the calculations of the early 1960s, that made him unelectable. Still, his name, his money, his golden-boy charisma, and his ambition all demanded respect, and the Kennedys watched him closely.

The reelection team was beginning to take shape, with brother-in-law Stephen Smith installed as campaign manager. Other key members of the team would include speechwriter Ted Sorensen, Kenny O'Donnell, Lawrence O'Brien, and, of course, the attorney general, Robert Kennedy. The president told these trusted advisors that he anticipated a tough reelection campaign, regardless of which Republican wound up opposing him.

As he prepared for 1964, Kennedy scheduled two political trips to the contentious South—one to Florida, and the other to his vice president's home state of Texas. Those two states were critical to his reelection if, as he suspected, some white voters in the solid South turned history on its head by deserting the Democrats and embracing the Republicans because of racial politics.

And the struggle for civil rights continued to produce horrifying headlines.

On Sunday morning, September 15, 1963, members of the 16th Street Baptist Church in Birmingham, Alabama, gathered for a morning service. The worshippers were black, and they were elated over the desegregation of the state's schools earlier in the week.

A bomb went off at ten thirty. Four girls, none older than fourteen, were killed. Kennedy formally expressed his outrage and privately told Martin Luther King that he and other civil rights leaders, along with the federal government, had to "keep their nerve."

Even as Kennedy attended to these awful events, never-ending crises abroad continued to force their way onto his agenda.

On November 1, 1963, a group of South Vietnamese army officers staged a carefully planned coup against the nation's president, Ngo Dinh Diem, and his brother and chief advisor, Ngo Dinh Nhu. Diem had been falling out of favor in Washington because of his repressive policies toward South Vietnam's Buddhists, the vast majority of the country's population. (Diem himself was a Roman Catholic.) The Kennedy administration already had committed about seventeen thousand troops to defend the Diem regime against a Communist insurgency, but now Diem had become an embarrassment—and the escalating conflict in Vietnam was becoming front-page news as the president's reelection campaign neared.

Kennedy decided that Diem and Nhu had to go. The coup was carried out with the knowledge, cooperation, and encouragement of U.S. officials in South Vietnam and Washington.

But events very quickly spun out of Kennedy's control.

Diem and Nhu were arrested and taken prisoner. Amid talk of a possible U.S.-arranged exile for the two leaders, some of the plotters of the coup took matters into their own hands. Diem and Nhu were murdered, their deaths described by the South Vietnamese military as a double-suicide.

Kennedy was stunned. Apparently, he had persuaded himself that the plot against Diem and Nhu would not end in bloodshed, although it is hard to imagine any other conclusion. He called the murders "abhorrent" and blamed himself for not anticipating such a dreadful turn of events.

In mid-November, State Department officials announced that U.S. and Vietnamese officials would meet in Hawaii to discuss the future of American involvement in South Vietnam. The Hawaii meetings were scheduled to begin on November 20.

The president was in campaign mode on November 18 when he flew to Tampa and Miami as part of his strategy to hold the two most important states in the South. Then, on November 21, he left Andrews Air Force Base for a flight to San Antonio, Texas.

The Lone Star state was source of some concern among Democrats as 1964 approached. Kennedy noted that while donors from states like New York and Massachusetts were doing their part for the party and his reelection bid, Texas seemed to be in a less charitable mood. He was determined to change that. He wanted the state's Democratic governor, John Connally, to intervene on his behalf with rich Texas Democrats. Kennedy also wanted to meet with the state's leading Democrats, where he planned to remind them that good things happen when state party leaders turn out the vote—and bad things happen when they do not.

Connally, a conservative Democrat who would later switch to the Republican Party, was not particularly enthusiastic. What's more, he was engaged in a bitter feud with his fellow Texan, U.S. Senator Ralph Yarborough, who was more liberal than the governor. Vice President Johnson was aligned with Connally, adding to the intrigue.

Traveling with the ever-popular Jackie in tow—the first lady's presence could be counted on to break some of the anticipated political tension, the president visited San Antonio and Houston on November 21. One of the several speeches he gave that day took place at the opening of an aerospace medical facility in San Antonio. It gave Kennedy a welcome opportunity to return to one of his favorite themes—the new frontier of space exploration.

For John Kennedy, the United States still had not quite reached its manifest destiny. The phrase from school textbooks referred to the dream of a continental United States—a dream that had been achieved, a dream that belonged to the ages.

The old frontier was long closed, but for Americans born in the twentieth century, history had provided a new frontier—not just in space, but on earth as well. American power, ideals, knowledge, and benevolence no longer were constrained by oceans and isolation. Destiny had called the United States to assume a new role in the affairs of humankind, and surely, that role was part of the new frontier. U.S. troops were garrisoned in the old cities of Europe, and in emerging nations in Asia. U.S. wealth was spread across the globe, no longer restricted to Wall Street and Main Street. U.S. scientists were winning battles against disease and premature death. U.S. thinkers and writers were exploring the values and vices of our common humanity.

John Kennedy's New Frontier was not just about the stars, not just about the race for the moon. It was about ideas, and ideals, and the new role the United States was assuming in the world.

In San Antonio, he reminded his audience that he had been speaking about the New Frontier for three years. "This is not a partisan term, and it is not the exclusive property of Republicans or Democrats," he said. "It refers, instead, to this nation's place in history, to the fact that we do stand on the edge of a great new era, filled with both crisis and opportunity, an era to be characterized by achievement and by challenge. It is an era which calls for action and for the best efforts of all those who would test the unknown and the uncertain in every phase of human endeavor. It is a time for pathfinders and pioneers."

The following day, John Kennedy's life came to an end in Dallas.

In a speech he was scheduled to deliver at the Dallas Trade Mart on the afternoon of November 22, 1963, Kennedy planned to offer another glimpse of that city on a hill he spoke of years earlier, as he left Massachusetts for the White House. But he would never speak these words. They would have to speak for themselves:

"We in this country, in this generation, are—by destiny rather than choice—the watchmen on the walls of world freedom. We ask, therefore, that we may be worthy of our power and responsibility, that we may exercise our strength with wisdom and restraint, and that we may achieve in our time and for all time the ancient vision of 'peace on earth, goodwill toward men.' That must always be our goal, and the righteousness of our cause must always underlie our strength. For as was written long ago, 'except the Lord keep the city, the watchman waketh but in vain.'"

Dreaming Things That Never Were
SPEECHES BY ROBERT AND
EDWARD KENNEDY

*Robert F. Kennedy's Tribute
to John F. Kennedy*
August 27, 1964

TRACK 32

*Robert F. Kennedy's Statement
on the Assassination of Martin Luther King Jr.*
April 4, 1968

TRACK 33

Edward Kennedy's Tribute to Robert F. Kennedy
June 8, 1968

TRACK 34

PRESIDENT KENNEDY'S TWO BROTHERS WENT ON TO DELIVER SEVERAL memorable speeches of their own. Three in particular remind us of the traumatic times that followed the murder of President Kennedy, times that led to tragedy and heartbreak for the nation as a whole, and for the Kennedy family. We have included, as an audio postscript, two speeches by Robert F. Kennedy and one by Edward Kennedy.

The first (track 32), by RFK, was delivered at the Democratic National Convention in Atlantic City in 1964. The Democrats gathered less than a year after the President's assassination to nominate Lyndon Johnson to a full term. The dramatic highlight of the convention took place on August 27, when Robert Kennedy stepped to the podium to deliver a tribute to the fallen president.

Like his brother's speeches, Robert Kennedy's was filled with references to America's past and its great leaders and heroes. He said his brother delighted in telling how "Thomas Jefferson and James Madison made up the Hudson River in 1800 on a botanical expedition searching for butterflies; that they ended up down in New York City and that they formed the Democratic Party."

And like his brother, Robert was capable of poetic turns of phrase. "When I think of President Kennedy," he said, "I think of what Shakespeare said in *Romeo and Juliet*:

When he shall die take him and cut him out into stars and he shall make the face of heaven so fine that all the world will be in love with night and pay no worship to the garish sun."

Nightfall, however, would not be so romantic as the glow of Camelot faded into the darkness of the mid-1960s. Within four years, the nation was so torn apart by the Vietnam War that JFK's successor, Johnson, turned down the chance to run for a second full term. Robert Kennedy entered the 1968 presidential race on an anti-war platform.

On the night of April 4, 1968, RFK was campaigning in Indianapolis when he learned the awful news that Dr. Martin Luther King Jr. had been murdered in Memphis, Tennessee. The candidate was scheduled to speak at a campaign rally that night to a mostly African American audience. The Kennedy supporters did not know about King's murder.

An obviously shaken Robert Kennedy decided to address the crowd (track 33), telling them what had happened, and appealing to them to stay calm and, somehow, hopeful. Speaking without notes, he said: "For those of you who are black and are tempted to be filled with hatred and distrust at the injustice of such an act, against all white people, I can only say that I feel in my own heart the same kind of feeling. I had a member of my family killed, but he was killed by a white man. But we have to make an effort in the United States, we have to make an effort to understand, to go beyond these rather difficult times."

He then quoted, from memory, a verse from the Greek poet Aeschylus. "In our sleep, pain which cannot forget falls drop by drop upon the heart until, in our own despair, against our will, comes wisdom through the awful grace of God."

A month later, Robert F. Kennedy was killed by an assassin's bullet in Los Angeles, seconds after he declared victory in the 1968 Democratic presidential primary in California.

On June 8, 1968, the Kennedy family assembled to mourn yet another fallen son, brother, husband, and uncle. For the first time, the youngest Kennedy male, Edward, was cast into the national spotlight as he delivered his brother's eulogy (track 34) in St. Patrick's Cathedral in New York.

With President Johnson, whose feud with Robert Kennedy had reached epic proportions in 1968, in attendance, the young senator from Massachusetts recalled his brother "as a good and decent man who saw wrong and tried to right it, saw suffering and tried to heal it, saw war and tried to stop it."

Edward Kennedy quoted a line from George Bernard Shaw, the Irish playwright whom John Kennedy himself had quoted during his memorable speech to the Irish Parliament in 1963. "Some men see things as they are and say why. I dream things that never were and say why not."

Notes

Introduction

Biographer Robert Dallek: Dallek, *An Unfinished Life*, 52.
"Democracy sleeps":   ibid., 113.
Kennedy's longtime friend: ibid., 193.
In this piece: ibid., 223.

Part One

Chapter One

He responded: Dallek, *An Unfinished Life*, 244.
By then, he said: ibid., 232.
That would take: ibid., 236.
In reply: ibid., 234.
He told a reporter: ibid., 246.
"There's only one problem: Thomas Maier, *The Kennedys: America's Emerald Kings*, 333.
"I am a Catholic: Dallek, *An Unfinished Life*, 253.

Chapter Two

As he watched: Dallek, *An Unfinished Life*, 266.

Chapter Four

I wondered: Robert Slayton, *Empire Statesman: The Rise and Redemption of Al Smith*, 258.
Even as he reaffirmed: Slayton, ibid., 303.
In 1927:   William V. Shannon, *The American Irish*, 179.
"They're mostly Republicans: Dallek, *An Unfinished Life*, 283.
Kennedy was determined: Dallek, ibid., 282.
His brother Bobby: Maier, *The Kennedys*, 240.
Two months before: Maier, ibid., 345.

Another Baptist preacher: Maier, ibid., 346.

A minister in: Maier, ibid., 340.

As historian Robert Slayton: Slayton, *Empire Statesman*, 33.

In his 1928:   Slayton, ibid., 303.

According to Thomas Maier's: Maier, *The Kennedys*, 344.

"I think it's so: Maier, ibid., 306.

Chapter Five

Nixon would later write: Richard Nixon, *RN: Memoirs of Richard Nixon*, 219.

Chapter Six

"I immediately took: Nixon, *RN*, 219.

Journalist Tom Wicker: Tom Wicker, *One of Us*, 238.

Two months before: Arthur Schlesinger Jr., *Robert Kennedy and His Times*, 309.

Wofford, who would: Schlesinger, ibid., 309.

But now he would: Wicker, *One of Us*, 241.

"Imagine Martin Luther King: Schlesinger, *Robert Kennedy and His Times*, 235.

Chapter Seven

Years later: Nixon, *RN*, 220.

Kennedy commented on: Theodore C. Sorensen, ed. *Let the Word Go Forth*, 25.

"It can be and has been: Wicker, *One of Us*, 235.

Chapter Eight

As he later lamented: Nixon, *RN*, 220.

In the statement: Wicker, *One of Us*, 232.

"His statement: Nixon, *RN*, 220.

Wicker added: Wicker, *One of Us*, 232.

Nixon said that: Nixon, *RN*, 221.

"Whether it was: Wicker, *One of Us*, 234.

Part Two

Chapter Twelve

But, he added: Schlesinger, *Robert Kennedy and His Times*, 509.

After he finished: Dallek, An *Unfinished Life*, 341.

"It's because they: Dallek, ibid., 469.

Castro told a journalist: Schlesinger, *Robert Kennedy and His Times*, 622.

On November 18, 1963:   Schlesinger, ibid., 624.

Chapter Thirteen

In late March: Richard Reeves, *President Kennedy: Profile of Power*, 76.

"I want to say: Reeves, ibid., 86.

She left a message: Nixon, *RN*, 234.

The White House: Arthur Schlesinger Jr., *A Thousand Days: John F. Kennedy in the White House*, 289–290.

Behind the scenes: Reeves, *President Kennedy*, 99.

"It's like Eisenhower: Dallek, *An Unfinished Life*, 371.

"Well," he said: Sorenson, *Let the Word Go Forth*, 30.

"It's the sort of proposal: Sorenson, ibid., 74.

Chapter Fourteen

"Well," he replied: Sorensen, *Let the Word Go Forth*, 31.

"All he has: Dallek, *An Unfinished Life*, 363.

"What the hell: Dallek, ibid., 363.

"We're going to have: Reeves, *President Kennedy*, 101.

Chapter Fifteen

Only weeks before: Reeves, *President Kennedy*, 100.

"I built a swimming pool: Reeves, ibid., 180.

Chapter Sixteen

In the summer of 1961:   Dallek, *An Unfinished Life*, 424.

"I hope you get: Dallek, ibid., 406.

"Khrushchev's presentation: John C. Ausland, *Kennedy, Khrushchev, and the Berlin-Cuba Crisis*, 4.

Khrushchev, he later: Dallek, *An Unfinished Life*, 413.

"Then, Mr. Chairman: Dallek, ibid., 413.

"The whole position: Dallek, ibid., 419.

Alsop's ensuing story: Reeves, *President Kennedy*, 179.

Chapter Seventeen
"We are not there: Reeves, *President Kennedy*, 597.
He asked for: Dallek, *An Unfinished Life*, 686.

Part Three

Chapter Eighteen
"Bobby and I: Bill Adler and Tom Folsom, eds., *The Uncommon Wisdom of JFK*, 141.
Truman despised: David McCullough, *Truman*, 970.
"Senator, are you: McCullough, ibid, 973.
Kennedy's chief economic advisor: Reeves, *President Kennedy*, 294.

Chapter Nineteen
"You double-crossed: Dallek, *An Unfinished Presidency*, 484.
In late 1961: Dallek, ibid., 483.
"I've been screwed: Dallek, ibid., 484.
A Kennedy aide: Dallek, ibid., 484.

Chapter Twenty
When John F. Kennedy was: Michael Waldman, *My Fellow Americans*, 84.

Chapter Twenty-One
Eisenhower had said: Dallek, *An Unfinished Life*, 393.
"The country should: Reeves, *President Kennedy*, 139.
That was all: Reeves, ibid., 139.
Kennedy greeted King: Reeves, ibid., 100.
"The President is going on TV tonight: Schlesinger, *Robert Kennedy and His Times*, 360.
"Is this ready to be fired: May, Ernest R. and Philip D. Zelikow, eds., *The Kennedy Tapes*, 49.

Chapter Twenty-Two
He later explained: Schlesinger, *Robert Kennedy and His Times*, 341.
"Sending in troops: Schlesinger, ibid., 343.
At one point: Schlesinger, ibid., 342.

In his biography: Schlesinger, ibid., 347.

"I haven't had: Dallek, *An Unfinished Life,* 517.

"People are dying: Reeves, *President Kennedy,* 363.

"No wonder it's: Reeves, ibid., 363.

The president called: Dallek, *An Unfinished Life,* 544.

Kennedy said afterwards: Dallek, ibid., 553.

He told the president: May and Zelikow, *The Kennedy Tapes,* 182, 178.

Afterwards, the president: Dallek, *An Unfinished Life,* 555.

"If I'd known: Dallek, ibid., 557.

Months later: Sorensen, *Let the Word Go Forth,* 31.

At one point: Reeves, *President Kennedy,* 411.

Years later, Khrushchev: Nikita Khrushchev, *Khrushchev Remembers: The Last Testament,* 329.

"I see the possibility: Reeves, *President Kennedy,* 477.

Kennedy summoned Cousins: Reeves, ibid., 440.

"One thing the President and I: Reeves, ibid., 440.

Part Four
Chapter Twenty-Four

"If this planet: Dallek, *An Unfinished Life,* 505.

Kennedy once asked: Reeves, *President Kennedy,* 227.

Rusk told the president: Reeves, ibid., 512.

When Cousins spoke: Reeves, ibid., 511.

"The moment is now: Dallek, *An Unfinished Life,* 612.

Less than two weeks: Dallek, ibid., 621.

Chapter Twenty-Five

"Domestic policy can only: Adler, *The Uncommon Wisdom of JFK,* 57.

According to Richard Reeves': Reeves, *President Kennedy,* 515.

Wallace read a statement: Reeves, ibid., 520.

In late May: Reeves, ibid., 501.

He told Sorenson: Dallek, *An Unfinished Life,* 602.

His brother Bobby: Dallek, ibid., 605.

"He looks like: Reeves, *President Kennedy,* 535.

Chapter Twenty-Six

The speech's power: Michael R. Beschloss, *The Crisis Years: Kennedy and Khrushchev, 1960-63*, 605.

A memo prepared: Reeves, *President Kennedy*, 534.

Polke told Kennedy: Reeves, ibid., 535.

He said he believed: Reeves, ibid., 536.

As he left Germany: Beschloss, *The Crisis Years*, 604.

Chapter Twenty-Seven

A decade earlier: Maier, *The Kennedys*, 114.

"When I say: Reeves, *President Kennedy*, 532.

"The bastards: Dallek, *An Unfinished Life*, 429.

Chapter Twenty-Eight

But in a: Beschloss, *The Crisis Years*, 396.

A correspondent for: Beschloss, ibid., 396.

Khrushchev, even as he: Reeves, *President Kennedy*, 547.

Chapter Twenty-Nine

Upon returning: Dallek, *An Unfinished Life*, 540.

"Why did Frost: Dallek, ibid., 540.

In fact,: Reeves, *President Kennedy*, 475.

During a trip: Dallek, *An Unfinished Life*, 400.

Kennedy formally expressed: Reeves, 600.

Chapter Thirty

"Don't waste any: Reeves, *President Kennedy*, 655.

That, he said: Dallek, *An Unfinished Life*, 685.

Bibliography

Adler, Bill and Tom Folsom, ed. *The Uncommon Wisdom of JFK*. New York: Rugged Land, 2003.

Ambrose, Stephen E. *Eisenhower and Berlin 1945*. New York: W.W. Norton & Company, 2000.

Ausland, John C. *Kennedy, Khrushchev and the Berlin-Cuba Crisis, 1961-1964*. Oslo, Norway: Scandinavian University Press, 1996.

Beschloss, Michael R. *The Crisis Years: Kennedy and Khrushchev, 1960-1963*. New York: HarperCollins, 1991.

Clarke, Thurston. *Ask Not: The Inauguration of John F. Kennedy and the Speech That Changed America*. New York: Henry Holt, 2004.

Coffey, Michael and Terry Golway. *The Irish in America*. New York: Hyperion, 1997.

Dallek, Robert. *An Unfinished Life: John F. Kennedy, 1917-1963*. Boston: Little, Brown, 2003.

Fisher, James T. *Dr. America: The Lives of Thomas A. Dooley*. Amherst: University of Massachusetts Press, 1998.

Goodwin, Doris Kearns. *The Fitzgeralds and the Kennedys*. New York: Simon & Schuster, 1987.

Kennedy, John F. *Profiles in Courage*. New York: Harper, 1956.

Kennedy, John F. *The Strategy of Peace*. New York: Harper and Brothers, 1960.

Khrushchev, Nikita S. *Khrushchev Remembers: The Last Testament*. Boston: Little, Brown, 1974.

Maier, Thomas. *The Kennedys: America's Emerald Kings*. New York: Basic Books, 2003.

May, Ernest R. and Philip D. Zelikow. *The Kennedy Tapes*. Cambridge, MA: Harvard University Press, 1997.

McCullough, David. *Truman*. New York: Simon & Schuster, 1992.

Morris, Charles. *American Catholic*. New York: Times Books, 1997.

Nixon, Richard. *RN: Memoirs of Richard Nixon*. New York: Grosset & Dunlap, 1978.

Reeves, Richard. *President Kennedy: Profile of Power*. New York: Simon & Schuster, 1993.

Schlesinger, Arthur M. Jr. *A Thousand Days: John F. Kennedy in the White*

House. Boston: Houghton Mifflin, 1965.

Schlesinger, Arthur M. Jr. *Robert Kennedy and His Times*. New York: Ballantine Books, 1979.

Shannon, William V. *The American Irish*. New York: Macmillan, 1963.

Slayton, Robert A. *Empire Statesman: The Rise and Redemption of Al Smith*. New York: The Free Press, 2001.

Smyser, W.R. *From Yalta to Berlin*. New York: St. Martin's Press, 1990.

Sorensen, Theodore C. *Kennedy*. New York: Harper & Row, 1965.

Sorensen, Theodore C., ed. *Let the Word Go Forth*. New York: Dell, 1988.

Thomas, Evan. *Robert Kennedy: His Life*. New York: Simon & Schuster, 2000.

Tofel, Richard J. *Sounding the Trumpet: The Making of John F. Kennedy's Inaugural Address*. Chicago: Ivan R. Dee, 2005.

Tuchman, Barbara. *The Guns of August*. New York: Dell, 1962.

Waldman, Michael. *My Fellow Americans*. Naperville, Ill.: Sourcebooks, 2003.

White, Theodore C. *The Making of the President, 1960*. New York: Atheneum Publishers, 1961.

Wicker, Tom. *One of Us*. New York: Random House, 1991.

Index

Credits

Audio and photos have been obtained with the kind assistance of the John F. Kennedy Library and Museum (located in Boston, MA) and the Library of Congress.

Audio segments have been edited for time and content. In the interest of clarity and accuracy, all edits within each speech are made apparent by the fading out of the audio, then the fading in of the next segment. While we have attempted to achieve the best possible quality on this archival material, some audio quality is the result of source limitations. Audio denoising by Christian Pawola at Music & Sound Company, DeKalb, Illinois.

For full versions of most of the speeches featured in this book, plus a wealth of other information about the president, visit the website of the John F. Kennedy Library at www.jfklibrary.org.

About Sourcebooks MediaFusion

Launched with the 1998 *New York Times* bestseller *We Interrupt This Broadcast* and formally founded in 2000, Sourcebooks MediaFusion is the nation's leading publisher of mixed-media books. This revolutionary imprint is dedicated to creating original content—be it audio, video, CD-ROM, or Web—that is fully integrated with the books we create. The result, we hope, is a new, richer, eye-opening, thrilling experience with books for our readers. Our experiential books have become both bestsellers and classics in their subjects, including poetry *(Poetry Speaks)*, children's books *(Poetry Speaks to Children)*, history *(We Shall Overcome)*, sports *(And The Crowd Goes Wild)*, the plays of William Shakespeare, and more. See what's new from us at www.sourcebooks.com.

Acknowledgments

Our thanks go to the staff at the John F. Kennedy Library, especially James Hill, Colleen Cooney, Laurie Austin, and Jessica Sims. Thanks, also, to Alan Joyce for his photo research. Thanks to Tom Glad at the National Press Club and the staff at the Recorded Sound Division of the Library of Congress.

Our editor, Hillel Black, was a constant source of enthusiasm. We are grateful for the talents of Todd Stocke, Samantha Raue, Anne LoCascio, Heather Moore, and the publicity staff of Sourcebooks.

John Wright, our agent and friend, was an inspiration, as always. Thank you for making the project possible.

About the Authors

© Geraldine Dallek

Robert Dallek was a winner of the Bancroft Prize for his book *FDR and American Foreign Policy*. He is also the author of *An Unfinished Life: John F. Kennedy, 1917–1963*. He lives in Washington, D.C.

© William Tomlin

Terry Golway is also the author of *Washington's General*, a biography of Nathanael Green. He writes for the *New York Times*, *American Heritage*, and the *New York Observer*. He lives in Maplewood, New Jersey.